THE DOMINION
OF NEW ENGLAND

AMERICAN CLASSICS

THE DOMINION
OF NEW ENGLAND

A Study in British Colonial Policy

VIOLA FLORENCE BARNES

Professor Emeritus of History, Mount Holyoke College

FREDERICK UNGAR PUBLISHING CO.
NEW YORK

TO
D. G. B.

PREFACE

The purpose of this study is to show that the most complete expression of the British colonial policy in the seventeenth century was the Dominion of New England. By it England attempted to define the status of the New England colonies, to bring them into a closer relationship with the mother country, and to reform the colonial policy in matters of trade and defense. The establishment of Dominion government was variously received by the different parties and factions. The moderates, although supporting it at the outset, objected to the great concentration of power in the hands of the governor and council and to their extensive interference with long-established precedents and traditions. The strict Puritans hated it because it destroyed their theocracy and brought a remodeling of their institutions on the English pattern. Before the reforms which the moderates demanded could be granted, the theocrats, taking advantage of the revolution in England of 1688, overthrew the Dominion government and seized the power. In spite of the petitions of the moderates for the re-establishment of the Dominion, William III, the new ruler, lacking familiarity with England's colonial problems, abandoned the policy of consolidation and restored the charter governments in New England, with, however, certain restrictions on the self-government which Massachusetts had enjoyed before 1684. The effect of this decision on subsequent relations between New England and the mother country was far-reaching.

It was my intention originally to treat the subject of this study as a chapter introductory to a book on the relations between England and Massachusetts in the eighteenth century, but I soon discovered that it would be necessary first to make a thorough investigation of the Dominion experiment. I have therefore limited the subject of this essay entirely to the Dominion of New England. In its preparation I have received valuable assistance from Professor Charles M. Andrews, to whom I am indebted for the inspiration and guidance which he has given me, both while I was a student in his seminary at Yale and in my work since that time. I wish also to acknowledge my gratitude to Dr. N. Neilson, of Mount Holyoke College, who has given me most helpful assistance in preparing the manuscript for publication. Others to whom I am under obligations are Mr. Albert Matthews, editor of the transactions and collections of the Colonial Society of Massachusetts, who kindly permitted me to use transcripts of British sources which he had gathered for publication, Mr. Julius H. Tuttle, of the Massachusetts Historical Society, and Mr. John H. Edmonds of the Massachusetts State Archives department at Boston.

VIOLA F. BARNES.

January 26, 1923.

CONTENTS

CONTENTS

INTRODUCTION

INTRODUCTION: BRITISH COLONIAL POLICY TO 1665

Before 1660, England had no definite colonial policy, although her later interest in the commercial development of the colonies was foreshadowed in the passage of the ordinance of 1651 and the establishment of councils of trade and plantations. The restoration of the monarchy, which ended the internal dissension over religious and constitutional questions, gave to both the government and the merchants an opportunity to interest themselves in trade expansion. In the light of this new commercial interest, England viewed the colonies no longer as mere outlets for restlessness at home, but as potential markets and commodity producers. Since colonies were necessary for her commercial development, she desired to increase their number and to draw them all into a closer relationship with the government at home. New Netherland was wrested from the Dutch, and the Carolinas and Bahamas were granted to proprietors to settle, but England found herself confronted with more serious obstacles when she attempted to direct the affairs of the older colonies. Because in the early seventeenth century she had been too poor to undertake colonization as a state enterprise, she granted to trading companies charters which contained not only the gift of territory but also very extensive powers of government in such colonies as they might found. They could choose the governor, make laws without other restriction than that the laws be conformable to those of England, and establish courts that were independent of the English judicial system.[1] However, the colonists soon outgrew the narrow control of the commercial oligarchies and demanded a share in government,[2] probably by virtue of their rights as Englishmen.[3] The establishment of representative assemblies in Virginia, Bermuda, and Massachusetts set the example for other colonies to follow, so that by 1663 every colony then existing had a house of deputies.[4] These representative institutions stood in the way of England's administration of government in the colonies, but they could not be abolished without danger of alienating the colonies completely. Therefore England adopted local self-government as an essential feature of the new colonial policy, intending for the future to exercise authority in the colonies by parliamentary enactments and by the king's supervision of laws and courts. During the first four years of the reign of Charles II, parliament passed navigation acts which gave to the mother country a measure of control of colonial shipping, products, and markets,

[1] In these charters the legislative power was given to the members of the company resident in England, not to the colonists. Thorpe, *Federal and State Constitutions*, III, 1832, 1853; VII, 3805-3806; Lefroy, *Memorials of the Discovery and Early Settlement of the Bermudas or Somers Islands*, 1515-1685, I, 90.

[2] In defending the Massachusetts charter of 1691, Cotton Mather reminded the disappointed theocrats that the first charter of Massachusetts "directed not an House of Deputies or Assembly of Representatives." *Andros Tracts*, III, 169.

[3] Hutchinson in his *History of Massachusetts* (2d ed.), I, 37, suggests that this was the case with the Massachusetts colonists. "There was, as has been observed, no express provision for it [house of representatives] in the charter; they supposed the natural rights of Englishmen, reserved to them, implied it."

[4] A share in the government was guaranteed to settlers in the proprietary grants to Lord Baltimore and to Sir Ferdinando Gorges. Thorpe, *Federal and State Consts.*, III, 1628, 1679.

while the king appointed councils of trade and plantations with general supervisory powers, and began cautiously but firmly to assert his right to inspect laws and to hear appeals.[5]

In comparison with the colonial systems of other countries that of England was remarkably liberal and quite unique in the amount of freedom of action allowed the colonies both in trade and government. However, they failed to appreciate its merits because they preferred no policy at all. Through England's early indifference to them they had been able to develop their political institutions unhampered by outside authority and consequently they had quite a different conception of their relationship with the mother country from that held by England herself. Particularly in New England, the colonists were scarcely aware of any connection. Therefore, in that region one would expect to find a challenge to England's right to introduce startling governmental and commercial innovations.

[5] See the secret instructions given to the royal commissioners who were sent to New England by Charles II in 1664. Among other things they were "to peruse the collection of the lawes published in those Colonies during the late usurping Government or at any time before or since; to the end that upon examination thereof you may discerne both the indecent expressions and materiall points and determinations in them which are contrary to our dignity and to the lawes and customes of this realme, and to the justice thereof; all which they have obliged themselves to cancell and repeale." *Documents Relative to the Colonial History of New York*, III, 57-58. A special commission was likewise given them to hear and "determine complaints & appeals in all cases and matters as well military as criminal & civill." *Ibid.*, 64-65.

CHAPTER I

THE REFUSAL OF MASSACHUSETTS TO BECOME A PART OF THE BRITISH COLONIAL SYSTEM

Of all the colonies, Massachusetts was the one most reluctant to submit to the new colonial policy. Outside of New England, all were either royal or proprietary and were therefore easier to control than those of the corporation type. Moreover, the southern and island colonies developed economically in such a way as to cause them to fit naturally into their places in the commercial system. Of the New England group, Maine and New Hampshire were, after 1652, governed by Massachusetts, while Connecticut and Rhode Island, having before 1662 and 1663 no legal right to exist as political communities, could not afford to antagonize the mother country. The granting by Charles II of very liberal charters in 1662 and 1663[1] was taken by these colonies to be a pledge of good

---

[1] There seems to be no very satisfactory explanation of the king's action in creating two such independent corporations at a time when the policy of the English government was to draw the colonies into a closer relationship with the mother country. If Roger Williams was correctly informed concerning the circumstances surrounding the grant, the statesmen in charge of the colonial policy evidently suffered a great shock when they heard of the king's intention. Williams wrote to Mason in 1663, "This his Majesty's grant, was startled at by his Majesty's high officers of state who were to view it in course before the sealing, but, fearing the lion's roaring, they crouched against their wills in obedience to his Majesty's pleasure." Cited in Weeden, *Early Rhode Island*, pp. 70-71. Perhaps the seeming inconsistency in policy as shown by these liberal charters and the contrast in the instructions to the royal commissioners of 1664 is due to the fact that the first was

faith, after which time they were slow to oppose the mother country, although in an inconspicuous way they governed themselve; quite independently.[2] Massachusetts, hav'ng begun her existence as a trading company with a very liberal charter, gained even greater governmental freedom by the transference of the charter and company to New England. The development of the trading company into a theocracy increased the spirit of independence which freedom of government had given, for the Puritans thought of themselves as being divinely called to settle a state in the wilderness and deemed their connection with the mother country a mere means to an end, to be broken when no longer useful. Civil war in England gave to Massachusetts the opportunity to sever the tie. Since her sympathies were with the parliamentary party, she assumed that its successful revolt against the king released her from her charter obligations and gave her independence. In 1652, therefore, she declared herself a commonwealth, petitioned Cromwell to recognize her as such, and began to exercise the prerogatives of sovereignty in every way as though she were an independent state.[3] When the monarchy was restored, she almost refused to recognize the king's sovereignty, but was saved from a declaration of independence by the influence

the work of the king, the second of the lords of his Privy Council in charge of colonial policy. A similar lack of harmony appears later in the reign.

[2] The difference between the attitude of Massachusetts and that of the other New England colonies, particularly Connecticut, is shown in a letter from England to a colonist of Massachusetts: "Our last packet from England brings us news of two very loyal addresses to his Majesty, one from New Plymouth and the other from Connecticut, which were both very graciously received, by which I suspect you of the Massachusetts are more whiggish and your neighbors more toryish, to express it in the language of late in use." Hutchinson, *History of Massachusetts Bay* (2d ed.), I, 343, note.

[3] *Calendar of State Papers, Colonial,* 1660-1668, §1103; Hutchinson, *Collection of Original Papers,* Prince Society, II, 213-214, 232.

of the moderate Puritans and by the fear of revolt on the part of the non-Puritan, pro-English inhabitants of the colony.[4]

The first attempt to bring Massachusetts into line was made when the royal commissioners were sent over to capture New Netherland in 1664. They were instructed to investigate conditions in New England and, if possible, to persuade the colonies there to allow the king to appoint their governors from a list nominated by each colonial government. They were also required to make a careful inspection of colonial laws and of the way those laws were interpreted in the courts, and for this purpose to demand the right of hearing appeals. The resistance expected from Massachusetts was forthcoming. She defied the commissioners, denying that parliament could legislate for the colonies or the king supervise her laws and courts, and claiming that as long as she met the requirements laid down in her charter, namely, the payment of the fifth of all gold and silver ore found in the colony, she was "not obliged to the king but by civility."[5] The king ordered her to send at once agents who should explain her action. Again the Puritans would have defied the king but for the moderates and prominent non-Puritans, who sent to the General Court of Massachusetts very insistent petitions that the royal demands be complied with. Instead of the defiant letter which had been prepared, the General Court presented the king with masts for the royal navy, hoping that in consequence of

[4] Lechford wrote that many people complained that they were ruled like slaves and would soon have no more privileges than heathen unless the church discipline were amended. "It is feared," he continued, "that elections cannot be safe there long, either in Church or Commonwealth, so that some melancholy men think it a great deal safer to be in the midst of troubles in a settled Commonwealth, or in hope easily to be settled, then in mutinies there so far off from Succours." 3 Massachusetts Historical Society *Collections*, III, 95; *Cal. State Pap. Col.*, 1677-1680, §811.

[5] *Cal. State Pap. Col.*, 1660-1668, §1103.

this gift he would overlook the fact that agents had not been dispatched.[6]

No vigorous action having been taken against her, Massachusetts continued to resist the attempts of the mother country to draw her into the colonial system. Down to 1675, the principal charges against her were her ignoring of the navigation acts, denying the power of parliament to legislate for the colony, making laws contrary to the laws of England, usurping powers not granted by the charter,—such as taxing those not free of the company, laying imposts on English goods, coining money, and extending her jurisdiction over Maine and New Hampshire,—and refusing to grant the suffrage and liberty of conscience to dissenters. Very early in her history the colony had become a theocracy, in which citizenship and church membership were synonymous and those who were not Puritans were unwelcome. Conspicuous malcontents were driven out of the colony, but there were many non-Puritans who quietly conformed to the religious and political demands, attending church and paying the ministers' rates, although excluded from communion, and submitting to taxation, although allowed to take no part in the government which levied the taxes.

Among the disfranchised were many men of wealth and social position who were making their fortunes in commerce during the period of prosperity which the colony was enjoying.[7] They dwelt in the large coast towns,

[6] 2 Mass. Hist. Soc. *Col.*, VIII, 103-108, 110; *Massachusetts Colony Records* IV, pt. 2, 317-318.

[7] Among them were such men as Richard Wharton, Thomas Brattle, Nicholas Page, John Foster, Anthony Checkley, John Eyre, Nathaniel Oliver, Simon Lynde, Nathaniel Byfield, Francis Foxcroft, Charles Lidgett, Humphrey Liscombe, Captain Anthony Howard, Francis Burroughs, Benjamin Alford, Edward Shippen, Peter Sergeant, William Taylor, Philip English, and many others. On the Boston tax list for 1687, there were only thirty men whose tax on trade came to fifty pence per annum or above in a single country rate. Of these, twenty-two were non-freemen, of whom five were

where they formed a strong party of opposition to Puritan policy and ideals. They preferred that the colony maintain a closer relationship with the mother country and were not at all in sympathy with the theocratic policy of defiance and independence. Had the suffrage been based on property qualifications, non-freemen of this class would have had a share in government while many of the "meaner sort" of Puritan theocrats would have been excluded from public office. The British government, realizing this fact, thought that if the non-free, who were in the majority in the colony, could be given political influence, the colony would lose its peculiarly theocratic and independent flavor and would probably come into line with the other English colonies, taking her place as a willing part of the commercial system. Consequently, the king demanded that the suffrage be no longer limited to church members in full standing. But the theocrats in charge of the government, though making a pretense at complying, refused to weaken "the hedge" and placed such heavy restrictions on the ballot that only a very few who were not church members could qualify.

Happily, not all the Puritans approved of this treatment of the non-free or of the colony's independent attitude toward England. Especially in the larger towns, there was noticeable a decided moderation in the stern and uncompromising spirit created by the early Puritan fathers. The principal factor in bringing about this change in the character of the life of the colony was the commercial prosperity and the rise to prominence of a merchant class. The change was especially manifest in the younger generation and caused the Puritan founders much anxiety, since it threatened the loss of all that for

given the franchise in 1689-1690, when the old freemen were compelled to extend the suffrage in order to win support for the revolution. *Report of the Boston Record Commissioners*, I, 91-127.

which they had sacrificed so much. The General Court attempted to check this growing laxity by legislation prohibiting indulgence in the vanities of the times, but the laws seem to have had no deterring effect. Out of these changing conditions which accompanied the rise of the second generation arose a moderate group among the Puritans themselves, men with a less stern attitude toward life and a broader vision of external relationships, who, responding to the influence of the expanding trade of the colony, disapproved of the narrow policy of isolation which the older generation of Puritans had insisted upon. In this group were William Stoughton, Joseph Dudley, William Browne, Jr., Wait Winthrop, Jonathan and Edward Tyng, Simon Bradstreet and his son Dudley, Samuel Shrimpton, Bartholomew Gedney, and Peter Bulkley. Their interests were more like those of the leading non-free, and as time went on these two groups tended to draw more closely together until they formed what might be called a moderate party. This party exercised a restraining influence upon the republican tendencies of the Puritan administration and supported the movement which had as its object the "royalizing" of the colony.[8]

Of all the charges brought against the Puritan commonwealth, the most serious were those which concerned trade. Massachusetts made no attempt to enforce the navigation acts and refused to recognize them as binding

---

[8] Edward Randolph, in his report of 1676, gave the impression that large numbers of the prominent people in Boston complained of the oppression of the magistrates and hoped the king would "free them from this bondage by establishing your own royall authority among them and govern them according to your Majesties lawes." *Hutchinson Papers*, Prince Soc., II, 246-247. Culpeper likewise informed the Lords of Trade that when he was in New England he noticed that the generality of the people were very weary of the government of the magistrates. *Cal. State Pap. Col.*, 1681-1685, §74. See also Captain Wyborne's statement that some of the magistrates and principal merchants desired a royal government. *Ibid.*, 1675-1676, §721.

on the colony unless re-enacted by the General Court.[9] She had built her own system of commerce during the Puritan Revolution and did not care to see the prosperity which she was enjoying interfered with. Her trade was expanding in every direction, and she was becoming for the American colonies what England wanted to be for the whole colonial world, the centre of the trading system.

England did not interfere with the commercial activity of the colonies as long as it was limited to colonial exchanges, but when the enumerated articles were taken directly to European ports and the products of those countries brought back contrary to the Staple Act then the English government complained. Not only were colonial markets spoiled for the British merchants but their Continental markets were also interfered with. Objections to these infringements were made on two grounds: hindrance to the trade of England and impairment of the king's revenue. As a remedy the act of 1673 was passed, which provided that colonial shippers, taking on any of the enumerated articles, must give bond to carry the goods either to some other colony or to England, Ireland, or Berwick-on-Tweed, and, in case of the former, must pay at the lading port the same duties that would have been paid had the goods been imported into England.[10] Since there was an extensive coastwise trade, it was probably supposed that the enforcement of this act would increase the king's revenue, but its main purpose was the better regulation of colonial commerce.[11] In the first place, it was designed to draw more enumerated articles to England, thereby decreasing the coastwise trade, because traders would find it cheaper to go directly to England with their goods and pay one duty than to go indirectly

[9] *Cal. State Pap. Col.*, 1681-1685, §953, p. 407.
[10] *Statutes of the Realm*, V, 792-793, 25 Charles II, c. 7, secs. ii, iii, iv.
[11] *Cal. State Pap. Col.*, 1675-1676, §900; 1689-1692, §2065.

and pay the duty twice. In the second place, it would make illicit trade with Europe less profitable. The addition of a duty to the costs of production and transportation would increase the price of sale in the foreign markets, where the colonial traders had been underselling the English merchants. If, after paying the colonial duty, the goods were carried illegally to European ports, the English merchants would have a slight advantage over the colonial, owing to a rebate of the import duty allowed them on re-exportation from English ports. If the goods were carried legally, the English merchants would have a much greater advantage, for the colonial merchants had to pay the import duty at English ports, as well as the export duty in America. If the goods were re-exported from England, the rebate was only on the English duty. The duties from the act of 1673 were the first England ever collected in the colonies and required an administrative official establishment resident there. Until this establishment was provided for, the act was unenforced.

After the appointment in 1675 of the Lords of Trade, an expert committee of the Privy Council succeeding the earlier Council for Trade and Plantations, complaints concerning breaches of the navigation acts in Massachusetts were received with even greater frequency than before. English merchants reported that colonial shippers continually traded contrary to the acts of 1663 and 1673. Not only was merchandise imported directly from Europe into New England but it was carried from there to all of the other colonies, where it was sold at far cheaper rates than those at which the English merchants could afford to sell the produce of England. Moreover, the commodities of the plantations were transported to Europe without first coming to England, "so that New England is become the great mart and staple, by which

means the navigation of the kingdom is greatly prejudiced, the King's revenue inexpressibly impaired, the
price of home and foreign commodities lessened, trade
decreased and the King's subjects much impoverished.''
The committee begged that Massachusetts be reduced to
a royal colony or compelled to trade according to the laws
prescribed.[12] Mercers and silk weavers of London likewise petitioned the king that the colonies be forced to
recognize the navigation acts, complaining that New England traders imported into the American colonies, directly from the Continent, silks and stuffs as well as
brandy, sugar, oil, and other commodities.

The Lords of Trade, thinking the time had come ''to
do something effectual for the better regulation of that
Government, or else all hope of it may be hereafter lost,''
began a systematic investigation to find out exactly what
trade laws applied to the colonies and the extent of the
violation. They first asked the opinion of the Commissioners of Customs on these points and were informed
that the law of 1673 had been designed to put a stop to
New England's direct trade to Europe, but was evaded,
to the detriment of the king's revenue and to the menace
of England's position as the centre of trade with the
colonies. The commissioners advised that all governors
be required to take the oath for executing the law and
be instructed also to see that ship-masters give bonds for
transporting the goods according to the terms of the acts.
This advice was accepted, and new instructions and lists
of queries were accordingly sent to the governors. At the
same time a proclamation was issued informing the colonies of the trade laws which applied to them.[13]

The committee went further and sought for other
sources of information concerning trade conditions in

---

[12] *Cal. State Pap. Col.*, 1675-1676, §§ 787, 789, 797, 879, 884.
[13] *Ibid.*, 1675-1676, §§ 556, 568, 694, 695, 713; 1676-1677, §848.

the colonies. The merchants who complained were ordered to appear and make good their statements, and depositions were taken from ship-captains and from New Englanders who happened to be in London.[14] The charges against Massachusetts were of so serious a nature that the Lords of Trade thought it wise to dispatch a special agent, Edward Randolph, to New England to get first-hand information. Upon his return, Randolph reported that there existed in Massachusetts an utter disregard of the acts of trade, and that when he remonstrated against this condition of affairs, the government denied that parliament had any right to make laws for the colony or the king to hear appeals from its courts. He also reported that the faction in control continued to oppress the non-free, who longed for the establishment of royal authority in Massachusetts.[15]

Randolph advised an immediate regulation of the colony by forcibly cutting off trade, but the Lords of Trade thought such action too stringent. They decided to recommend the issue of a supplementary charter which should define the relationship of Massachusetts to England, reserving to the king certain rights which Massachusetts refused to recognize, and granting to that colony privileges which she had already presumed to exercise as rights. They made known their decision to the agents whom Massachusetts had sent after a long delay, assuring them that there was no intention on England's part to annul the charter. They informed the agents of the charges against the colony, some of which, they said, were errors of attitude, some errors of action. They tried to explain the former, and to make clear that the latter,

14 *Cal. State Pap. Col.*, 1675-1676, §§721, 871, 880, 881, 889, 898.

15 *Ibid.*, 1675-1676, §§953, 1037, 1067; *Hutchinson Papers*, Prince Soc., II, 219, 235, 247.

especially breaches of the trade laws, must be corrected at once.[16]

The Lords of Trade were much impressed with the deportment of the agents, who were able to convince them that the attitude of Massachusetts was due to ignorance of her obligations to England. They were led to expect that she would accept the supplementary charter gracefully and correct the error of her ways. But they were doomed to disappointment, for Massachusetts took no notice "of those points which were soe fairly and with soe much softness, intimated here to the agents."[17]

At this juncture, the lords became convinced that no settlement could be made by conciliation. The colony must have a royal governor, and the charter of 1629, if it stood in the way, must be vacated. Their first task, therefore, was to ascertain the legal security of the patent, for which purpose they sought the opinion of the attorney-general and the solicitor-general. They asked concerning the validity of the charter as originally granted, its status after the *quo warranto* of 1635, and the effect of the corporation's recent maladministration on its legality. The crown lawyers replied that the *quo warranto* had not been effective, but that the action of Massachusetts was sufficient to justify the annulment of the charter. This gave the Lords of Trade a legal basis for procedure, but before any action could be taken on this report, the Popish Plot intervened and a settlement was postponed.[18]

Up to this time, England had made no attempt to enforce the acts of trade in New England except through the local machinery. Customs officials, previously considered unnecessary because the northern colonies had none of the enumerated commodities, were now ap-

[16] *Cal. State Pap. Col.*, 1675-1676, §953; 1677-1680, §§41, 289, 290, 294, 295; Toppan, *Edward Randolph*, II, 277-280, 283-284.

[17] Toppan, *Randolph*, II, 289-298.

[18] *Ibid.*, 295; III, 3-5; *Cal. State Pap. Col.*, 1677-1680, §996.

pointed to take duties arising from the act of 1673, and the threat of boycotting the plantation trade was held over the colonies if they refused to admit them. Randolph was appointed collector, surveyor, and searcher of the customs for New England with his office at Boston, and well-defined instructions were given to him concerning the laws in force and his duties in administering them.[19] The office of surveyor-general of the customs, provided for by the act of 1673, was established and William Dyre was made the incumbent.[20]

Massachusetts was quite concerned over these signs that the navigation acts were to be enforced. She first instructed her agents in England to petition for free trade[21] and then began to pass laws designed to preserve the control of the shipping and trade in her own hands. If the British commercial system must be recognized, there was no reason why the colony should concede to the mother country the political right to control its administration. Therefore, the General Court adopted enactments for the observance of the British laws, but left it to the governor and council to ''imploy such persons in the severall ports as they shall see meet.''[22] By

[19] The instructions to Randolph are printed in 3 Mass. Hist. Soc. *Col.*, VII, 129.

[20] *Mass. Col. Rec.*, V, 530; Toppan, *Randolph*, III, 339.

[21] See a letter of John Hull, the treasurer of Massachusetts, to the colony's agents in England, cited in Hanscom, *Heart of the Puritan*, pp. 147-148.

[22] This attitude is well shown in the answer made by the General Court to the charges of the Lords of Trade against them, in October, 1678. ''That for the acts passed in Parliament for encouraging trade & navigation, wee humbly conceive, according to the usual sayings of the learned in the lawe that the lawes of England are bounded within the fower seas, and doe not reach America. The subjects of his majtie here being not represented in Parliament, so wee have not looked at ourselves to be impeded in our trade by them, nor yett wee abated in our relative allegiance to his majtie. However, so soone as wee understood his Maj'ties pleasure, that those acts should be observed by his maj'ties subjects of the Massachusetts, which

these arrangements, Randolph's commission was ignored.

Randolph met with every possible obstruction in the performance of his duty. The General Court issued an order, October 27, 1680, that all outward-bound vessels of more than twelve tons should have a permit from the governor or his appointee, an arrangement which allowed ships to go out without Randolph's inspection of their lading.[23] As long as Leverett, who represented "the faction," was governor, Randolph could expect no aid from him, for he refused to take the oath for enforcement of the navigation laws. Finding that his first commission as collector was almost useless, Randolph asked for and obtained one under the great seal, for which he thought they would have more respect.[24] Bradstreet, who became acting governor on Leverett's death in 1680, belonged to the moderate party and was much more favorably disposed. He urged that Randolph's new commission be recognized, but "the faction" maintained that it was against their charter right of choosing their own officers.[25]

could not be w'thout invading the liberties and propperties of the subject, until the General Court made provission therein by a law, which they did in Oct. 1677, and shall be strictly attended from time to time, altho the same be a discouragement to trade, and a great damage to his maj'ties plantation, untill wee shall obteyne his majesties gracious favour for that liberty of trade wch wee are not w'thout hopes but his maj'tie will see just occasion to grant to us." *Mass. Col. Rec.*, V, 200-201.

23 *Mass. Col. Rec.*, V, 290.

24 Toppan, *Randolph*, III, 66-67. In one of the rebutting arguments in a seizure trial, it was maintained "that the Commissioners of the Customs had no power to depute an officer to act in that country." *Cal. State Pap. Col.*, 1677-1680, §1383; 1681-1685, §580.

25 When Randolph arrived at Boston with the new commission, he was not allowed to read it openly in court. His deputies were imprisoned for acting by virtue of the commission, and an old law was revived by the General Court to try him for his life for acting under the commission before it was allowed by them, on the charge that he was attempting the subversion

Ignoring this second commission, the General Court, through the efforts of "the faction" passed an act, establishing a naval office for the enforcement of the British acts of trade. James Russell, who was already the colony's collector of the duty on wines, was appointed to the place with a deputy at Salem. The moderates opposed the measure, but without success. The governor refused to swear in the naval officer, whereupon the oath was administered by Danforth, the deputy governor.[26] This brought about a conflict of jurisdictions, and Randolph found it quite impossible to enforce the acts of trade when the entries were made only at the naval office. The governor refused to recognize Russell, and would give no passes to ships outward bound until the masters produced Randolph's certificate that he had visited them. His action met with the disapproval of "the faction," who disciplined him by ordering his salary paid in corn at three shillings six pence a bushel, which was above the market price.[27]

The Naval Office Act was an application of the colony's theory that the laws of the British parliament did not apply to Massachusetts unless re-enacted by the General Court. It provided for the publishing of the navigation acts of 1660 and 1663, but omitted mention of all the others. In place of the act of 1673, to which the chief objections were raised, a similar measure was passed, but more favorable to the colony's trading interests. This measure released all vessels carrying on a coastwise trade from the requirement to give bond, provided they did not take on board more than one ton of each of the enumerated commodities.[28]

of the government. *Cal. State Pap. Col.*, 1681-1685, §580; Toppan, *Randolph*, III, 150.

[26] *Cal. State Pap. Col.*, 1681-1685, §§526, 579, 580.

[27] *Ibid*, 1681-1685, §580.

[28] *Mass. Col. Rec.*, V, 337-338. The commission to James Russell as naval

To preserve further the colony's right to administer the trade laws within its own limits, the Naval Office Act provided that the royal officers and informers could ask the governor, deputy governor, or magistrates to issue warrants to constables and marshals for assistance in the prosecution of the acts of trade. Without a warrant, no seizures could be made.[29] By an addition to the act, made a year later, Randolph was empowered to seize any ship suspected of illegal trading, to search all outward-bound vessels, and to put waiters on board all ships inward bound. By this act, the colony was apparently conferring power, but in reality not, Randolph being helpless as long as he did not have access to the records at the naval office.[30]

Randolph also found it difficult to get a fair trial of breaches of the acts in the court of assistants which sat as an admiralty court, and because the jurors were often interested parties condemnations were rare. If Randolph asked for a special session of the court, in order that a case might be tried immediately, he was required to deposit a security against damages. When decisions were rendered against him, as they usually were, he was denied the right of appeal to England. Most annoying of all, owners of vessels that had been seized and acquitted often retaliated by suing him for damages.[31]

officer is printed in the same volume, p. 338. *Cal. State Pap. Col.*, 1681-1685, §579.

[29] Although the court of assistants, in a seizure trial, declared that Randolph's deputation and instructions from the commissioners of the customs were valid, and his letters patent sufficient for searching and seizing without any authority from the colony government unless he or his deputies requested it, the General Court insisted that the king's officers could not make seizures in the colony without a warrant. *Cal. State Pap. Col.*, 1681-1685, §580; Toppan, *Randolph*, III, 150.

[30] Whitmore, *The Colonial Laws of Massachusetts* (1887), p. 298. This edition is a reprint from the 1672 edition, with additions to 1686. *Mass. Col. Rec.*, V, 383-384.

[31] The king in a letter to the Governor and Company, Oct. 21, 1681, told

When the Lords of Trade again took up the matter of reforming Massachusetts, they found that her misdemeanors had increased and her manner had become even more insolent. She had continued to disobey the navigation acts, had appropriated to her own use the funds due the king from fines and forfeitures, had not extended her suffrage, although continuing to tax the non-freemen, had bought Maine of the Gorges heirs, knowing that the king desired to purchase it, continued to deny the right of the crown to supervise her laws and courts, and had again ignored the king's demands to send agents to England, empowered to treat regarding a regulation of the charter.[32] In a letter of October 21, 1681, the Lords of Trade threatened the colony with a *quo warranto* if agents were not dispatched at once, authorized to accept, in the name of the colony, a supplementary charter.[33]

Massachusetts dared not procrastinate any longer.

them that they must allow prosecution of appeals of offenders under the acts of trade without charge, as in England, and must admit appeals about revenue. *Cal. State Pap. Col.*, 1681-1685, §§264, i. See also, *ibid.*, 1681-1685, §§45, 122, p. 60, 1383, 1494, 1529; Toppan, *Randolph*, III, 185.

One cannot help feeling a little sympathy for Randolph's discouragement because of his inability to make much headway in enforcing the acts of trade. He admitted to Southwell in 1685 that he had slackened his prosecutions because he could never obtain a conviction for his majesty in Boston courts. Moreover, he had never been allowed one penny toward all the charges and expenses he had been at in prosecuting. No wonder he ''was tired out with tedious journeys and no profit which could not be expected should be otherwise till the Govt was altered & new laws made there to prevent that trade complained of.'' *Ibid.*, IV, 5. Nevertheless our sympathy for the man is bound to be tempered somewhat by the unmistakable infirmities of disposition and judgment that characterized his relations with all those with whom he came into official contact. He got on no better with Copley in Maryland than with the Puritans in Massachusetts.

[32] Hutchinson, *Hist. of Mass.*, I, 334; 4 Mass. Hist. Soc. *Col.*, V, 56; *Cal. State Pap. Col.*, 1685-1688, §580.

[33] Public Record Office, Colonial Office, Class 1, vol. 47, no. 79; an extract of this letter is in *Cal. State Pap. Col.*, 1681-1685, §266. The letter is a history of the misdeeds of the colony from its earliest settlement.

Agents were chosen, but were instructed by the General Court to take no steps in the matter of the charter. When the agents arrived in England, the Lords of Trade told them to get instructions or the *quo warranto* would proceed. Again and again the General Court instructed them not to act concerning the points in question,—extension of the suffrage, religious liberty, and such matters. Finally they were told that if the lords insisted on charter changes or on the right to hear appeals they were to bargain for non-intervention by an offer of Maine. If objections were made to practices in which the charter did not protect them, they were to promise reform.[34]

This action brought matters to a head. When the lords found out that again the agents had only limited powers, they recommended that a writ of *quo warranto* be issued at once. Their report was confirmed by order in council, June 3, 1683.[35] Fearing lest "the faction" might stir up a revolt, the king issued a declaration promising to respect all private interests in spite of the *quo warranto* and to regulate the charter liberally if the colony would submit without further ado. At the same time, he forbade the spending of public money for defense of the charter

[34] *Mass. Col. Rec.*, V, 333-334; 346-349, 370-371; 4 Mass. Hist. Soc. *Col.*, V, 82; *Cal. State Pap. Col.*, 1681-1685, §§416, 558, 527, 529, 662, 1024, 1032. Massachusetts seems temporarily to have managed her case with a great deal of skill, for Randolph wrote June 14, 1682, to Sir Leoline Jenkins, in great concern for fear no action would be taken. He said that the poor people were heavily taxed to pay the expenses of the agents, and that the last ones in England brought £4,000 to account, "part of which was disposed of to persons of great station at Court by whose help together with that of their Counsel, the Attorney General, Sir William Jones, they averted the King's intended alterations in their government." He added grimly, "I will stake my good reputation that if the agents come back with an olive branch, that branch will be a fatal tree for me." *Ibid.*, §559.

[35] 4 Mass. Hist. Soc. *Col.*, II, 293-294; *Cal. State Pap. Col.*, 1681-1685, §§1120, 1124, 1134, 1142, 1152, 1159, 1165, 1677.

and the taxing for this purpose of those who were willing to submit.[36]

The *quo warranto* and the declaration stirred to flame the factional fires that had long been smoldering in the colony. In the General Court, the council, where the moderates were strong, favored submission, because regulation seemed inevitable and immediate acquiescence promised a more satisfactory settlement. In the House of Deputies, however, "the faction" who were in control fought bitterly against acceptance and were finally successful in getting a vote to employ an agent for defending the charter at law.[37]

Outside the General Court, the colony was in a turmoil. The non-free were petitioning the king for a royal government,[38] while the Puritans in Boston, under the leadership of the ministers and elders, campaigned to win the support of public opinion in favor of a defense of the charter. Mather attended the town meeting, and after the non-free had been expelled made a great emotional appeal which brought a unanimous vote against submission.[39] "The faction" carried the battle into the next election where they fought to oust from office the moderates who had voted for surrender. Although Governor Bradstreet was re-elected, Dudley, Browne, and Gedney were left out of the magistracy, whereupon Bulkley and Stoughton resigned. A great display was made of their action, for they were conducted to their homes by a mounted procession of about seventy prominent merchants and gentlemen. Randolph was pleased to see this

36 *Ibid.*, 1681-1685, §§1145, 1159; Toppan, *Randolph*, III, 243-244, 246-247.

37 *Mass. Col. Rec.*, V, 421-423, 424, 439-441; *Cal. State Pap. Col.*, 1681-1685, §§1145, 1445, 1566; Hutchinson, *Hist. of Mass.* (2d ed.), I, 338-339; Toppan, *Randolph*, III, 273-274.

38 *Cal. State Pap. Col.*, 1681-1685, §1135.

39 *Ibid.*, §1589; Toppan, *Randolph*, III, 283-284.

parting of the ways between "the faction" and the moderate Puritans, for he thought the latter could now be counted upon, with the leading non-freemen, to support a royal government.[40]

Meanwhile the authorities in England were becoming weary of the delays Massachusetts was causing. Since the sheriffs of London objected to returning a summons on the ground that their letter was not delivered until after the return of the *quo warranto* was due, the attorney-general advised proceeding by a *scire facias* against the company for the repeal of the patent. A writ was sued out from the Court of Chancery directed to the sheriffs of London and returnable in Easter term, 1684.[41] The governor and company not appearing at the appointed time, another writ similar to the last was issued, returnable in Trinity term. The governor and company appeared by their constituted attorney and counsel, but refused to plead, asking time to send to New England. Although contrary to the rules of the court, a concession was made, allowing them until the first day of Michaelmas term. If they failed, judgment was to be entered by default. They did not plead, so on October 23, 1684, the charter was declared null and void.[42]

A copy of the judgment against the charter arrived in

[40] Toppan, *Randolph*, III, 310-311, 317; *Cal. State Pap. Col.*, 1681-1685, §§1670, 1589, 1808.

[41] *Cal. State Pap. Col.*, 1681-1685, §1677. News of this change reached Massachusetts in September, 1684, by a private letter to Joseph Dudley. The General Court wrote at once to Humfreys that they were "amased" at the new measures taken at court, and had called a special session to consider what to do. When it met, an address to the king was prepared, in which they begged the continuance of the charter and its privileges, having just heard that a *scire facias* had been issued out of chancery against them, returnable in six weeks, without legal notice, and judgment entered thereon. *Mass. Col. Rec.*, V, 458.

[42] *Cal. State Pap. Col.*, §§1681-1685, 1742, 1755, 1762, 1902, 1928; *Andros Tracts*, I, 33-34; Kimball, *Joseph Dudley*, pp. 20-21.

Boston on July 1,[43] while the General Court was in session. There does not seem to have been the slightest idea of forcible resistance, for the question which immediately came up, was whether the General Court should surrender the government at once, or wait until the king's commission came establishing the new administration. The matter was as usual left to the elders to decide, and they advised waiting.[44] Their counsel was accepted, and the General Court voted adjournment. From this time on, until the arrival of the commission for the royal governor in May, 1686, the old government proceeded to exercise all of its functions, although it had no legal basis for existence. For "the faction," it was a period of great depression and of bitter hostility toward the moderates who had been in favor of submission. They were looked upon as traitors and some of them received

[43] Rumors that the charter had been vacated reached the colony before January, 1685. Moved by these reports, the governor and company sent a very humble address to the king, complaining that they had never had any legal notice of the *scire facias* against their charter and could not possibly appear in the allotted time to defend it. They protested having intention of doing anything contrary to the king's prerogative or oppressing his subjects. They implored pardon for all errors and asked for a continuation of the liberties granted in their charter. This was probably due to the influence of the moderate party, for Bradstreet at the same time wrote Randolph implying that they hoped the king would pardon them and continue the government "in such a way as is intimated in his Majesty's gracious declaration to which myself and several of the magistrates voted a submission." An address of this date to the king is given in 2 Mass. Hist. Soc. *Proc.*, XIII, 331, which, as is there stated, was probably offered by John Richards as a substitute for the one adopted by the General Court. This letter is given in *Diary of Samuel Sewall*, 1674-1729 (5 Mass. Hist. Soc. *Col.*, V VII), I, 79-80, and was drawn up by a committee of the General Court consisting of Samuel Sewall and Elisha Cooke. *Mass. Col. Rec.*, V, 466-467; Toppan, *Randolph*, III, 337; Sewall, *Diary*, I, 85.

[44] *Mass. Col. Rec.*, V, 492, 494. Several ministers present expressed dissent to this, saying that Mr. Hubbard was not authorized to speak for all of them. Sewall, *Diary*, I, 89; Mass. Hist. Soc. *Proc.*, 1871-1873, pp. 105-107 and note.

public marks of popular disapprobation. "Black boxes" were sent to Stoughton and Dudley, who were later "grossly abused on the road" by a crowd of people.[45]

Too much has been made of the annulment of the charter as a punitive measure. There was very little of that in it. It was simply England's last resort when Massachusetts refused to adapt herself to England's commercial scheme. She was fast becoming a formidable commercial rival and competitor, and was drifting away from a close political and institutional relationship with the mother country. She faced two paths: either to accept the restrictions and privileges of her colonial position or to sever her connections with England. The latter path she was not ready to take in 1660, as appears from the acceptance by the theocrats of the pro-English point of view of the moderates. She preferred to fall back on her charter as a guarantee against the interference of the mother country, denying that the laws of parliament applied to her, and that the king could inspect her laws and hear appeals from her courts. England had never surrendered the right to legislate for her colonies, and she now claimed the supervising power over laws and courts, on the grounds of the charter provision that the laws must be conformable to those of England.

Massachusetts went still further. She had, during the period of her virtual independence, usurped powers not granted in the charter. England was justified in asking that she either give these up or accept a supplementary charter, which would grant her many of the powers she had already illegally exercised and which would also define her relationship to the mother country. When Massachusetts refused to conform to her charter, to accept a supplementary one, to recognize the right of the

45 Mass. Hist. Soc. *Proc.*, 1871-1873, pp. 78-79, 100, 101.

mother country to control her trade in the interests of
her economic empire, or to share the government with
the pro-English element, England could do nothing else
than withdraw the charter.

CHAPTER II

AN EXPERIMENT IN CONSOLIDATION

The appointment in 1675 of the special committee of
the Privy Council as a board of trade and plantations
was a recognition on the part of the British government
of the need of greater attention and more vigorous action
in matters of colonial policy. This committee immediately
took up the task of defining and establishing the relationships of the various New England colonies to the
mother country. The position of Massachusetts was, of
course, the greatest problem, but while attempting to
persuade her to accept an explanatory charter, the lords
examined also the claims of the Mason and Gorges heirs
to New Hampshire and Maine respectively and offered
Plymouth a royal charter which would give that colony
a legal right to exist and extend her boundaries to include
the territory called Mount Hope, won from the Indians
in King Philip's War.[1]

The claims of the Mason and Gorges heirs were based
on the royal charters supposed to have been granted
after the New England Council had surrendered its
patent in 1635. These claims the Lords of Trade referred
to the chief justice of the king's bench, who reported
that as regards Maine, the charter had been issued to
Gorges, giving him the possession of the territory and

[1] *Records of the Colony of New Plymouth in New England*, VI, 36-37;
4 Mass. Hist. Soc. Col., V, 181, 323.

the right to govern it,[2] but that as regards New Hampshire, the charter had never passed the seals, and, consequently, the government of the province never having been given to Mason, only his proprietary claims to the soil could be recognized.[3] Since the chief justice dismissed, with scant attention, the claims of Massachusetts that both colonies were included within her charter grant, the colonies were by this decision left without provision of government. Consequently, New Hampshire was made a royal province under the temporary administration of a native council,[4] while Maine was turned over to the Gorges heirs, whose claims the king tried to buy out, intending to give the province to his son, the Duke of Monmouth. While he was dallying with the negotiations, Massachusetts bought the province and proceeded to govern it as a propriety, much to the chagrin of the king.

The offer of a charter to Plymouth had been made at a time when the Lords of Trade hoped to regulate Massachusetts without taking away her charter, but as the conviction grew that this was impossible they thought it wise to grant no more charters giving such complete powers of government to a colony. Consequently Blathwayt wrote the General Court of Plymouth in 1683 that it was not probable anything further would be decided upon "until His Majesty forsee an issue of proceedings in relation to the Massachusetts colony," and that if Massachusetts were brought under a direct dependence on the crown, Plymouth would be also.[5]

The failure of the Lords of Trade to persuade Massa-

2 *Cal. State Pap. Col.*, 1681-1685, §1955; *Acts of the Privy Council of England, Colonial Series*, I, §1159.

3 *Acts, Privy Coun. Col.*, §§1199, 1284; *Cal. State Pap. Col.*, 1677-1680, §1045.

4 *Laws of New Hampshire*, I, 1-8; *Cal. State Pap. Col.*, 1677-1680, §§912, 1031; *Acts, Privy Coun. Col.*, I, §1293.

5 4 *Mass. Hist. Soc. Col.*, V, 91, 93; Toppan, *Randolph*, III, 317.

chusetts to accept a supplementary charter shook their
confidence in the possibility of enforcing any colonial
policy in the colonies having charters. They were particularly concerned over the fact that wherever the king
had granted away his right of government it seemed
almost impossible to enforce the acts of trade. Circular
letters on the subject were sent to all governors of proprietary and corporate as well as royal colonies, but
where the governors were not directly responsible to the
king, very little attention was paid to them. The lords
were soon convinced that unless there was more direct
control of the colonies, England could never develop her
commercial plans. There seemed to be only one course to
follow, and that was to vacate the charters. Consequently,
quo warrantos were issued against Connecticut, Rhode
Island,[6] the Jerseys,[7] Pennsylvania,[8] Maryland,[9] the
Carolinas,[10] the Bahamas,[11] and Bermuda.[12]

One great difficulty stood in the way of reducing all of
the colonies to governments of the royal type, and that
was expense. England could not afford to maintain a
separate establishment in each of the colonies, nor could
the colonies themselves bear the burden of expense which

[6] On May 5, 1865, the Lords of Trade ordered Randolph to "prepare a
paper containing all such particulars upon which a Quo Warranto may bee
grounded against their Charters." Upon his report, an order in council
was issued July 17, 1685, which commissioned the attorney-general to bring
in writs of *quo warranto* against the two colonies. Toppan, *Randolph*, IV,
18-19, 26; *Acts, Privy Coun. Col.*, II, §194; *Cal. State Pap. Col.*, 1685-1688,
§§632, 645.

[7] *Cal. State Pap. Col.*, 1685-1688, §§283, 632, 645, 411; *Acts, Privy Coun.
Col.*, II, §195; *Records of the Colony of Rhode Island and Providence Plantations in New England*, III, 176, 177, 178.

[8] Toppan, *Randolph*, IV, 4-5; *Acts, Privy Coun. Col.*, II, §209.

[9] *Ibid.*, §88; Toppan, *Randolph*, IV, 4-5, 26-27; *Cal. State Pap. Col.*,
1685-1688, §§320, 632, 645.

[10] *Ibid.*, 1685-1688, §767; *Acts, Privy Coun. Col.*, II, §209.

[11] *Ibid.*, §209.

[12] *Ibid.*, I, §§1317, 1333; II, §§25, 136.

the introduction of English officials in each would involve. Cranfield, the governor of New Hampshire, complained bitterly about Mason's misrepresentations concerning the ability of that province to support a royal government,[13] while Dongan, the governor of New York, frequently reported that the revenues of that colony were insufficient for the maintenance of government there.[14] Connecticut and Rhode Island were too small to attract a desirable governor, while the poverty of Maine and Plymouth was so evident that it would be difficult to find appointees willing to accept posts as poor as these promised to be.[15] Consequently, a reduction in the number of governors was inevitable.

While considering the case of Massachusetts, the lords came to see what great advantages could be gained by the union of all of the New England colonies under one governor.[16] Royalization, it is true, would make possible the enforcement of the acts of trade, thereby removing a dangerous competitor in the foreign and colonial markets and augmenting the king's revenues, but union would offer greater opportunities for the development of a constructive commercial programme for the turning of trade into new channels and for the production of staples such as England herself needed and desired. The Lords of Trade were particularly interested in the development of naval stores, which England wanted more than anything else from her colonies, in order that she might be freed from dependence on the northern

[13] Goodrick, *Randolph,* VI, 120.

[14] *Cal. State Pap. Col.,* 1685-1688, §§1429-III, 1638, 1479.

[15] *Hutchinson Papers,* Prince Soc., II, 145.

[16] The lords reported to the Council in 1681 that in their opinion New England could not be brought to a perfect settlement unless a general governor be sent over and maintained there at the king's charge. *Cal. State Pap. Col.,* 1681-1685, §82.

crowns.[17] Such a policy would require considerable effort, for control of the woods was necessary to prevent the ruthless destruction of small trees, and efforts must be made to encourage the manufacture of naval products and the raising of hemp. These things could be done wisely only by some one who thoroughly understood conditions in all parts of New England and who was in a position to direct the production according to the needs and ability of each locality.[18] A great interest also was taken at this time in mining. Bloomeries were worked successfully in New England, and there were prospects of the development of lead and copper. For all this, capital was needed, which prominent English financiers were willing to furnish, providing there was a stable government in that part of the colonial world which would give all possible encouragement to local enterprises.[19]

Union was needed also for defense. It was quite evident that the colonies, acting as separate units, could not adequately protect themselves against possible aggression from the Dutch, the French, and the Indians.[20] After the third Dutch War, 1673-1674, rivalry with Holland

[17] Toppan, *Randolph*, IV, 34, 42, 93; *Cal. State Pap. Col.*, 1675-1676, §721; 1681-1685, §91.

[18] The necessity of co-operation on the part of all the New England colonies in the production of naval stores was appreciated by the colonists themselves, as is shown by the action of the general courts of Massachusetts and Plymouth when Richard Wharton, prime mover in a company formed in 1671 for developing naval stores, applied for monopoly privileges. Each colony granted them on condition that he be given similar privileges by the other colonies of the federation. *Plymouth Col. Rec.*, V, 65; *New England Historical Register*, IX, 339.

[19] C. O. 5: 855, no. 90; *Hutchinson Papers*, Prince Soc., II, 145, 222; Toppan, *Randolph*, IV, 4, 221; *Cal. State Pap. Col.*, 1685-1688, §§901, 1629, 1809, 1839, 1840, 1850, 1855, 1859, 1863; *Andros Tracts*, III, 6-8; 6 Mass. Hist. Soc. *Col.*, V, 14-15.

[20] Toppan, *Randolph*, II, 303-304; *Cal. State Pap. Col.*, 1677-1680, §357; 1681-1685, §91.

was no longer a matter of much concern, but the menace of France as England's greatest rival in the colonizing world was already in evidence. King Philip's War had proven that the colonies were unable to conduct with efficiency military campaigns on a large scale, while the threatening attitude taken by the French toward New York, the Newfoundland fisheries, and the West Indies rendered the prospect of war in the near future a matter of serious concern.[21] A single governmental establishment would greatly simplify also the supervision of colonial laws and the maintenance of legal practices consistent with the laws of England. The governor and council would constitute a central court of appeals where justice could be obtained by those against whom the local courts had shown prejudice, and a court of original jurisdiction for the trial of cases involving matters of more than local concern.[22]

With these considerations in view, the lords were anxious to try the experiment of consolidating all the New England colonies under a single head, and an opportunity was soon offered by the success of the proceedings against the Massachusetts Bay charter. They agreed at the outset to annex Maine, New Hampshire, Plymouth, and the Narragansett Country to Massachusetts, and to

[21] *Hutchinson Papers*, Prince Soc., II, 246; Toppan, *Randolph*, II, 303; *Cal. State Pap. Col.*, 1685-1688, §925. Richard Wharton wrote in 1676 to a friend in England that "except God give greater wisdom to their rulers or put it into the King's heart to rule and relieve them, the colonies will soon be ruined and they reduced to the necessity of subjecting upon any terms to any one that will protect them." *Cal. State Pap. Col.*, 1675-1676, §816.

[22] Richard Wharton and others petitioned the king in 1680 to erect a court of claims in New England to determine all private claims and pretensions and to ascertain bounds between the colonies. Randolph had previously pointed out the necessity of erecting a "Great Council" from all the colonies with a president as a court of appeal from the several judicatures. *Cal. State Pap. Col.*, 1677-1680, §1532; Toppan, *Randolph*, III, 57, 263.

add Connecticut and Rhode Island as soon as the charters of these colonies could be vacated by the *quo warranto* proceedings instituted against them.[23]

These plans for the unification of New England were quite in keeping with the ideas of the Duke of York concerning the middle colonies. In 1664, he had been granted an extensive territory reaching from the Connecticut River to the Delaware, and he intended to make it a model propriety by developing it in conformity with England's new commercial and colonial policy, at the same time endeavoring to augment his personal income by profit from trade and the customs revenues. He planned to make New York City the chief port of trade for all of the colonies, as well as the distributing centre for the back country to the northward, and hoped, with the help of the Five Nations, to draw to that city the Indian trade in peltry from the vast country around the Great Lakes and the St. Lawrence River. A large revenue was expected from an export duty on furs and from a ten percent import duty on other products.

Several factors contributed to thwart these expectations. In the first place the Duke of York unwisely subleased the Jerseys to two of his friends without reserving governmental control, thereby allowing them to develop the commerce of their proprieties to their own

[23] Toppan, *Randolph*, III, 324-325. At this time New Hampshire was a royal colony, New Plymouth was independent and self-governing, but without a charter, while Maine was still governed by Massachusetts. The annexation of the Narragansett Country brought to an end a long series of disputes over possession of the land and jurisdiction. The land had been claimed by Connecticut and Rhode Island, by the Atherton Company of Massachusetts, and by the Earl of Arran, representing the original Hamilton grant. Commissioners appointed by the king in 1684 to inquire into these claims reported their opinion that the jurisdiction belonged to Connecticut and the soil to the Atherton Company, whereupon the Lords of Trade advised adding it to the Dominion. *Cal. State Pap. Col.*, 1681-1685, §§1986, 2017.

advantage. East Jersey especially contributed to the decay of trade at New York, because her chief port of entry, Perth Amboy, was a free port, and goods coming up the river were landed in New Jersey without paying customs, and then smuggled into New York. This freedom of trade not only attracted immigrants from England, but tended to draw New York inhabitants into New Jersey.[24] The granting of Pennsylvania to William Penn completed the ruin of his enterprise, for the peltry trade with the Five Nations was diverted down the Susquehanna and the Delaware, to the detriment of the fur trade of New York and the loss of the duke's revenues.[25] Once having realized his mistake, the duke tried to get the East Jersey proprietors to agree to a governmental union with New York, but they refused, and because they had legal possession by grant from himself, which had been confirmed by the king, he could do nothing except instruct the governor of New York to make every effort to prevent the Jerseys and Pennsylvania from "obstructing the peltry trade."[26] Another discouragement was the loss of the land west of the Connecticut River, due to the priority of Connecticut's title to the territory, based on an earlier royal charter.[27] The duke and his representatives in the propriety hoped to raise foodstuffs in this region and to produce a few staples to be used in an exchange trade with England and Massachusetts for manufactured articles. Stripped of all these contributing parts of the original grant, New York had small chance of economic development unless, by reciprocal trade agreements, a larger economic unit could be formed

[24] *Cal. State Pap. Col.*, 1681-1685, §§1847, 2078; 1685-1688, §§1014, 1160, p. 327.

[25] *Ibid.*, 1685-1688, §1160, pp. 327, 334-335.

[26] *Ibid.*, 1681-1685, §§1583, 1841, 1848; *New York Col. Docs.*, III, 330.

[27] *Cal. State Pap. Col.*, 1677-1680, §222; 1675-1676, §795; 1685-1688, §1160, pp. 326, 334.

which would bind together the lost provinces for commercial purposes. It was very doubtful if such an economic co-operation could ever be arranged without political union, because of the commercial restrictions imposed
by neighboring colonies.

In his political plans also the duke was disappointed.
He desired to pattern the government of his propriety
after that of the French colonies, where there was a
strongly centralized administration without self-governing institutions, but when the Jersey colonists received a
representative assembly from their proprietors, those
of New York demanded one also. This the duke agreed
to give, if the colonists would guarantee a permanent
fund for the support of the government, so that he need
not depend upon a popular assembly for appropriations.
The matter having been arranged, Governor Dongan,
who was sent over at this juncture, was instructed to call
an assembly. It met in 1683, and drew up a ''Charter of
Liberties and Privileges,'' which was sent to the duke's
commissioners for approval. Thus after having tried for
nearly twenty years to govern without a popular assembly, James was apparently driven to the point of granting one. The situation was saved by the death of Charles
II and the accession of the Duke of York as king of
England, whereupon the colony automatically changed
its status to that of a royal province. This gave James his
opportunity to attempt the reunion of the lost provinces
in the interests of trade and revenue.[28]

Under James II, the plans for consolidation went on
rapidly and began to assume larger proportions. Accord-

[28] *New York Col. Docs.*, III, 317, 231-232, 341, 348, 354, 355. An entry
in the journal of the Lords of Trade for March 3, 1685, states that the
charter of New York was considered, but that his Majesty ''doth not think
fitt to confirm the same. And as to the government of New York, his Majesty
is pleased to direct that it be assimilated to the Constitution that shall be
agreed on for New England.'' *Ibid.*, III, 357.

ing to these plans two groups and possibly three were to be formed, the first to include the New England colonies, the second, the territories comprised in the duke's grant of 1664,—New York and the Jerseys,—and Delaware, which had been given to William Penn.[29] There is insufficient evidence to prove the existence of a plan to add the southern colonies also, but it is reasonable to suppose that such was the case, since *quo warrantos* were issued against the southern proprietors as well as those of the north.[30] The delay in carrying out this plan was no doubt due to the difficulty in bringing about a vacation of the charters. Baltimore, Penn, and the Carolina proprietors all seem to have made a successful defense before the law.

Evidently Charles II had intended to add Connecticut and Rhode Island to the northern New England group where they naturally belonged, since their interests, especially those of Connecticut, were very similar to the interests of the other New England colonies,[31] but the representatives of James II wished to join them to the middle group, because they were badly needed there for the de-

---

[29] *Cal. State Pap. Col.*, 1685-1688, §§1014, 1250, 1342; *Rhode Island Col. Rec.*, III, 176; *Public Records of the Colony of Connecticut*, III, 359.

[30] *Cal. State Pap. Col.*, 1685-1688, §§520, 566, 974, 1152. John Saffin wrote to the secretary of Connecticut in June, 1687, ''Sr it is generally received without hesitation that all these parts of America pertaineing to the Crown of England from New Carrolina round about with the sun, (takeing in all the Islands) till it come to the French towards the east, will be brought under a more imediate dependency and subjection to his Majesty, so that all maner of Charters granted to the greatest Favorites & persons of the most notable extraction and highest degree, who consequently have the greatest interest at court, both by their persons and purses, must veile thereto sooner or later, yea and that in a very short time, the most part haveing done it already.'' *Conn. Col. Rec.*, III, 382.

[31] *Conn. Col. Rec.*, III, 363; Toppan, *Randolph*, III, 325; IV, 151, 154; *Cal. State Pap. Col.*, 1685-1668, §925, p. 261.

velopment of New York's agricultural interests.[32] After
Rhode Island had received the writ of *quo warranto*
June 22, 1686, she decided not to stand suit but petitioned
for a continuation of her charter privileges and liberties,
asking especially that "no persons be imposed over them
that suit not the nature and constitution" of the inhabitants. As soon as this petition was received in England,
Andros was instructed to annex Rhode Island to the
Dominion.[33]

If Connecticut ever thought of resisting annexation,
she must have seen very soon the futility of such action,
for it is inconceivable that she could have maintained a
separate and independent existence located as she would
have been between the two large royal colonies. Union
with one group or the other, or division of her territory
at the Connecticut River, was inevitable.[34] Owing to New
York influence, a number of towns in western Connecticut
favored union with the middle group.[35] Commissioners

[32] *Cal. State Pap. Col.*, 1685-1688, §§186, 1160, pp. 326, 327, 330, §§1262,
1270; *New York Col. Docs.*, III, 340-341.

[33] *Rhode Island Col. Rec.*, III, 176-177, 190, 193, 194, 195, 203-204; *Cal.
State Pap. Col.*, 1685-1688, §§750, 844, 857, 902.

[34] Dudley pointed out this fact to Governor Treat in a letter dated July
21, 1686, as follows: "and for that we know that the consideration of the
new modelling and perfect settlement of all his Majesty's Provinces from
Pennsylvania to New York is now lying before his Majesty and probable
to have a sudden and lasting dispatch, and that your parts as lying between
the two seats of government, may be the more easily poysed either way."
Conn. Col. Rec., III, 359. It is difficult to tell whether or not the Lords of
Trade ever seriously considered dividing Connecticut into two parts. The
colony's agent in England wrote that "it was discoursed at Whitehall" to
annex all west of Connecticut to New York. Randolph mentioned the possibility in a letter to Governor Treat, urging the necessity of the colony's
surrender to avoid such a division. Treat wrote at once to Governor Dongan
to inquire if he thought there was any truth in Randolph's threat. A special
session of the General Court was held on July 28, 1686, and a letter sent to
the king begging that the colony be not divided, but disposed of as a whole.
Ibid., 362; *Cal. State Pap. Col.*, 1685-1688, §1237.

[35] *Cal. State Pap. Col.*, 1685-1688, §1237; *Hutchinson Papers*, Prince

from New York attended the General Court at Hartford[36] and persuaded the deputies to surrender their charter and be annexed to New York, but before the letter to the king asking for the union was signed, some of the clergy appeared in the house and exhorted the deputies not to surrender the patent.[37] Meanwhile the council, whose members preferred union with the New England colonies, took matters into its own hands and wrote to the secretary of state that the colony would submit to regulation according to the king's wishes.[38] Consequently Connecticut was added to the New England group, to the great disappointment of the New Yorkers.[39]

During the overtures made by New York to Connecticut, the increasingly hostile and aggressive attitude of the French was causing great alarm in New York. The rivalry over the control of the fur trade of North America had developed into a campaign on the part of the French to win from the English the allegiance of the Five Nations, whose friendship was of great importance because of their location in central and northern New

Soc., II, 298. Even Treat seems to have been not averse to such a union, for he told Dongan that ''It may be as easie for us to fall that way as Eastward. I think I may say that by any of Mr. Randolph says to move us to encline eastward hath not all prejudiced us against yor honor or yor Government.'' Conn. Col. Rec., III, 354.

[36] Cal. State Pap. Col., 1685-1688, §1262.

[37] Ibid., §1270.

[38] Ibid., §1237.

[39] Three writs of quo warranto were issued against Connecticut, the first dated July 17, 1685, the second issued about April 21, 1686, while the third was ordered October 23, 1686, and was received in December. Quo warranto proceedings against the charter were, however, never completed, the colony having surrendered without further action against it. With the arrival of the letter of the council, the Lords of Trade advised that Andros be empowered to accept the colony's submission and take it under his government, and that Treat, the governor, and Allyn, the secretary, be added to the council of the Dominion. An order in Council followed and a letter was dispatched to Andros. Ibid., §§807, 933, 1237, 1308, 1301, 1473, 1497, 1638, p. 499; Laws of New Hampshire, I, 171-172.

York. The French were sending priests among the Indians, building forts in their territory, and attacking those among them who seemed disinclined to accept the French allegiance.[40] Should these schemes succeed, the English would certainly lose the peltry trade, as well as all opportunity for expansion to the north and west.[41] Dongan recommended building forts at strategic places, and garrisoning them with English troops, the expense of which could be borne by the colony if united with Connecticut and the Jerseys. If this union did not take place, he said, New York would be unable to wage war against French aggression, for the revenue of the province had decreased each year until it was scarcely sufficient for paying the expenses of government.[42] At this critical stage, he heard of the annexation of Connecticut to the Dominion of New England. Feeling certain that the addition of the Jerseys to New York would not bring enough revenue to support the civil establishment and furnish means of resisting the encroachments of the French, he urged that New York be likewise added to the New England group.[43] His suggestion was adopted, and a new commission uniting under one government all of the colonies from Pemaquid to Pennsylvania was issued to the governor of New England in 1688.[44] The plan to form two or three administrative units thus came to naught, owing partly to the need of immediate provision for defense, and partly to the inability of the crown to effect the vacation of the charters of the other proprieties.[45]

[40] *Cal. State Pap. Col.*, 1685-1688, §§1146-V, 1262, 1479.

[41] *Ibid.*, §§1494, 1638.

[42] *Ibid.*, §§1146-V, 1429-III, 1494, 1638.

[43] *Ibid.*, §1479.

[44] *Ibid.*, §§1674, 1688.

[45] Without doubt, this union of the New England and the middle colonies would make the English in America appear much more formidable to the French. That the British statesmen so intended it to be is shown by Blathwayt's letter to Randolph, March 11, 1688: ''If the union of all New

The constitution of the Dominion of New England was determined by the commission and instructions which were issued to Governor Andros and modeled on those given to the governors of the first royal colony, Virginia. In the draft of the commission prepared by the Lords of Trade, provision was made for a governor and council to be chosen by the king, and a representative assembly whose members were to be elected by the people.[46] When this draft was sent to the king for his approval, he ordered that no mention be made of the assembly,[47] evi-

England under one governor be acceptable on your side the water, what will the joining and annexing to the same government be, of all the English territories in America, from Delaware-bay to Nova Scotia. This is already determined by his Majesty and a commission is in hand, constituting Sir Edmund Andros governor also of New York as united to New England. And for the two Jerseys, scire facias are expecting towards their union. This, besides other advantages will be terrible to the French, and make them proceed with more caution than they have lately done.'' Cited in Hutchinson, *Hist. of Mass.* (2d ed.), I, 371, note.

[46] *Cal. State Pap. Col.*, 1681-1685, §1928; Toppan, *Randolph*, III, 325.

[47] Toppan, *Randolph*, III, 332; *Cal. State Pap. Col.*, 1681-1685, §1953. It is probable that the Duke of York was more responsible for this decision than anyone else. He had expressed his opinion to Andros in January, 1676, while the latter was governor of New York, that he could not but ''suspect an assembly would be of dangerous consequences, nothing being more known than the aptness of such bodies to assume privileges destructive to the peace of the Government.'' He did not ''see any use of them which is not as well provided for while the Governor & Council govern according to English laws established.'' *Cal. State Pap. Col.*, 1675-1676, §795. At the cabinet council held the last of November, 1684, it was debated whether provincial assemblies should be established, or powers vested in governor and council. The Marquis of Halifax contended that ''there could be no doubt whatever but that the Same laws which are in force in England should also be established in a country inhabited by Englishmen.'' His speech was opposed by the other ministers, and especially by Lord Jeffreys, who maintained that ''whoso capitulateth, rebelleth.'' As a result, it was decided not to require the governor and council to convoke general assemblies of the people. It is easy to see which side the duke was on, for it was said that he made use of the incident to convince his brother ''of the inconsistency and danger involved in employing one so opposed to the interests of monarchy as Halifax.'' Foxcroft, *Life and Letters of Sir George Saville*,

dently intending to experiment on a larger scale with the system of colonial administration which he had tried in New York. The commission was, therefore, drawn up in accordance with his wishes, for no one seemed able to dissuade him from his decision. In the final draft, provision was made for a government entirely in the hands of a governor and council chosen by the king, who were to have the power to make laws, levy taxes, establish courts of justice, and themselves sit as a court of record. The governor alone was to control military affairs and make appointments. All laws were to be sent to England for approval, and appeal to the king's courts was to be allowed in all cases over three hundred pounds. All land henceforth granted, was to be held of the king by payment of a quit-rent of two shillings and six pence per hundred acres, while the conditions on which confirmation of the old grants should be made were left to the judgment of the governor. Liberty of conscience was to be granted to all sects, but particular countenance was to be given to the Church of England.[48]

The most important constitutional change in the new government was the abolition of a representative assembly, which many writers, overlooking the practical aspects of the question, like to ascribe entirely to Stuart absolutism. Such a conclusion is manifestly unfair both to Charles II and James II and to the interest they took in the welfare of the colonies. The Restoration period

I, 428. There are other proofs of his attitude. As long as New York was not prospering without an assembly, when all of the surrounding colonies had one, he was willing to make concessions, but as soon as he became king, procedure toward granting one came to an abrupt stop, and he ordered that the government of New York be ''assimilated'' to that of New England. In 1688 Lord Sunderland claimed to have been responsible for the origin of the idea of abolishing assemblies in New England and to have persuaded James to adopt the policy. *Andros Tracts*, II, 10.

[48] *Cal. State Pap. Col.*, 1681-1685, §§1941, 1953, 2017; Toppan, *Randolph*, III, 334.

was teeming with new political theories, especially concerning the government of colonies, and much attention was being paid to concessions to popular interests, but always with the idea of their being *privileges* not rights. The king had recognized and preserved existing representative institutions in the colonies as a part of England's colonial policy, but he later had reason to doubt the wisdom of that decision. In all the colonies there was trouble with the popular assembly, and it was a grave question whether or not the interests of the whole could be best served by allowing the unfit to have a share in the government. This was especially true of New England. The abolition of the assembly in Massachusetts was the only way to break the power of the theocracy there, and to free that region from Puritan domination just as the restoration of the monarchy in 1660 had freed Old England from Cromwell and the Independents. Without such action, it would have been difficult to carry out successfully any new policy in commerce or government, for even with an extension of the suffrage, the Puritans would still have been in control. In contrast to the difficulties and failures of the English colonial policy, there was the example of the French colonies who seemed to be happily governed without representative assemblies. It is quite natural that James II, influenced by his brother's experience with popular government in England and by his own observance of the French colonial administrative policy, should have deemed representative bodies little more than clogs impeding governmental efficiency and progress.

That is one side of the story. There is much to be said on the other side, of course, for the king committed a great blunder when he failed to take the advice of those who knew colonial conditions better than himself. British officials, who had seen service in America, and the Lords of Trade, who had an intimate knowledge of colonial affairs, knew that representative government was essential to the happiness of Englishmen beyond the seas, who thought of themselves as English subjects and entitled to all the privileges which they would have had at home. Moreover, they had been too long indulged in self-government to make it wise to deprive them of it now. Consequently, an assembly was a necessary and essential part of every settlement of Englishmen in America. Instead of abolishing that institution, James II would have done better to regulate it in such a manner as to keep it under control, and so to make it an aid instead of a hindrance in carrying out his plans.

The second important innovation, the change in the system of land tenure, was connected with the question of revenue. The expense of the new royal provinces was not the least of the king's worries. It was very desirable, if possible, that the colonial establishments be made self-supporting, yet if the assemblies were abolished there was danger of insurrection should the colonial methods of direct taxation be continued, and, if they were not abolished, an equal danger of the assemblies using their control over finances to thwart the governor's activities. Consequently, the Lords of Trade favored the introduction of quit-rents for revenue purposes, and instructed the governor to reserve them in all future grants. Their policy regarding lands already granted was based on the need of wiping out irregularities in land-holding due to the slipshod way in which the colonies had originally made their grants. In New England, lawsuits due to conflicting titles were becoming more and more common, and were difficult of settlement without some definite legal test. Not only were titles defective, but tenure was uncertain and the king's ultimate ownership of the lands was denied. The Lords of Trade had no desire to introduce an oppressive system of land-holding, their object being to bring New England methods more into conformity with English law and customs, and at the same time to obtain a constant and certain source of income for the support of government.

The third important innovation, the granting of religious liberty, was a great step in advance. It was designed to free dissenters from Congregational control and give to all sects the right to worship as they saw fit. To encourage the establishment of an Anglican communion within the Puritan stronghold of Massachusetts was certain to arouse discontent, but it could hardly have been a menace, devoid as it was of any provision for the maintenance of an Anglican clergy. From the standpoint of ''the faction'' the introduction of liberty of conscience was an affront and a challenge, since by it the Puritan church was shorn of a part of its power, but when viewed from the standpoint of the general good, it was a wise measure.

Consolidation in its essential features was an improvement over the former governmental organization of the colonies, and, at the outset, was so considered by the moderate party throughout New England. That it failed to fulfil expectations was due partly to the omission of a representative assembly, for which the king was responsible, and partly to certain blunders committed by the Lords of Trade in drawing up the details of Andros's instructions and by Andros in carrying out these instructions too strictly. Extension of the Dominion in 1688 to include New York and the Jerseys probably weakened the effectiveness of the consolidation, because the area under one establishment was made much too large to cope with the existing difficulties of communication. Moreover, by extension, the Dominion ceased to be an economic and political unit, and in consequence any form of centralization was bound to be more or less artificial.

The success of the plan, with its far-reaching constitutional and tenurial innovations, depended a great deal upon the choice of a governor. The desirable appointee would need to be a man of forceful character, with military and administrative ability, tact, social standing, and colonial experience. Among those suggested, Lord Culpeper would perhaps have been the most satisfactory.[49] His political experience as governor of Virginia had acquainted him with colonial conditions and the trend of British colonial purpose. Besides, he had visited New England and had made good friends among the prominent moderates there. Edward Cranfield, the royal governor of New Hampshire, was also considered, but fortunately his name was never taken very seriously.[50] Colonel Percy Kirke was the choice of Charles II, but his commiss⸱⸱⸱ had not passed the seals when that monarch d⸱⸱⸱⸱ e appointment was confirmed by James II, but jus⸱ time when the people of New England were begin⸱ await his arrival, the rebellion of Argyle and ⸱⸱⸱uth broke out and his share in the suppression ⸱⸱⸱prising discredited him.[51] Randolph had never be⸱⸱⸱ ⸱ed with his selection, and wrote a friend that h⸱ it a "great pity.... that a great country of go⸱ ⸱⸱⸱ects should not have some time of trial" before they were "all at once condemned to the passion and avarice of an unreasonable man."[52] Randolph also suggested Dudley, but there was not much

---

[49] *Cal. State Pap. Col.*, 1681-1685, §91.

[50] Toppan, *Randolph*, I, 235, note; IV, 16-17; III, 155.

[51] *Ibid.*, I, 261; IV, 29, 35, 40-41, 60; *Cal. State Pap. Col.*, 1681-1685, §1928; 1685-1688, §190; 4 Mass. Hist. Soc. *Col.*, V, 142; Sewall, *Diary*, I, 134.

[52] *New England Historical and Genealogical Register*, XXXVII, 268-269; Toppan, *Randolph*, IV, 16-18, 40-41, 71-72; 4 Mass. Hist. Soc. *Col.*, V, 142.

enthusiasm for a native governor.[53] The final choice was
Sir Edmund Andros, a man of social position, personal
integrity, military training, and administrative experience in colonial affairs, but unfortunately lacking in tact,
adaptability, and imagination, particularly in matters
relating to commerce and finance.

[53] Toppan, *Randolph,* III, 317.

CHAPTER III

ESTABLISHMENT OF THE DOMINION OF NEW ENGLAND

The changes under consideration in the government of Massachusetts were of so drastic a character that the Lords of Trade proceeded very slowly in drawing up Andros's commission, a process which at best was a lengthy one. While the matter was under debate, the corporation of Massachusetts Bay continued to govern its colony and Maine, as though the charter had never been vacated. Randolph thought it most unwise to allow this, because of the danger to commerce through continued breaches of the navigation acts, and he urged again, what he had suggested to the Lords of Trade in 1681, the establishment of a provisional government under a temporary president and council, the administration of which should be in the hands of the moderates of the united colonies. Such an arrangement, he argued, would give the lords an opportunity to experiment with some of the more troublesome features of the reorganization.[1] His suggestion was accepted and on October 8,

[1] *Cal. State Pap. Col.*, 1681-1685, §§83, 91; 1685-1688, §319; Toppan, *Randolph*, III, 94; IV, 36-37. Randolph's suggestions for a temporary government are interesting because they represent a federation like that in the Leeward Islands, rather than a union. Realizing the extent of settlement and the great distances from the northern to the southern parts of New England, he advocated a government consisting of a president and deputy president with four councils and four assemblies—Massachusetts Bay, Charlestown Bay, New Plymouth, and Maine. *Cal. State Pap. Col.*, 1685-1688, §350. For the same reason he had, at an earlier date, advocated the

1685, a commission was issued to Joseph Dudley, as president, for the government of Massachusetts, Maine, New Hampshire, and the Narragansett Country.[2] In this commission liberty of conscience found place but there was no mention of a representative assembly, two features of the new system that boded ill for the success of the plan. Should, however, the colonists accept these innovations and at the same time submit to the enforcement of the trade laws, to which the attention of the president and council was especially called, then the royal government in its permanent form could be established without serious danger of revolt.

The organs of government provided for by the commission were a president and council, who were given power to pass laws on all matters except revenue, appoint civil and military officials, make provision for defense of the colony, and establish courts of justice.[3] A quorum of the council, which was seven besides the president, was to constitute a permanent court of record for all cases civil and criminal, and appeals to the crown were to be allowed in all suits above the value of £300.

Joseph Dudley was appointed president, with power to choose a deputy to preside in his absence. The Lords of Trade thought him the candidate most likely to be acceptable to all classes of people because, although identified with the moderates, he was the son of one of

establishment of two deputy governors in the permanent plan of the Dominion, "divided as the two Ridings in Yorkshire." Toppan, *Randolph*, III, 263-264. It is worthy of note that Randolph took it for granted that there would be popular assemblies under the new arrangement.

[2] Toppan, *Randolph*, IV, 40; *Cal. State Pap. Col.*, 1685-1688, §328. Dudley's commission is to be found in the *Laws of New Hampshire*, I, 92-99, and in the *Publications* of the Colonial Society of Massachusetts, II, 37-43.

[3] In Dudley's commission, as well as in that issued later for the permanent government, no mention was made of a popular assembly. *Cal. State Pap. Col.*, 1685-1688, §357.

the strictest of the colony's Puritan founders. Eighteen councilors were named, four of whom, Simon Bradstreet, John Pynchon, William Stoughton, and Nathaniel Saltonstall, were prominent officials in the Massachusetts government; eleven. Wait Winthrop, Richard Wharton, John Usher, Jonathan Tyng, Dudley Bradstreet, Peter Bulkley, Bartholomew Gedney, and the four above mentioned were residents of that colony; two, John Hinckes and Robert Mason, were residents of New Hampshire; two, Francis Champernoon, a nephew of Sir Ferdinando Gorges, and Edward Tyng, were residents of Maine; Fitz-John Winthrop[4] was from the Narragansett Country, and Edward Randolph represented English interests. With the exception of Randolph and Robert Mason, all were men of the moderate party, born in the colonies or long-time residents there. On their coming into office, the government lost its old Puritan theocratic character.[5]

The commission was brought over by Randolph, who was returning to his post of duty. He anticipated little trouble in the establishment of the new government, because he thought the treatment of the participants in the Monmouth and Argyle rebellion would tend to discourage any outbreak. Precautions were taken, however, to keep the "heady in awe," Captain George of H. M. S. *Rose* being ordered to continue on the coast for twelve months, unless the president should have occasion to send him home earlier with prisoners.[6]

Randolph brought, also, an exemplification of the judgment against the charter, copies of the *quo warrantos* against Rhode Island and Connecticut, and commissions for himself as secretary and register, surveyor of the

[4] Fitz-John Winthrop lived at New London, but he was selected to represent the Narragansett Country (King's Province), because of his proprietary interests there.

[5] The councilors are all named in Dudley's commission.

[6] Toppan, *Randolph*, IV, 64, 71, 73.

woods, collector of the customs, and deputy postmaster in New England.[7] These commissions show that the Lords of Trade had confidence in him and had accepted many of his ideas for the development of New England, and it is probable that no one connected with the colonies in the seventeenth century had greater vision than he regarding the future of this region. As secretary and register, he would have the custody of all records of land grants and so be able to judge of the advisability of using quit-rents as a source of revenue. As surveyor of the woods, he could make use of the vast forests of northern New England for the benefit of the English navy, by preserving the trees suitable for masts and making regular shipments of them to England. As collector of the customs, he could see that the navigation acts were enforced in the interests of commerce and the king's revenue. As deputy postmaster he could have an eye on the revenue possibilities of a postal system, and could formulate some plan of easy communication whereby the various parts of the Dominion could be more closely united.

Randolph arrived on May 14, 1686. With the reading of the commission, the old government was faced with the problem as to whether or not it would surrender. On May 20, Dudley, with seven of his council, attended the meeting of the General Court and announced the change in government. A few days later, the court answered that since there was no provision for a representative assembly, without which the citizens of Massachusetts were "abridged of their liberty as Englishmen, both in the matter of legislation and in the laying of taxes," it seemed worthy of consideration whether or

[7] Toppan, *Randolph*, IV, 49-50, 58-59, 67-68, 69, 71; *Cal. State Pap. Col.*, 1685-1688, §472. Randolph's commission as secretary and register is printed in the *Documents and Records Relating to the Province of New Hampshire*, II, 13-14, and in 3 Mass. Hist. Soc. *Col.*, VII, 161.

not the commission were "safe," either for those going
out or for those coming into power. If the president and
council persisted in taking over the government, the
members of the General Court could not give their consent, but would demean themselves as loyal subjects and
commit their cause to God for relief.[8] Aware that it probably would not meet again, the General Court adjourned
until the second Wednesday in October.

The unwillingness of the Puritans to submit to regulation and their reluctance to surrender the government
may seem unreasonable and impolitic, considering that
they had nothing to gain by such an attitude. The explanation is to be found in the very essence of their theocracy. They had always believed themselves to be God's
chosen people, especially called to carve out a Puritan
state in the wilderness. They had seen their own settlement prosper from the first, while the settlements of
others around them had seemingly failed. In 1635 when
their charter was threatened by legal attack from England, God had intervened to save them, and later by means
of a triumphant Puritan revolution in England had made
possible their setting up as a commonwealth. Then came
the Restoration, with the consequent danger of a strict
inquiry and regulation. This danger they had escaped
by procrastinating, until God again intervened with the
Dutch War. After 1675 the charter was again in danger,
but the Popish Plot drew the attention of the English
government elsewhere for a time. Instead of learning
caution from their narrow escape, they continued in their
ways with an even stronger faith in divine support, until
they were called to account by the Lords of Trade, who
were fast losing patience with their dilatory attitude.

8 Sewall, *Diary*, I, 137-139, 140; *Mass. Col. Rec.*, V, 515-516; Toppan,
Randolph, IV, 88, 104. At this same session, a committee was appointed to
safeguard all colonial papers relating to the charter and land titles, a pre-
caution which later caused Edward Randolph much inconvenience.

Had they submitted   xplanatory charter, which
would have defined   ions with the mother country, they need have   rther regulation, but they
would not do this, b   alteration in the charter,
such as would en   irist's kingdom in that
colony," would have   ad as the complete loss of
the charter. They now held out against regulation because they still had confidence that God would surely
intervene again. Their predecessors had not submitted
to attack, therefore they should follow their example
and so "trust in the God of their fathers, that they
shall see his salvation." If suffering should come "because they dare not comply with the wills of men against
the will of God, they suffer in a good cause and will be
accounted martyrs in the next generation and at the
great day." This conviction on their part accounts for
the fact that after 1680 they held out in the face of an
almost inevitable loss of the charter.[9]

Running athwart this confidence in God's support was
a growing fear that they had incurred His displeasure
and must suffer punishment for their sins. The tendency
of the younger generation to break away from the
rigidity of their fathers seemed to them to disclose only
deterioration in the moral fibre of the colony. They construed the Indian War, the failure of crops, the decline
in trade, the attacks on the charter, and a comet which
they saw in the heavens as evidences of God's wrath,
and they tried to show their contrition by prayers for
the rising generation and by specially appointed fast
days.[10] Then came the fall of the charter, which they
accepted as their just punishment, since God had not

[9] 3 Mass. Hist. Soc. *Col.*, I, 74-81; Toppan, *Randolph*, IV, 88; *Cal. State Pap. Col.*, 1681-1685, §1316.

[10] *Samuel Sewall's Letter Book* (6 Mass. Hist. Soc. *Col.*), I, 28, 52; *Mass. Col. Rec.*, V, 388, 463, 470, 484; 2 Mass. Hist. Soc. *Proc.*, XIII, 407, 409.

seen fit to save it.[11] Yet when month after month went by, during the years 1684, 1685, and 1686, and they were allowed to continue administering the government as before, they began again to expect God's intervention. What wonder is it that they rejoiced at news of Monmouth's rebellion, and thought it an answer to their prayers?[12] Yet in the end they were doomed to disappointment and were forced to witness the fall of all their hopes when Dudley and his council assumed control of the government.[13] Their only chance now lay in a complete spiritual reformation, which might move God to restore their theocracy. This hope must not be overlooked in explaining their readiness to revolt upon hearing the news of the landing of William of Orange. They thought the hour of their deliverance had come.[14]

The first session of the new council was held on May

[11] This belief is shown in Mathers' "Fables": "The Birds had maintained good order among themselves for Several years, under the shelter of charters by Jupiter granted to several flocks among them; But heaven, to chastise many faults too observable in its birds, left them to be deprived of their ancient settlements." 3 Mass. Hist. Soc. Col., I, 126.

[12] Randolph reported to the Lords of Trade that "During Monmouth's rebellion most of the ministers stirred up the people by saying that the time of deliverance was at hand. Not one of them prayed for the King, nor believe his letter reporting the overthrow of the rebels." Cal. State Pap. Col., 1685-1688, §794; Toppan, Randolph, IV, 102, 105.

[13] In one of his letters telling of his arrival at Boston, Randolph says, "The factious party were of opinion that (according to their prayers) God would never suffer me to land again in this country, and thereupon began in a most arbitrary manner to assert their power higher than at any time before." Toppan, Randolph, IV, 104.

[14] An address, probably prepared by the clergy, shows the expectation of a miracle. "We know not indeed what God may unexpectedly do for us if we sit still either by sudden turning the heart of the King to favor us, or other ways providentially diverting what is intended & resolved concerning us," but if "this Government and the people of the land will strenuously, wholly & presently rise up to the work of reformation .... we believe God would then yet graciously appear for this poor land." 2 Mass. Hist. Soc. Proc., XIII, 333; Rhode Island Col. Rec., III, 204.

25, when were read the "exemplification" of the judgment against the charter and the commission to Dudley.
The president and the councilors present then took the
oaths of allegiance and of office.[15] Four of those nominated in the commission declined to serve, Saltonstall,
Champernoon, and the Bradstreets, the last two because
they considered the commission "a thing contrived to
abridge them of their liberty and indeed against Magna
Charta."[16] Dudley expressed the keynote of his administration in his opening speech, when he assured those
who expected a great relaxation in civil and religious
control that his royal instructions and his own inclina-
tions were opposed to any such course and that the
"necessary alterations in the rule and form of administration" in the new government from the methods used
by the old "need be but a few."[17] These alterations he
would contrive to make as "plain and easy" as possible,
and would hasten to lay them before the king for confirmation. He considered that his chief duty was to conciliate "the faction" and to keep the Lords of Trade
informed concerning "what further methods and rules
may be judged necessary for the good government,
happy increase and growth" of the province. The address of the General Court made on May 20, 1686, the
day before that body ended its session, impressed him
very little, because neither he nor his councilors approved of the omission of a representative assembly, and

[15] 2 Mass Hist. Soc. *Proc.*, XIII, 225-226. "It was at first intended to
install the President and Council with some military pomp, and the Boston
Troop was to escort Dudley from his home in Roxbury, but the discontent
among the Soldiers was so great that the design was given up." *Ibid.*, 225.

[16] Goodrick, *Randolph*, VI, 171-172. Although the president and council
at once nominated eight persons from which the Lords of Trade should
fill the vacancies, no new members were added during Dudley's brief
administration. *Cal. State Pap. Col.*, 1685-1688, §735.

[17] 2 Mass. Hist. Soc. *Proc.*, XIII, 227.

fully expected the defect to be corrected as soon as the king received their memorial asking for its restoration.[18]

One of the first duties of the president and council was to appoint the necessary civil and military officials. William Stoughton was chosen deputy president and John Usher treasurer. Edward Randolph already held the post of secretary and register by commission from the king, with the power of deputation, but this was ignored by the council, who appointed clerks for Maine and New Hampshire. Local officers were confirmed, except justices of the peace, who were mostly new. The same policy was followed with the military offices. Dudley reported to the Lords of Trade that he had entrusted the militia to "persons well affected to His Majesty, the chiefest whereof being members of the Council," but as a rule the under officers were continued in command under a new commission. The artillery election was held on June 5 as usual and the choice of officers confirmed by the president and council, but many refused to serve under the new government.[19]

Not much change was made in the judicial system. The president and council constituted a superior court of general assize and general gaol delivery for the Dominion, meeting three times a year at Boston. This court had jurisdiction in all cases of appeal from lower courts and original jurisdiction in all capital cases and important matters beyond the cognizance of the inferior courts. From this court appeal was allowed to the king in council. In each county and province was kept a court of pleas

[18] 2 Mass. Hist. Soc. *Proc.*, XIII, 237-239, 241, 244.

[19] *Ibid.*, 231, 235, 240, 252, 261, 262, 269; *Cal. State Pap. Col.*, 1685-1688, §2136. Sewall, who was captain of the South Company, resigned his commission because the cross had been introduced into the flag and he feared it might hinder his entrance into the Holy Land. Sewall, *Diary*, I, 143, 145, 147.

and of general sessions, consisting of a councilor or councilors resident in the county or province (not excluding
others of the council who might desire to attend), and
such justices of the peace as should be "particularly
commissioned thereunto." There were always to be at
least three judges, one of whom must be a councilor. The
county courts had jurisdiction in all civil causes and
pleas and in criminal cases not extending to life or limb.
In civil cases, appeal to the president and council was
allowed.[20] New justices of the peace chosen from among
the moderates were appointed in the counties and principal towns. Peter Bulkley, one of the councilors, was
commissioned provost marshal-general with power to
appoint the county marshals who paid him a part of their
fees. Jurors instead of being elected were now chosen in
each county by the marshal and justice of the peace.
Throughout the whole court system the spoils of office
fell to the moderates, so that while the courts themselves
remained much as before the personnel was changed.[21]
The office of probate of wills and granting administrations was directly under the control of the president, who
was given, by a council order, the power to appoint a
probate judge and clerk for the other provinces and the
"remote counties," the clerks to be accounted deputies
to the secretary and register. This method of handling
probate matters was unpopular, because people considered it a great inconvenience to have to travel so far to
a probate office and preferred the former custom of
having the county courts handle such matters.[22]

[20] *Laws of New Hampshire*, I, 102-106; 2 Mass. Hist. Soc. *Proc.*, XIII,
229-230, 232-233.

[21] 2 Mass. Hist. Soc. *Proc.*, XIII, 245; *Laws of New Hampshire*, I, 113.

[22] *Laws of New Hampshire*, I, 105; 2 Mass. Hist. Soc. *Proc.*, XIII, 234.
There was evidently some doubt in the minds of the councilors as to the
legality of the president's probate powers, for they desired Randolph to
ask Blathwayt, who had drafted the commission in England, "whether the

At the suggestion of Benjamin Bullivant, the attorney-general, an order was passed, May 28, authorizing certain men to serve as attorneys in the courts and requiring them to take a prescribed oath before entering upon their profession. Of the men named, Giles Masters, Anthony Checkley, Captain Nathaniel Thomas, John Watson, and Christopher Webb, only the last two had been freemen under the charter government, and considering that previously any one could practice in the courts, the colonists looked upon the change as a hardship. As a matter of fact it was a much-needed reform, for it was bound to raise the standards of the profession by placing the practice of the law in the hands of men acquainted with English legal customs.[23] As a guarantee against extortion in the taking of fees, a table was established with maximum prices for services in all trials and issues at law. Since the fees were thereby legally increased, the colonists complained bitterly and thought them much too high in spite of the fact that they were only the conventional ones charged in England and in the royal colonies. However, any one desiring to avoid the expense could plead his own case as formerly.[24]

The president and council immediately faced trouble in having to provide funds for the maintenance of the government, for they found the treasury empty and the country burdened with debt.[25] The commission did not give them the authority to pass new revenue laws, but empowered them only to continue in operation those

president is *virtute officii* the ordinary to grant administrations and to allow the probate of wills, he producing no authority from his Majesty's Lords of the Council, or from my Lord of London.'' Toppan, *Randolph*, IV, 100.

[23] *Laws of New Hampshire*, I, 105; Sewall, *Diary*, I, 216; Massachusetts Archives, vol. 126, p. 29. This material is in manuscript form in the public archives department of the State House at Boston.

[24] 2 Mass. Hist. Soc. *Proc.*, XIII, 242-243.

[25] *Ibid.*, 240; *Cal. State Pap. Col.*, 1685-1688, §925, p. 262.

of the former government. Technically speaking, this could not be done, because there were no revenue acts on the statute books when the president and council took over the reins of government. In 1683 when the loss of the Massachusetts charter appeared inevitable, the General Court repealed all revenue laws, evidently intending by so doing to use its constitutional right of voting taxes as a means wherewith to bend the new royal governor to its wishes, a method frequently employed later by assemblies in the royal colonies. Shortly thereafter, not hearing anything more definite about the charter and being quite short of funds, the General Court extended the Impost Act a year.[26] At the end of the year, in June, 1685, the act having expired, the only legal sources of revenue for the support of the government were fines,[27] forfeitures,[28] license money,[29] and tonnage duty.[30] These brought in very little, so the government was forced to levy a few rates according to the old "Charges Publick" Act, which they had previously repealed and did not now re-enact. But this means of raising money failed, because, with the arrival of news concerning the annulment of the

[26] *Mass. Col. Laws* (1887), pp. 304, 312; 4 Mass. Hist. Soc. *Col.*, V, 155; *Andros Tracts,* I, 81; Gay Manuscripts, *State Papers,* VI, 92. This material is now in the custody of the Massachusetts Historical Society, by whose courtesy I have used it.

[27] *Cal. State Pap. Col.*, 1677-1680, §373; Randolph said in 1682 that the fines amounted to about four hundred pounds per annum, but this is no doubt a high estimate. Toppan, *Randolph,* III, 171.

[28] From a half to a third of the value of the forfeiture was payable to the country treasurer.

[29] The license money did not amount to a great deal, because the law concerning licenses was not strictly enforced.

[30] A tonnage duty of twelve pence or one pound of powder per ton was levied on all ships over twelve tons burden, except those owned within the colony or by inhabitants of the confederate colonies. The proceeds were used to supply the castles and forts. *Mass. Col. Rec.*, V, 242-243. This tax was the cause of considerable complaint against the colony. *Cal. State Pap. Col.*, 1677-1680, §358, p. 130.

charter, many people, especially the non-free, refused to recognize the right of the old government to tax them.[31]

Since revenue had to be raised in some way, the president and council decided to revive the old import duty, the excise, and the tonnage.[32] They dared not adopt the act entitled "Charges Publick," because it concerned a direct tax, levied on polls, property, and income, collected annually in the form of a country rate, and Dudley well knew that there was nothing more apt to precipitate a revolution than an attempt to tax the people directly, when they were not represented in the government.[33] Even the revival of the indirect revenue acts was attended with some danger, but as it turned out no objection was made to them, probably because New Englanders cared less about an indirect tax than about one that was direct.

The second innovation, the granting of liberty of conscience to all, was designed by the Lords of Trade as a means whereby the political power of the Puritans might be overthrown. They desired to free dissenters from their obligations to the Congregational church and to make some provision for the Anglicans in New England, in order that this new royal province might gradually become, in religion as well as in other matters, more like England and the other royal colonies in America.[34] Yet they realized the danger of rousing the Puritans by going too far at the outset with the religious policy, and consequently made no provision for the establishment of

[31] *Mass. Col. Rec.*, V, 454, 505; Mass. Arch., vol. 126, p. 18.

[32] 2 Mass. Hist. Soc. *Proc.*, XIII, 241, 242.

[33] Goodrick, *Randolph*, VI, 181, 185.

[34] In 1683, a writer pointed out that "the Government of *New England* (both civil and Ecclesiastical) do so differ from that of his Majesties other Dominions that it is hard to say what may be the Consequence of it." *England's Guide to Industry* (London, 1683), pp. 75, 76, cited in Beer, *The Old Colonial System,* pt. I, vol. II, 268, note 2.

the Church of England as a state church, other than to instruct Dudley to give it special encouragement.

In fact, however, there was really very little that he could do, partly because his first concern was to conciliate "the faction," and partly because the public treasury was empty. Consequently, the Rev. Robert Ratcliffe, who had been sent over to Massachusetts by the Bishop of London, found himself entirely dependent on what his congregation contributed,[35] and Randolph, who thought it most unfair to expect the few Anglicans in Boston to bear the whole burden of the support of a minister, petitioned the council to make adequate provision for "an honorable maintenance and good encouragement, suitable for a minister of the Church of England."[36] The council, handicapped by a lack of funds, could do nothing more than order "that the contribution money collected in the church where he performs divine service, be solely applied to the maintenance of Mr. Ratcliffe,"[37] whereupon Randolph appealed to the Archbishop of Canterbury, suggesting that his Majesty grant them "his royal letters," requiring that the three meeting-houses in Boston, which severally collected about seven or eight pounds a Sunday, should pay the Anglican

[35] Toppan, *Randolph*, IV, 65, 82.

[36] *Ibid.*, 89-90; 2 Mass. Hist. Soc. *Proc.*, XIII, 253; Mass. Arch., vol. 126, p. 29.

[37] 2 Mass. Hist. Soc. *Proc.*, XIII, 256, 262. The Congregational ministers of Boston were paid by a weekly collection made in the several congregations by the elders, who gave the ministers what they thought fit. *Hutchinson Papers*, Prince Soc., II, 238. Nothing more could have been expected from the council at this juncture, for it was literally true that there was "nothing in the Treasury." As the president and council wrote to the Lords of Trade, "We have done our best for Mr. Ratcliffe. We suppose that his expectations exceeded your intentions and orders which were that we should assign him a maintenance out of the revenue." *Cal. State Pap. Col.*, 1685-1688, §925.

churchwarden twenty shillings a week each.[38] Nothing
came of this, however. The English authorities evidently
realized that to make such a demand would be playing
with fire.

The Anglicans had much the same trouble in finding
a place of worship. Through Mason and Randolph, they
asked to be allowed the use of one of the three Congregational meeting-houses in Boston, but again the council
dared not risk stirring up the Puritans, and instead
assigned to them the deputies' room in the town-house.[39]
They soon outgrew this, and moved to the Exchange,
for Ratcliffe's reputation as a preacher and the novelty
of the Church of England service drew large crowds.[40]
Randolph claimed that there were about four hundred
daily frequenters of the church, and that more would
come if they dared, but many merchants and tradesmen
were prevented from attending the service by the threats
of the Puritans to have them arrested for debt or discharged from their positions should they do so.[41] The
increasing numbers made the need of building a church
seem all the greater. Permission was asked of the council
to solicit voluntary gifts throughout New England, but
funds failed to come in during Dudley's administration[42]
in sufficient quantity to warrant a beginning.

Randolph was bitterly disappointed at the attitude of
the council toward the welfare of the Church of England.
He had expected that the new government would give the
church both financial aid and general encouragement, because he thought it would be controlled by Church of
England men. He had recommended Dudley for the presi-

[38] Toppan, *Randolph*, I, 290, 291, note; IV, 90, 109; Mass. Arch., vol. 126,
p. 29.

[39] Sewall, *Diary*, I, 141, 142.

[40] Toppan, *Randolph*, IV, 89, 105; 2 Mass. Hist. Soc. *Col.*, II, 106.

[41] Toppan, *Randolph*, IV, 131.

[42] *Ibid.*, I, 293-294, note; Sewall, *Diary*, I, 147.

dency, because the latter, although formerly a non-conformist minister, had, when in London, not only "set up for a King's Man" but had also given the impression that he had turned Anglican. Yet from the beginning of his administration, Dudley showed no inclination to favor the Church of England. The Anglicans thought it significant of the attitude of the president and council that, at the time of publishing Dudley's commission, the council refused to invite Ratcliffe to say grace, but instead conferred the honor upon Increase Mather. This manifest sympathy of the administration for the Puritans was the most important factor in preventing the new royal government from being unpopular, but at the same time it aided but little the cause of liberty of conscience, which the Lords of Trade had made so important a part of their policy.

With the provisional government as later with the Andros administration, trade was the dominant interest. The Lords of Trade had adopted the new policy principally for the purpose of encouraging commercial expansion, and naturally they expected the new royal province of New England to respond in some measure to the economic needs of the mother country. On the other hand, the president and council desired to restore to prosperity the commercial system which New England had already developed and which in many respects conflicted with the plans of those who were interested in the British scheme of trade. To reconcile these conflicting interests was the mission of the moderates in control of the government. Many of them were prominent merchants, who, while they were naturally not anxious to see England's commercial policy enforced strictly in American waters, were yet appreciative of England's position and knew that the colonies could not go on forever without commercial regulation of some sort. They realized that it would be better for Massachusetts to become a part of the larger commercial world, even with certain restrictions, than to be independent and enjoy free trade within a more limited area. Consequently, when they came into power, they saw to it that the navigation acts were enforced in the interest of the king's revenue, without too strict an adherence to the letter of the law, and then by petitions to the Lords of Trade sought to obtain a modification of the more stringent and inconvenient measures.

The great prosperity which Massachusetts enjoyed during the Puritan revolution and the Restoration period suffered a decline after 1675. The Indian war destroyed much property, checked agricultural expansion, and interfered with the Indian fur trade of the outlying towns. For many years the wheat crops in Massachusetts had suffered from an annual blight. The navigation act of 1673 seriously interfered with the re-exportation of the tobacco of Maryland, Virginia, and North Carolina, in requiring the payment at the port of lading of a duty similar in amount to that collected on importation into England. These double duties were a subject of much complaint and were an especial incentive to illicit trading with the European Continent. The new impositions of 1685 required the payment of additional duties on sugar and tobacco at English ports, and though intended to fall on the consumer brought great discouragement to trade. The permanent cutting off of the Irish trade with the colonies in 1685, the closing of the Massachusetts mint after the vacation of the charter, the interference by the French with the fisheries at Newfoundland and on the eastern coast, Randolph's attempts to enforce the English commercial system, all contributed to bring the once prosperous trade of the colony to a low ebb. For this result, the merchants in Massachusetts blamed the Puritans who had controlled the colonial government before the fall of the charter and who, they thought, lacked the ability to meet the problems of new routes, currency, relations with the mother country, and the like. They deemed even the local policy of the Puritans too narrow, for by unwise revenue tariffs the latter had discriminated against the goods of neighboring colonies, thereby rousing an antagonism which almost drove Connecticut and Rhode Island to seek union with New York. Had such a union been effected, those colonies would have been drawn into New York's commercial system, where a high export duty would have cut off their provision trade with Massachusetts, to the latter's very great detriment.

Immediately after coming into office, the council turned its attention to considerations of commerce. It sent a memorial to the Lords of Trade asking for the annexation of Connecticut and Rhode Island, for a rebate of the plantation duties on sugar and tobacco when imported into England, and for the establishment of a mint.[43] The two colonies were needed in order to give to the council complete control of New England commerce, the rebate on sugar and tobacco duties was necessary if legal trade with England were to be profitable, and a mint was essential in creating a more flexible medium of exchange. In order to make a careful study of trade conditions, a "grand and standing committee" was appointed, composed of merchants and leading citizens in Boston and the large coast towns.[44] Its members were to serve as local committees of trade in their respective

[43] 2 Mass. Hist. Soc. *Proc.*, XIII, 244-245. The rebate on tobacco was asked for only when shipped from New England to London. The amount was a penny a pound, and was levied by the act of 1673.

[44] Among the members of this committee were Blackwell and Lyndes of Boston, Russell and Sprague of Charlestown, Gedney and Browne of Salem, and Hinckes and Walden of Piscataqua. 2 Mass. Hist. Soc. *Proc.*, XIII, 248-249.

home towns, where they were to inform themselves concerning conditions and report the result of their investigations at the meeting of the general committee. One of the first recommendations made by this organization was that a bank of credit be established, but before the council could act on this suggestion Andros arrived and the provisional government came to an end.[45] It is true that the committee was continued by Andros, but it was not able to do anything effectual, its members having no influence with the men who dominated the new council.

Although the council was interested principally in the trade of New England, it dared not neglect the administration of the navigation acts, because it knew that the provisional government had been established in the main for that special purpose. Yet in all that it did, its aim was not so much to enforce the trade regulations as to appear to enforce them. It made, however, two reforms in the administrative system inherited from the former government of Massachusetts—the designation of four exclusive ports of entry, Boston, Salem, Ipswich, and Great Island,[46]—and the establishment of a vice-admiralty court.

Randolph was quite unable to understand the attitude of the council toward the navigation acts, for he had expected the provisional government to show a zeal similar to his own. Instead of that, he saw its members refusing to pass strict orders of regulation and giving him little aid in making seizures. He was angry with Dudley for encroaching upon his monopoly as an informer, by directing Captain George of the *Rose* frigate to act in that capacity and to make seizures while the *Rose* was

45 2 Mass. Hist. Soc. *Proc.*, XIII, 272; Mass. Arch., vol. 126, pp. 104-106.

46 Boston was named the head port of entry for Charlestown and Hull; Salem for Lynn, Gloucester, Cape Ann, and Marblehead; Ipswich for Salisbury and Rowley; and Great Island for the town of Hampton, Isle of Shoals, and Kittery in Maine. 2 Mass. Hist. Soc. *Proc.*, XIII, 264.

lying at anchor in Boston harbor. Since in case of condemnation, half of the forfeiture went to the king and
half to the informer, Randolph lost several pounds by
this infringement of his monopoly.[47] Moreover, Captain
George, who was not, like Randolph, incorruptible, connived at a certain amount of illicit trade, for which
reason the merchants preferred to have him examine
their cargoes.[48] The case of the *Friendship* is one of the
best examples of the friction which arose between Captain George and Randolph over the inspection of vessels
and their lading. The *Friendship* was a London boat,
hired by Penn Townshend, a prominent Boston merchant, to bring a cargo of salt from France, after which
it was to take a lading of fish to Bilbao. While riding at
Nantasket, the vessel was visited by Captain George's
men, who made a satisfactory report of the situation.
The captain thereupon withdrew his men and permitted
the boat to come into the harbor at Boston. Randolph,
who was suspicious of the cargo, seized the vessel and
forbade the taking out of any more of the lading until
security was given that it was all salt. Townshend, pretending to be very much surprised at the insinuation,
petitioned unsuccessfully for a release of the boat. The
case was tried in the vice-admiralty court, where the
jury, finding convincing evidence that wines, brandy, and
claret had been unloaded into a shallop near the Isle of
Shoals, condemned the vessel with all its appurtenances
and cargo.[49]

In spite of all opposition Randolph succeeded in making a number of seizures, and although many of the
vessels were released, there were enough condemnations
to cause considerable consternation among the mer-

[47] Toppan, *Randolph*, IV, 92, 93, 98.

[48] *Ibid.*, 125-128; 2 Mass. Hist. Soc. *Proc.*, XIII, 273-274; Mass. Arch.,
vol. 126, pp. 120-130.

[49] *Ibid.*, 25, 26, 32, 33, 282.

chants.[50] Most of the cases were tried in the new vice-
admiralty court, where, contrary to legal custom in England, decision was made by a jury returned by the
marshal and a justice of the peace, as in the ordinary
courts.[51] The High Court of Admiralty in England appointed Richard Wharton judge and Joseph Smith, one
of Randolph's deputies, marshal, but the latter's commission was withheld after its arrival in the colony, and
the regular marshals were allowed to act, probably because Smith was hostile to the party in power and perhaps favored a stricter enforcement of the acts of trade
than they did.[52] Although, before the fall of the Massachusetts charter, Randolph had been very friendly to
Wharton, who was then one of the most prominent of
the non-freemen, he now distrusted him, having discovered that Wharton was interested in illicit trade and suspected of collusion with pirates.[53] With his confidence in
the judge gone, Randolph ceased to consider the vice-
admiralty court an effective means of enforcing the trade
laws.[54]

To Randolph, the provisional government was a great
disappointment. It is plain that he expected himself to be
the power behind the throne and hoped that the president
and council, whom he had nominated to the Lords of
Trade, would be men through whom he could govern. He
found too late that he had been the tool of Dudley, who,
he now suspected, had duped him into getting the provisional government established, in order that the liberals

[50] Toppan, *Randolph*, I, 294, note; IV, 114; *Cal. State Pap. Col.*, 1685-
1688, §925; Sewall, *Letter Book*, I, 34.

[51] Sewall, *Letter Book*, I, 34. A list of the jurors in the case of the
Friendship is given in Mass. Arch., vol. 126, p. 32.

[52] 2 Mass. Hist. Soc. *Proc.*, XIII, 268; *Cal. State Pap. Col.*, 1685-1688,
§§468, 470.

[53] Toppan, *Randolph*, IV, 279.

[54] Late in Dudley's administration, trials were held in the ordinary courts
as well as in the admiralty courts. *Suffolk Deeds*, XIV, 110-111.

might be in a position to keep the control of affairs legally in their own hands, while they negotiated with the Lords of Trade for a government according to their desires. The truth seems to be that by affecting an intimacy with Randolph, by dictating to him the nomination of the members of the council, and by urging him to work for the provision in the commission against taxing by any other means than the colony's old revenue laws, Dudley planted in Randolph's mind ideas which the latter believed to be his own.[55] Once in office Dudley managed things as he pleased and took it for granted that the necessity of conciliating "the faction" would justify him in modifying his instructions.[56] For example, he did not levy a direct tax because representative government had been abolished, he did not encourage the Church of England because the people would resent it, and he did not enforce the navigation acts too strictly because to do so would kill trade to the detriment of the interests of the mother country as well as of New England. That he expected this course of action to satisfy the Lords of Trade is probable, if one may judge from the criticisms he was continually making in his letters to them. It was unfortunate for him and his moderate associates that they roused Randolph's antagonism and suspicions, for the latter made haste to undo, if he could, the work he

[55] Randolph wrote to Dudley, January, 1685, "I remember what you advise, that the government be, in the first place, transposed and committed to the care of fitting persons upon the place to prepare and accommodate affairs against the arrival of the governor. I am not wanting to press for liberty of conscience and confirmation of all your rights and possessions, and have nominated according to what was agreed betwixt you and myself, persons for the council, and dissuade all I can, from raising any rates upon the people to support government more than what has been usual with you." Toppan, *Randolph*, IV, 13.

[56] "I am treated by Mr. Dudley worse than by Mr. Danforth," Randolph complained to Blathwayt, "yet all under the pretence of friendship and is angry that I do not believe him." *Ibid.*, IV, 99, 107.

had accomplished in helping them into office. He urged the Lords of Trade to send over an English governor-general as soon as possible to "settle this distracted country," for "there must be something more than wax and parchment to reduce them to their perfect duty and obedience."[57] Because of his disquieting reports, the Lords of Trade hastened the work on Andros's commission and soon prepared to bring the career of the council to an end before the latter had achieved the reforms upon which it had been engaged.

From the standpoint of the Lords of Trade, the provisional government accomplished practically all for which it had been created, with the exception of the enforcement of the acts of trade. It had "unhinged the commonwealth"[58] and prepared for the coming of a royal governor; it had broken the power of the theocracy, because the abolition of a representative assembly had stripped the Congregational church of its political authority and the granting of religious liberty had destroyed its monopoly of religion. All this it had done without rousing the colony to revolt. The Dominion of New England having thus been firmly established under the administration of the president and council, the Lords of Trade thought that the time was now ripe for the sending of Andros, under whose direction the completed plan of union could be put into operation. Andros arrived on December 20, 1686, and immediately took up the reins of office. By his commission he united under one government all of the New England colonies except Connecticut and Rhode Island. These colonies had not surrendered their charters, but the latter had submitted, so Andros displayed his additional instructions from the king to annex it and treat it as a part of the Dominion.

57 Toppan, *Randolph*, IV, 106-107; *Rhode Island Col. Rec.*, III, 204.
58 Toppan, *Randolph*, IV, 114.

Connecticut and the County of Cornwall, the territory between the St. Croix and the Kennebec, at that time a part of New York, were added in the spring.

Andros faced difficulties of administration that were greater than those of Dudley, because of the increased size of the territory under his rule. Moreover, he was called upon to proceed more boldly with the innovations which the former administration had handled very cautiously. The Puritans had passively accepted Dudley's government without a representative assembly, but would they tolerate any attempt on the part of Andros's government to make new laws for them and to tax them? They had not resisted the establishment of liberty of conscience, but would they permit any encouragement of the Church of England? Would they be resigned to the enforcement of the British laws of trade and to the regulation of their land system? Answers to these and other similar questions lay in the future.

CHAPTER IV

LEGISLATION AND TAXATION

The most effective instrument in the hands of the British authorities for the enforcement of a uniform colonial policy was the control of legislation on both sides of the water. Acceptance by the colonists of all acts of parliament that applied directly to them, acknowledgment of the king's right to approve and confirm acts of colonial assemblies, and recognition of the royal privilege of hearing appeals from colonial courts, in matters both civil and marine, were, as far as the colonies were concerned, essential to this end. Wherever popular assemblies existed in the royal colonies complete control of legislation was impossible, because these assemblies evaded if they could the acts of parliament and thwarted by one means or another the king's will as expressed in the royal disallowance. James, as duke, had already expressed his opinion of such assemblies in no uncertain terms, and now, as king, he evidently wished to continue the experiment, begun under Andros and his predecessors in New York, of governing a colony without a popular body. Consequently in his commission to Andros of June, 1686, he vested in the hands of the governor the power to make laws, with the advice and consent of the major part of his council, and in his instructions of the September following indicated in great detail the matters concerning which legislation was needed. Laws were to be sent to England for the king's approval within three

months of the time they were passed and appeals to the
king in council were to be allowed.[1]

The new government was highly centralized and oli-
garchic in character, for but very few men held the principal offices, civil and military. The council was not only
the lawmaking body but also the chief administrative
organ of government, and it sat as a court to interpret
the laws it had made. Its members, besides serving as
councilors, filled important military and administrative
positions also, which they looked upon as offering them
opportunities for remuneration, since they received no
salary and, after March, 1687, not even their expenses.
John Usher, who was treasurer of the Dominion during
the administration of the president and council, was continued in that office.[2] Edward Randolph was appointed
secretary and register for New England, by letters-
patent from the king, but he met with so much opposition
that on Andros's advice he leased the office for four years
to John West of New York.[3] No deputy governor was
chosen until after the incorporation of New York and
the Jerseys, when Francis Nicholson was named for the
office.[4]

That the interests of the various parts of the Dominion might be represented, most of the councilors were
chosen from among those holding office under former

[1] Andros's commissions and instructions are printed in *Laws of New
Hampshire*, vol. I, 144-182, 226-244. The commissions are also to be found
in the *Publications* of the Colonial Society of Massachusetts, II, 44-68, and
elsewhere.

[2] Usher's commission, which came from England, is to be found in Mass.
Arch., vol. 126, p. 320, and in printed form in Goodrick, *Randolph*, VI, 177;
Cf. also *Cal. State Pap. Col.*, 1685-1688, §1235.

[3] *Cal. State Pap. Col.*, 1685-1688, §1234; Toppan, *Randolph*, IV, 155, 162-
163; Amer. Antiq. Soc. *Proc.*, N. S., XIII, 464, 497.

[4] C. O. 389: 9, p. 468; Mass. Arch., vol. 126, p. 320. Nicholson was sworn
a member of the council in August, 1687, and became lieutenant governor
in April, 1688.

colonial governments. In the case of Massachusetts, those selected represented, not the charter government, but that of the president and council, since otherwise the Puritans would have been given too much power. There were seven from Massachusetts,[5] one from New Hampshire,[6] two from Maine, six from Plymouth, one from the Narragansett Country,[7] seven from Rhode Island,[8] two from Connecticut,[9] and, after the addition of New York and the Jerseys, eight from the former and none from the latter. Besides the native councilors, there were Randolph, Mason, and Francis Nicholson, who was sent from England in command of the redcoats serving as Andros's bodyguard.[10]

There were many elements of friction in the council, not only because its members came from colonies which had been rivals, but also because they represented very different class interests. Those of Massachusetts were of the aristocracy, while those of Plymouth had the point

[5] Further additions to the council were made by the Lords of Trade in November, 1687, from Randolph's list of nominations, and mandamuses were sent to Andros to swear in the new members. Three of these, Samuel Shrimpton, William Browne, Jr., and Simon Lynde, were citizens of Massachusetts, while the fourth, Richard Smith, was from the Narragansett Country. They took office in the spring of 1688, except Lynde, who died shortly before. *Cal. State Pap. Col.*, 1685-1688, p. 464, §1685; *Laws of New Hampshire*, I, 173; C. O. 5: 904, p. 365.

[6] *Laws of New Hampshire*, I, 93, note.

[7] The Narragansett Country is the same as the King's Province.

[8] Rhode Island had not been included in Andros's commission, but having submitted before the instructions were completed, councilors from that colony were named.

[9] Connecticut and the County of Cornwall, the territory between the St. Croix and the Kennebec, formerly a part of New York, were added to the Dominion in the spring of 1687. Two councilors were named from Connecticut, Robert Treat, the former governor, and John Allyn, the secretary. Mass. Hist. Soc. *Col.*, II, 297; *Laws of New Hampshire*, I, 171-172; Amer. Antiq. Soc. *Proc.*, N. S., XIII, 483.

[10] C. O. 389: 9, p. 434; Amer. Antiq. Soc. *Proc.*, N. S., XIII, 475; *Andros Tracts*, III, 73.

of view of the poverty-stricken farmers of that colony. The councilors of Connecticut and Plymouth were Puritans, more in sympathy with the theocrats who had formerly controlled the government of Massachusetts than with the moderate element representing the Bay colony at this time. The councilors from Rhode Island were looked down upon by all, because of the position which that colony had always occupied in the eyes of its neighbors. It had been considered beyond the pale because it had harbored religious and political fanatics whom the other colonies had driven out. On their part, the Rhode Island councilors returned the dislike with interest. They could not easily forget the long feud over the Narragansett Country which had ended with the defeat of Rhode Island, the government going to Connecticut and the soil to the Massachusetts proprietors who claimed it, three of whom now sat as councilors from Massachusetts.

Within the circle of the Massachusetts councilors, who comprised the largest group, there was anything but harmony. A part of them were large landowners, "grandees," as Randolph called them, while the rest were wealthy merchants, and they usually disagreed on all economic questions. Among the large landowners were the Winthrops, the Tyngs, Dudley, Stoughton, Bulkley, and Pynchon, while Gedney, Wharton, and Usher were merchants of considerable standing. The Winthrops held extensive inherited estates, and were interested in many of the large land ventures of the day, such as the enterprises of the Atherton Company and the "Million Purchase." Stoughton, Dudley, and Wharton were also parties in these enterprises. Pynchon's interests lay in the Connecticut Valley, where his father had founded Springfield, and he himself was largely responsible for the settlement of Enfield. Gedney, although possessing large holdings in Maine, was interested in mercantile

affairs at Salem. Wharton seems to have been the most
conspicuous of the Boston captains of industry, for in
one capacity or another he was associated with nearly
every financial undertaking of the times, agrarian and
commercial. He, like the Winthrops, was a member of
the Atherton and "Million Purchase" companies, and
was engaged in laying out for himself a large manor in
Maine. He was the prime mover in one company for the
production of salt, which sought to acquire a monopoly
of all New England markets, in another for the manufacture of naval stores, and in a third organized for
mining ore.[11] Evidently, he considered his land ventures
the most important of all his enterprises, for he usually
cast his vote with the landowners. Perhaps he was drawn
toward them because of family connections, for he was
related to the Winthrops, the Tyngs, and Dudley.[12]
Usher was one of the most prominent figures in Boston
because of the wealth which he had acquired in mercantile pursuits. Although he followed the trade of his
father, Hezekiah Usher, who had kept a bookshop, he
was a general merchant, doing business on a large scale.
He possessed several ships and wharves and carried on
an extensive foreign trade. His father had not been a
freeman, and for that reason he had a different background from that of the Puritans of the second generation; and though a freeman himself he was generally
disliked because not in sympathy with Puritan life and
government and was scornful of anything that seemed

11 6 Mass. Hist. Soc. *Col.*, V, 11-15; *New England Hist. Reg.*, IX, 339;
Plym. Col. Rec., V, 65; *Mass. Col. Rec.*, IV-2, 505.

12 Wharton's first wife was Bethia Tyng, cousin of Jonathan and Edward, and their sister Rebecca was Joseph Dudley's wife. Three sons were
born of this union. His second wife was the daughter of the Rev. John
Higginson of Salem, by whom he had four daughters, and his third wife
was Martha Winthrop, daughter of Gov. John Winthrop and sister of Fitz-
John and Wait Winthrop. By her he had three sons and a daughter.
Savage, *Genealogical Dictionary*, IV, 13, 356-358, 413, 494, 612.

un-English. In all the administrative conflicts that arose, he usually sided with those who stood for prerogative interests.[13] The one thing, however, which held the Massachusetts councilors together was the fact that they were all of the moderate party, being either moderate Puritans or former non-freemen.

Besides the native councilors, there were Randolph, Mason, and later, Nicholson. These men, with Andros, stood for the king and the prerogative. Randolph, who by this time was thoroughly hated by all the native councilors, was respected by Andros because of his knowledge of British policy. Mason was unpopular in Massachusetts and New Hampshire, principally because he had successfully pressed his claims to the soil of the latter province.[14] Nicholson was looked upon with suspicion by the New England councilors, because, being captain of the governor's footguard, he stood for what must have seemed the military side of the Dominion government. The colonists were unaccustomed to the idea of a standing force in times of peace, and consequently associated the redcoats with oppression.

Andros, the new royal governor, was not unknown. Already as governor of New York, he had come into contact, sometimes not always in a friendly way, with the Massachusetts authorities, over boundaries and other similar matters. He had no sympathy with the stricter Puritans, but was on cordial terms with some of the moderates. He had had pleasant associations with the Winthrops while he was governor of New York, for Fitz-John Winthrop had held Fishers Island of the Duke of

[13] 2 Mass. Hist. Soc. *Col.*, II, 102; Toppan, *Randolph*, IV, 99, 161; VI, 177.

[14] Randolph was worried about Mason's appointment, and asked Southwell to "advise him to moderation for I fear when he comes to be mated with some of his former antagonists twill transport his passion and put all into a ferment." Toppan, *Randolph*, IV, 48.

York on payment of a quit-rent of a lamb a year, a relationship which occasioned the exchange of many friendly letters. He had also solicited at court in England in their behalf and performed other kindly offices.[15]

In the last analysis, in spite of intercolonial and party disputes, lines of division in the council were generally drawn primarily between the native members on the one hand and those representing prerogative interests on the other. Matters of difference were often decided after long and bitter discussion, not on the merits of the debate, but on Andros's personal interpretation of his instructions. Andros preferred to persuade the councilors to his way of thinking, if possible, but if that were not possible, he, being a conscientious servant of the crown, would always follow his instructions. For that reason his attitude frequently appeared to be highhanded and arbitrary.[16]

The making of laws was vested exclusively in the governor, with the advice and consent of the major part of his council, and the king's will in regard to legislation was expressed by instructions to the governor, general and specific, concerning the type of laws objected to and the matters touching which laws were needed.[17] Since the old laws in each colony were to continue in force until

15 6 Mass. Hist. Soc. *Col.*, III, 460, 462-463, 464, 469.

16 At the first council meeting, Andros encouraged the members to freedom in debate, but he evidently regretted this later. The five councilors who wrote a pamphlet criticizing Andros after the revolution complained that the ''Debates in Council were not so free as ought to have been, but too much over ruled, and a great deal of harshness continually expressed against Persons and Opinions that did not please.'' Andros was also accused of objecting to the council's share in initiating legislation, having the bills drawn up in private and unexpectedly brought into council, so that their discussions and objections were usually against a bill ''too far promoted and engaged in already.'' Amer. Antiq. Soc. *Proc.*, N. S., XIII, 243, note; *Andros Tracts*, I, 138, 140-141.

17 *Laws of New Hampshire*, I, 157-158, 165.

superseded by new legislation,[18] the first task of the government was to bring about uniformity in the legal system by a thorough revision and codification of the laws of the various colonies. A committee was appointed for this purpose, consisting of four councilors from Massachusetts, two from Plymouth, and two from Rhode Island.[19]

The council in its legislative capacity seems to have met quarterly, as had the old General Court, and at these times a full attendance was expected.[20] For executive business, it met weekly, and seven were considered a quorum.[21] In order to insure the attendance of at least this number, there were always to be among the councilors seven who lived in or near Boston. Since after March 22, 1687, the councilors did not even get their expenses paid, those living at a distance rarely came, except when summoned for a general session.[22] As a

[18] The Lords of Trade in 1685 asked the opinion of the law officers whether or not the laws made in Massachusetts before the vacation of the charter were still in force. The attorney-general reported that they were. *Cal. State Pap. Col.*, 1685-1688, §50.

[19] *Amer. Antiq. Soc. Proc.*, N. S., XIII, 245-246. The committee consisted of Dudley, Stoughton, Hinckley, Winthrop, Clarke, Coggeshall, Walley, and Bulkley. The secretary was also to attend, and Wharton to be present as often as possible. *Ibid.*

[20] The five councilors mentioned in note 16 said that "after a little while there were no set times appointed or given notice of for the making of Laws, that so the Members of the Council might attend in a fuller number to be helpful therein." *Andros Tracts*, I, 140-141. The records show that a general meeting was held on December 30 and 31 and on January 3 and 4; another was held on February 23, adjourning on March 8 to the first Wednesday in May. It met as planned on May 4 and sat until May 9. The last general session was held on June 22 and continued until June 24, after which usually no more than the quorum attended. *Amer. Antiq. Soc. Proc.*, N. S., XIII, 242, 243, 244, 246, 248, 251, 261, 463, 465, 468, 469; 4 *Mass. Hist. Soc. Col.*, V, 176.

[21] By Andros's commission, five constituted a quorum, but by his instructions seven were required. *Andros Tracts*, I, 51-52.

[22] *Mass. Arch.*, vol. 126, p. 369; Toppan, *Randolph*, IV, 163.

result, only the Boston members, Randolph, Usher, Dudley, Stoughton, Wait Winthrop, Mason, West and Nicholson, attended regularly. It was unfortunate that the majority of these men were the most unpopular members of the council, for people then spoke of them, as writers have done since, in terms of reproach, calling them Andros's "tools" and "henchmen," and so coloring very unjustly their own interpretations of the period. Andros was even accused of trying to discourage attendance at council, in order that he might the more easily have things his own way, whereas in matter of fact he was often greatly inconvenienced by his inability to get together even the required quorum of seven.[23]

The committee on laws began at once its work of codification. Instead of waiting until the complete revision was ready to present to the council, this committee at the beginning of each general session reported the laws it had prepared up to date, and these laws were announced to the people at large with much ceremony at the close of the session. On March 8, 1687, a proclamation was issued which declared that all laws not yet revised would remain in force until further orders. It is clear, then, that during Andros's administration, the laws of Massachusetts were in a state of transition, some, new or revised, being uniform for the entire province, while others, old and often local in character, differing in different places and partaking of the nature of custom, were survivals from the earlier period.[24]

[23] Mass. Arch., vol. 126, p. 369; *Andros Tracts*, I, 16-17, 51-52, 138-139, 140-141. In May, 1687, Randolph wrote in great irritation to Blathwayt that "His Excellency has to do with a perverse people. Here is none of the council at hand except Mr. Mason and myself, and Mr. B. [Bulkley] and Mr. Usher who appear lively for his Majesty's Interest." Toppan, *Randolph*, IV, 160-161.

[24] Amer. Antiq. Soc. *Proc.*, N. S., XIII, 245, 246, 257, 258, 259, 261, 264, 464, 465, 466; *Cal. State Pap. Col.*, 1685-1688, p. 340, §§1183, 1671; Toppan,

Of all the laws passed by the Dominion council, those
that related to courts, revenue, and local government
were the ones effecting the greatest changes in the constitutional and political order. The first introduced a
much-needed reform into the administration of justice;
the second brought to a head the question raised by the
colonists and left unanswered by the Lords of Trade,
as to the right of the new government to legislate on
taxation without a representative assembly; the third
brought to an end the normal functioning of the organs
of local government. All merit special attention, since
they roused fatal opposition to the administration.[25]

. Andros's commission empowered him, with the advice
of his council, to tax the inhabitants for the support of
the government, but directed him to continue in force
the existing revenue laws until better methods of taxing
could be agreed upon.[26] The Lords of Trade thought it
unwise to introduce at the outset innovations in taxation,
lest the resentment of the taxpayers be roused against
the new government, and for this reason, though the
treasury was empty, Andros deemed it better to continue
the former laws until a thorough study could be made
of economic and financial conditions in the Dominion and
a new scheme of taxation worked out. In the meantime,
his salary was to be paid out of the English exchequer,
although the lords had repeatedly stated it to be the
king's intention that all colonial governments should be
self-supporting.[27]

Randolph, IV, 150-151, 153; Andros Tracts, I, 139; Conn. Col. Rec., III,
441.

[25] This was particularly true of the revenue act, which was listed in a
revolutionary pamphlet as one of the laws destroying the liberty of subjects.
Andros Tracts, I, 79-81.

[26] Cal. State Pap. Col., 1685-1688, §680; Laws of New Hampshire, I, 158-
159; Andros Tracts, II, 210.

[27] Cal. State Pap. Col., 1685-1688, §712.

Had there been any former revenue laws to continue, Andros need not have touched the subject of taxation until the necessary study of conditions had been made.[28] But no revenue laws were any longer in operation, and in consequence a new measure had to be passed, in order that Massachusetts should bear her share of the financial burdens of the Dominion. The council, therefore, not being able to pass a law applying to Massachusetts alone, began work on a general revenue bill for the whole Dominion.[29]

The bill reported by the committee, in spite of the stipulations in Andros's commission, bore little resemblance to the revenue laws of the former New England colonies. It provided for a heavy tax on rum, wine, brandy, and other strong waters imported into, or distilled in, the Dominion, and a penny in the pound duty on imported merchandise.[30] The character of the bill was no mere accident, for it was drawn up by a committee, the members of which were little interested in trade. The

[28] Upon his arrival, Andros ordered that all such duties and imposts ''as now Setled in this Town of Boston and other parts of this Government are hereby continued till further Order.'' Amer. Antiq. Soc. *Proc.*, N. S., XIII, 240.

[29] *Cal. State Pap. Col.*, 1685-1688, §1093.

[30] A draft of the act is entered in the Massachusetts Archives, vol. 126, pp. 41-44, under date of July, 1686. This is, of course, an error. There is no evidence to show that the president and council ever attempted to adopt any new revenue legislation. Besides, the act shows by internal evidence that it belongs to the Andros administration. It reads, ''that from and after the tenth January instant,'' etc. Since Dudley's government lasted from May 17 to December 19 only, the act could not have been a measure of that administration. Furthermore, it is word for word like the draft given under date of January 6 (pp. 191-198), except that the latter has a paragraph concerning the collection of the excise ''through this his Ma'tyes Government,'' added without doubt after the issue of an order of February 26, providing for the inclusion of an excise duty in the revenue act. It is this draft of January 6, with the paragraph of February 26, which is incorrectly printed in the *Laws of New Hampshire*, I, 127-130, as having been passed on July 30, 1686.

three Massachusetts members were all of the class of large landowners, "the grandees," and for years had viewed with alarm the growing insistence in the colony on the taxation of unimproved lands held in propriety. They were naturally anxious to have the burden shifted from land to imports. The same was true of the Rhode Island members, while those from Plymouth favored any form of taxation that would fall lightly on the poverty-stricken agricultural inhabitants of their colony.

The bill occasioned much debate in council, and on that account further action on it was postponed until the February session. But while it was in the process of being amended by the committee, a new bill of an entirely different character was introduced, evidently at the instigation of Andros. The latter measure was rushed through, in spite of the committee's attempt to delay its passage, and in spite of opposition in the council from the large landowners and small farmers.[31] This bill was a re-enactment of two former acts of Massachusetts entitled "Charges Publick" and "Imposts."[32] It provided for the raising of funds by a country rate, by impost duties on wines, liquors, merchandise, and provisions, by an excise, and by a tonnage duty. The law of 1641 had specified that the country rate should be collected on "lands of all Sorts, as well broken up as other (Except such as Doeth or Shall lye Com'on)," but there had been so much complaint that "sundry Gentlemen, Merchants and others, having great Tracts of land, bounded out to them in Propriety, pay not to Publick Charges," that a law was passed in 1682 taxing such lands two shillings for every hundred acres.[33] No mention of this supplemental law is made in the Andros act, probably because

[31] *Andros Tracts,* I, 139-140; *Cal. State Pap. Col.,* 1685-1688, §1676; Toppan, *Randolph,* IV, 151; Amer. Antiq. Soc. *Proc.,* N. S., XIII, 256.

[32] *Mass. Col. Laws* (1887), pp. 22-26, 67-71.

[33] *Mass. Col. Laws,* p. 296 b; *Mass. Col. Rec.,* V, 375-376.

Randolph, in copying the provisions of the old law, failed to notice the additions that had been made. The imposts on liquors, merchandise, and provisions were continued unchanged. The excise duties remained the same, except that by the definition of retail, a restriction was placed on the unlicensed sale of small amounts, no person being allowed to sell less than five gallons of strong water or a quarter cask of wine at one time without a license. There was no change in the tonnage duty, but conditions in the Dominion made very different its application, because the consolidation of the colonies automatically lifted the tax on ships which had formerly been outside the jurisdiction of Massachusetts, and strict enforcement of the acts of trade reduced the number of foreign vessels trading illegally in that colony.[34]

The reason why Andros insisted on the re-enactment of the revenue law of Massachusetts is probably to be found in his interpretation of his commission, for he "expressed not a little heat and positiveness alledging his instructions and held the Council together unreasonably a very long time about it."[35] This explanation was not, however, acceptable to the councilors, particularly to those who were large landowners or small farmers. For one thing, they found the rating of cattle far too high in proportion to existing values. They objected also to Andros's method of rushing the bill through in spite of their objections, and then allowing it to be entered on the records as passed "nemine contradicte."[36] But more

[34] *Laws of New Hampshire*, I, 184-190.

[35] *Andros Tracts*, I, 139-140; Amer. Antiq. Soc. *Proc.*, N. S., XIII, 256; Mass. Arch., vol. 126, pp. 213, 377. When Andros reported to the Lords of Trade concerning the act of revenue, he said that it would not be sufficient to defray the ordinary expenses of government without Connecticut, but that it was found to be in accordance with his instructions. *Cal. State Pap. Col.*, 1685-1688, §1197.

[36] Amer. Antiq. Soc. *Proc.*, N. S., XIII, 256, 258.

than anything else, they feared that the levying of a direct tax might precipitate trouble, by calling into question the right of the council to legislate on taxation.

The new revenue act was intended as a temporary measure only,[37] but it was retained permanently and another act added later to supplement it. Andros, according to instructions, sent a very complete "State of Revenue" to the Lords of Trade in August, 1687, in which he estimated that the first revenue act would not bring in enough funds to pay the expenses of government.[38] Some other source of revenue must, therefore, be sought. Randolph had often recommended to the president and council, as well as to the Lords of Trade, the raising of a revenue for the support of the government from import duties and quit-rents, a combination which he thought ought to equalize fairly well the burden of taxation, though, he admitted, he had always found the councilors "cold and backward" on the subject. The Lords of Trade had already decided to introduce quit-rents, and instructed Andros not only to reserve a rent of two shillings, six pence for every hundred acres on all grants of vacant land which had reverted to the king upon the fall of the charter, but also to ask whatever rent seemed advisable on previously granted lands needing the king's confirmation. As quit-rents could not be counted on as a source of immediate revenue, Andros favored increasing the import duties, because funds could be obtained from that source at once. For this reason, in his report to the king, he asked permission to increase the customs on wine and the excise on rum, brandy, and strong waters. His

37 The bill was engrossed with the proviso that the act of revenue continue until the governor and council should "agree on and Settle Such other Rates, Taxes and Impositions as shall be Sufficient for his Majesty's Government here." Amer. Antiq. Soc. Proc., N. S., XIII, 256.

38 Laws of New Hampshire, I, 175-178; Toppan, Randolph, IV, 183-186; Andros Tracts, III, 71-72, 73; Cal. State Pap. Col., 1685-1688, §1414.

request was granted, and a bill to that effect was accordingly passed in February, 1688.[39]

The first revenue act imposed burdens on the large landowners and the small farmers, especially those of Plymouth, who were unaccustomed to a poll tax; the new impost bill of February, 1688, fell heavily upon the merchants. In passing these acts Andros thought he had satisfactorily equalized taxation in accordance with his instructions, but unfortunately he had adopted a system which proved unpopular with all classes and pleased none. Since the tax was indirect, the merchants could, of course, shift the burden to the consumer, but not without a certain amount of interference with trade at a time when business was at a low ebb.

The test of the revenue acts, of the legislative power of the council, and, indeed, of the stability of the new government, came, as was expected, when the first country rate fell due. By the first act, the rate was to be levied automatically and collected according to former law and custom in Massachusetts. The treasurer was to send warrants in July, 1688, to the constable and selectmen in every town, requiring the former to call together the inhabitants, who were to choose a commissioner. The next month the commissioner and the selectmen were to make a list of all male persons from sixteen years and upward and an estimation of all real and personal estates. Then the commissioners of the several towns were to gather at their shire town in September, bringing the lists thus prepared. These lists were to be discussed and corrected according to the judgment of the major part, after which they were to be transmitted under the hands of the committee to the treasurer. Upon receiving them,

[39] *Laws of New Hampshire*, I, 153, 159-160, 175-178, 215-218; *Cal. State Pap. Col.*, 1685-1688, §§1502, 1684; Toppan, *Randolph*, III, 334; Andros's "Answers to Instructions," C. O. 5: 855, no. 90.

the treasurer was to give warrants to the constables to distribute the returns among the taxpayers who were to pay the assessments to the treasurer before November 20.[40]

Since the new revenue act was to go into effect at once, a rate was due in July. John Usher, the treasurer, sent warrants in that month to the constables, but in so doing, used the old printed form of the colony. No mention was made in it of the king or governor and council, which was contrary to Andros's instructions, requiring that all writs be issued in the king's name.[41] The Boston selectmen were the first to call attention to this irregularity, but succeeded only in arousing the ire of Andros, who bade them "make the Rates upon their P[er?]iel."[42] They evidently obeyed. The first real defiance came from Taunton. Upon receipt of the warrant, a "seditious writing" was sent to Usher, for which the town clerk was arrested and bound over to answer for the same at the next superior court at Bristol. The constables were accorded the same treatment for neglect of duty, while one of the justices was suspended from office because he made no effort to dissuade the voters at town meeting from drawing up the remonstrance.[43]

40 *Laws of New Hampshire*, I, 184-186; *Mass. Col. Laws* (1887), p. 23.
41 *Laws of New Hampshire*, I, 184-190; *Andros Tracts*, I, 154, 156; C. O. 5: 855, no. 90.
42 *Andros Tracts*, I, 152.
43 Amer. Antiq. Soc. *Proc.*, N. S., XIII, 476. Among the Hinckley papers was found one in Hinckley's handwriting evidently written for the Taunton remonstrators, containing the plea they offered in defense of their actions. Objection to the rate was based, first, on the ground that it was contrary to a "statute of 25 Ed. I de Tallagio non concedendo that says 'Taxes shall not be imposed without consent of the Commons' "; secondly, that it was contrary to the letter of the title of the revenue act itself, which purported to be a law continuing former rates, as Andros's commission had directed, and, therefore, since there never had been such a method of raising taxes in Plymouth, was not legally binding on them; and thirdly,

Mutiny against the writ broke out in Essex county and spread like an epidemic. All the towns except Salem, Marblehead, and Newbury refused to obey the law. At a meeting of the selectmen of Ipswich the warrant was read and condemned because it "did abridge them of their liberty as Englishmen." Among those present was the Rev. John Wise, the pastor of Chebacco, who spoke against the raising of money without an assembly. The next day, another meeting was held, at which the moderator, John Andrews, and the clerk, John Appleton, expressed themselves vehemently. Wise spoke again and urged them to stand up for their privileges, whereupon a paper was read, containing the town's refusal to choose a commissioner for participation in a tax levied contrary to Magna Carta without the consent of an assembly. This refusal was accepted as the vote of the town and forwarded to Usher. In answer, the ringleaders were apprehended and brought before the governor and council for examination.[44]

News of the vote at Ipswich spread to other towns, where it served as the kindling spark to the flammable discontent. At Rowley, Haverhill, and Salisbury, the inhabitants refused to elect their commissioners, and in consequence the selectmen were ordered to appear before the governor and council and "answer the contempt thereby put upon yr Excellency's government." The commissioners of Andover and Bradford went to Salem, the shire town, but after participating in the discussion there as to the legality of the form of the writs, refused to complete their lists. They also were arrested.[45]

The various selectmen, officers, and others, twenty-

that it omitted the king's name and consequently was illegal. 4 Mass. Hist. Soc. *Col.*, V, 165.

[44] *Cal. State Pap. Col.*, 1685-1688, §1534; Sewall, *Diary*, I, 190, note 1.

[45] Mass. Arch., vol. 127, pp. 116, 145, 180, 201, 202, 236; vol. 35, pp. 130, 143, 146, 148 a.

eight in all, committed from the county of Essex for "refusing to pay their rates pursuant to the Treasurers warrant & making and publishing factious & seditious votes & writings against the same," were examined before the governor and council on September 21. This formidable arraignment, as was intended, cowed most of them into submission, but Wise took the same bold stand shown in the town meeting, "asserting the priviledges of Englishmen according to Magna Charta." John West is reputed to have answered that they "had no further privilege reserved saveing to be exempted from being sold for slaves."[46]

As a result of the examination, the "insurrectioners" were divided into three groups according to the seriousness of their offenses. The men in the first group were ordered to be committed until the time of their trials at Boston by a special commission of oyer and terminer. Those in the next group were ordered bound over for two hundred pounds each, with surety, to appear at the next superior court to be held in the county of Essex, and in the meantime to be of good behavior. Those of the third group, consisting of men "appearing more ingenious and less culpable then the others," were discharged

[46] Amer. Antiq. Soc. *Proc.*, N. S., XIII, 477. West's remark is commonly thought to have been made by Dudley, but the following petition of Francis Wainwright to the governor and council, asking pardon "for unadvised words," would indicate that it was John West who made the statement. "Whereas yor Petitioner hath inconsiderately rehearsed & repeated some words or expressions proceeding from Mr. John Wise which he declared to have passed from John West Esq. at the time of sd Wise his Examination before yor Excellencey and Councill, upon his asserting the priviledges of Englishmen according to Magna Charta It was replyed to him that wee had no further privilege reserved saveing to be exempted from being Sold for Slaves, or to like Effect, Yor Petitioner is heartily sorry that he Should be so imprudent and unadvised as to receive and repeat any such Report or expressions not considering the evill consequences or tendency thereof." Mass. Arch., vol. 127, p. 162.

upon their humble submission and acknowledgment and the payment of their fees.[47]

A few days of close confinement wrought a great change in many of those imprisoned. They began to petition Andros for pardon, promising to acquiesce in the treasurer's orders. Andros at first ignored these petitions, thinking it advisable to make the punishment severe and to keep the ringleaders where they could do no harm until the people had quieted down. Meanwhile, in order that the returns might be completed, he commanded the high sheriff and the justices of the peace of Essex county to summon the inhabitants of the towns to meet together and bring in accounts of their estates as by law directed, and to instruct the constables to make a list of the taxables, returning the list to the treasurer with all speed. Ipswich chose her tax commissioner and paid her rate by November 24.[48]

Public attention centred upon the trial of the six Ipswich "insurrectioners" at the special court of oyer and terminer, held at Boston early in October. The judges were Dudley, Stoughton, Usher, and Randolph.[49] In their defense, the prisoners pleaded the repeal of the Massachusetts law of assessment and the privilege of Englishmen, secured by Magna Carta and the statute laws, not to be taxed without their consent. Dudley, who was familiar with English law and the legal point of view on this matter, replied that they must not think the laws of England followed them to the ends of the earth. The case

[47] Amer. Antiq. Soc. *Proc.*, N. S., XIII, 477-478.

[48] Mass. Arch., vol. 127, pp. 109, 127, 147, 148, 164, 166, 170, 180, 184, 208 a, 209, 209 a, 236; Amer. Antiq. Soc. *Proc.*, N. S., XIII, 478.

[49] Ten commissioners, all councilors, were appointed: Joseph Dudley, William Stoughton, Peter Bulkley, Robert Mason, Wait Winthrop, John Usher, Bartholomew Gedney, John Hinckes, Edward Randolph, and Francis Nicholson. According to the commission, any three could act, provided one of the three was Dudley, Stoughton, or Bulkley. Mass. Arch., vol. 126, pp. 167-169.

was committed to the jury, who pronounced the accused guilty of high misdemeanor. After the rendering of the verdict they were remanded to prison and kept there for judgment, which when it came seemed overwhelmingly severe to the transgressors, who had hoped for a pardon. Wise and Appleton were fined fifty pounds in money, charged the costs, and required to give a one-thousand-pound bond for good behavior for one year. Appleton was disqualified from holding office and Wise was suspended from the ministerial function, although later Andros remitted this part of his sentence. The other four had similar judgments, except that the fines were made smaller and the amount of the bond was reduced. The fees were heavy, the prison charges considerable, and the time lost from business and profession was an added expense. A further grievance was the conviction on the part of the accused that a prejudiced jury had been especially chosen to try them, a conviction based on the fact that, contrary to the provisions of a former law of Massachusetts, some of the jurymen were not freeholders.[50]

By prompt and vigorous action, the new government had weathered a storm that might have wrecked it, since the lack of a representative assembly offered a very vulnerable point of attack. At the request of the Lords of Trade, the English attorney-general, in 1685, had expressed his opinion that to govern New England without an assembly was illegal, and the colonists themselves claimed that the right of representative government was guaranteed to Englishmen by Magna Carta. The irregularity in the form of the writ gave another opportunity for complaint,[51] and it is not surprising that the Puritans,

[50] Toppan, *Randolph*, IV, 171-183; *Andros Tracts*, I, 82, 84, 85.

[51] This point was especially emphasized in the revolutionary propaganda. At the time of the remonstrances, the emphasis was placed on the illegality of taxation without a representative assembly, but later, in the charges drawn up by the committee in December, 1689, Usher, as treasurer, was

accustomed as they were to question and nullify the acts of their own assemblies whenever they thought them unjust or inconvenient, should have raised the question of the constitutionality of the council's right to levy a tax.[52] If Andros were to put an end to this pernicious habit and to make the people respect and fear the new government, it was necessary that he deal severely with the objectors.

The law was unpopular in other respects also, for certain of its provisions worked unfavorably for the towns and the rural communities. As far as Massachusetts was concerned it should have made little difference, for it was in the main but a re-enactment of two of that colony's laws, but it differed from those laws in two particulars: the valuation of cattle and the abolition of the discount on cash payments. The tax on polls and land was the same that it had been, but, owing to Randolph's error in copying the form of the new act from an obsolete edition of the laws of Massachusetts, cattle were rated too high. Oxen four years old or more, had been valued by the act of 1646[53] at five pounds, but had been reduced in 1683 to three pounds in order to keep pace with the drop in prices. They were now listed at five pounds. Horses of three years and upwards had dropped from five to

arraigned for having issued a ''Warrant not in His Majestyes Name (who had advice from Sir Edmund so to doe as said Usher declared) and was a maine reason why some Ipswich people and others did not at first pay their Rates, But when he Issued out his warrant in his Majesties name they Readily paid their rates, this is true although there is none sworn to it yet. There was formerly orders from England that all warrants should runn in his Majesties name, and oh the very great damage the omission of this hath done.'' *Andros Tracts*, I, 156.

[52] The colonial governments frequently had trouble in collecting rates, in persuading towns to send representatives, and in securing obedience to orders regarding the militia.

[53] This act was renewed in 1647, 1651, and in 1657. *Mass. Col. Laws* (1887), p. 23.

three pounds in 1677, but were now re-rated at five
pounds. Other animals were valued as in the earlier
acts.[54] This high rating fell heavily on the little agricultural communities, which still made up the greater part
of the country. In their turn, the towns were just as
seriously affected by another provision of the act, the
withdrawal of the discount formerly allowed for cash
payments. According to former custom, the country rate,
unless otherwise specified in the levy, could be paid either
in kind or in money, but in order to draw money into the
treasury for the payment of salaries and other expenses,
a discount of one-third was allowed when the rate was
paid in cash. The inhabitants of the large towns generally
found it easier to pay the country rate in money, since
as a rule they were not farmers and had no farm products
to offer. The withdrawal of the discount for cash had the
effect of increasing their taxes, in proportion to those of
other classes, at least one-third.[55]

Although the impost act of 1688[56] could not so easily
be charged with unconstitutionality, as it levied only an
indirect tax, yet its economic effect was such as to make
it most unpopular with certain classes. The duty on wines
was more than doubled, as a result of which many people
ceased to buy the expensive drinks and began to use home
brews, to the detriment of the interests of wine vintners
and tavern keepers. The excise, also, was greatly increased, and the license requirement for the sale of small
quantities of liquor, being strictly enforced, affected a
class of people who had formerly escaped it. Here and
there a little liquor had been sold, without a license, by
families who had more than was needed for home consumption. This practice had always been winked at by

[54] 4 Mass. Hist. Soc. *Col.*, V, 154-156; *Laws of New Hampshire*, I, 185.

[55] Another class affected by the new revenue act was the clergy, who had
formerly been free from taxation. Only councilors were now exempt.

[56] *Laws of New Hampshire*, I, 215-218.

the officials, because it seemed to do very little harm, but under Andros, the collection of the excise in most parts of the Dominion was put into the hands of commissioners, who took great pains to ferret out these little irregularities. They were given authority to collect the fines for breaches as well as the duties, which was a dangerous delegation of power, and one apt to be taken advantage of by unscrupulous and grasping officials.[57]

Taxes were lower during Andros's administration than they had been in Massachusetts for many years past or were to be for many years to come. After the passage of the revenue act in the spring of 1687, there were no other country rates than the one levied under the provisions of the act, and consequently the poorer people, who had always felt very severely the reduplicated poll tax, enjoyed considerable relief. The act fell lightly also on the great landowners, who usually carried a burden on real estate of several country rates a year. During the year 1690, after the charter government had been resumed in Massachusetts, thirty-two and a half single country rates were levied and the duties on imports increased.[58] But these heavy taxes were borne much more

[57] Mass. Arch., vol. 35, pp. 133, 135, 182; vol. 128, p. 244; vol. 129, pp. 35-38, 273; John Usher's Accounts (Massachusetts Historical Society); *Andros Tracts*, III, 196. One Boston merchant petitioned Andros in 1688 saying that he could not possibly live and "maintain any attendance Suitable for such an Imploy" with the high rates for excise. Mass. Arch., vol. 35, p. 37.

[58] The rates levied from 1676 to 1686 were as follows: 1676, 6; 1677, 3; 1678, 3; 1679, 5½; 1680, 4; 1681, 2¾; 1682, 3½; 1683, 3½; 1684, 2½; 1685, 1½; *Mass. Col. Rec.*, V, 120, 156, 195, 219-220, 245, 296, 307, 324, 341, 376, 417, 426, 443, 454, 505. Ten rates were ordered on March 14, 1690, two and one-half on July 15, and twenty in November. If the fiscal year, dating from March 25 is taken, the same figures apply because the rates were all collected in 1690. The writs of the treasurer for the ten rates are recorded in the *Boston Town Records* as received on July 23. *Laws of New Hampshire*, I, 335, 367, 433, 450, 463, 467; *Boston Town Records*, 1660-1701, pp. 203, 205, 208; *Andros Tracts*, II, 210.

willingly by the followers of "the faction" than had been the lighter taxes of the Andros administration, because they were voted by an assembly composed of the representatives of the people.[59]

The effects of the revenue acts were the same in Maine and New Hampshire as they had been in Massachusetts, for both had been under the Massachusetts jurisdiction, and also in Connecticut, whose revenue system had been modeled on that of the Bay colony.[60] Rhode Island had a country rate, but not in combination with the poll tax and income tax as in Massachusetts and Connecticut, and she was not accustomed to excise and import dues. The inhabitants, however, adapted themselves more readily to the new law than did Plymouth, whose revenue policy had been to impose light burdens upon the inhabitants, because in general they were very poor. The government of Plymouth had been supported by means of a direct tax on improved lands and on produce and by import and export dues.[61] The sums raised by these methods had been very small, but nevertheless sufficient to meet the needs of government, which had been only one hundred pounds a year, fifty of which went to the governor and fifty to the assistants, among whom it was equally divided. For Plymouth Andros's revenue act was a positive hardship, both as to the form and the amount of taxation. The poll tax fell heavily on the poor, who often had large families, with sons above sixteen still working for the father. But worst of all was the over-

[59] *Andros Tracts*, I, 206.

[60] John Pynchon requested Andros to send him copies of the laws passed, that he might have them to show to the people when they inquired, having found it most convenient to have in his possession the act about rates "to the satisfying of several Connecticut men who herd reports of its being otherwise, but by it I convinced them that it was noe otherwise then formerly." Mass. Arch., vol. 126, p. 377.

[61] 4 Mass. Hist. Soc. *Col.*, V, 155.

rating of the cattle and horses which made the tax about
five times higher than it ought to have been.[62]

Neither of the revenue laws was extended to New York
and New Jersey. When Andros received his new commission in 1688 he went at once to New York to assume
the government and issued a proclamation continuing
the existing revenue measures and confirming all public
officers in their posts. He did the same with New Jersey.
The revenues of these provinces were thereafter managed separately, so there was no change from the existing
systems and consequently no opposition to the collection
of the taxes.[63]

Scarcely less hated than the revenue act was that
which regulated town meetings. At first local government was left unchanged by the Andros administration,[64]
because the legislative committee and the council were too
much occupied with the passage of laws of more immediate importance to take it under consideration. All local
officials were directed to proceed, until further orders,
in the execution of their respective duties according to
such laws and usages of the provisional government and
of the colonies not included in that government, as were
not repugnant to the laws of England, the Declaration
of Indulgence, Andros's commission, and the laws of the

[62] 4 Mass. Hist. Soc. *Col.*, V, 154-157, 165, 168, 173-175.

[63] *Cal. State Pap. Col.*, 1685-1688, §1901; Amer. Antiq. Soc. *Proc.*, N. S.,
XIII, 498. Andros in his "Answers to Instructions," sent to the Lords of
Trade, says, "And on the Annexation of New-Yorke the like Comittee [on
laws] was appoynted upon whose report Courts of Judicature were estab-
lished, And Circuits appoynted for that as for all other parts of the Govt.
And Prudentiall Locall Acts before passed, Confirmed and Inforced & the
Revenue Only Continued as before Established there." C. O. 5: 855, no. 90.

[64] An order was issued on January 3 that "all Selectmen, Constables,
Overseers of the poor and all other Town officers for manageing the Pru-
dentiall Affaires thereof be Continued and elected and are to act in all
Town Affairs in their Severall bounds as formerly." Amer. Antiq. Soc.
Proc., N. S., XIII, 244.

governor and council.[65] Unfortunately, before the council
had time to legislate on local government, the Essex
revolt occurred. As this revolt had taken place in town
meeting, the last stronghold of the theocracy, Andros
considered it necessary to reduce the extensive governmental powers which the towns enjoyed, particularly as
the towns were no longer responsible for many matters
formerly handled in their meetings. The central government had already assumed in the name of the king full
control of the undivided commons, and had made provision for the care of the poor,[66] while in establishing liberty of conscience, it had annulled all local laws on ministers' rates. Consequently, Andros brought about the
passage of a law restricting the number of town meetings to one a year, to be held for the election of officers[67]
and forbidding the inhabitants to convene at any other
time upon any pretense whatsoever. Because this law
deprived the theocrats of the control of local affairs,
just as effectively as abolishing the assembly shut them
out from the central government, they were filled with a
panic of fear lest the administration should be planning
to destroy Puritanism in New England.[68]

The anger of the theocrats at the loss of self-government was concentrated on these two most unpopular of
all the Dominion laws, passed by a government in which
they had no share. The revenue act was not oppressive,
either in the form of taxation or in the amount. Nor was
it an arbitrary act of Andros, for it was based on his instructions and passed by his council. When it was put into

[65] Amer. Antiq. Soc. *Proc.*, N. S., XIII, 261.

[66] By an order, Nov. 30, 1687, the justices of the peace were to provide
for the necessary relief and maintenance of the poor ''in such manner as
by the laws and statutes of England is directed.'' *Ibid.*, 486.

[67] *Ibid.*, 478, 485, 494; Sewall, *Diary*, I, 206.

[68] Toppan, *Randolph*, IV, 150-151; *Andros Tracts*, I, 80, 139, 141; III,
197.

operation, its legality was attacked, as was also Andros's commission of government, on the ground that both were contrary to Magna Carta, which guaranteed taxation by representatives of the people. One cannot help questioning the consistency of the theocrats in so violently asserting their right of sharing in taxation, when they, the voting citizens of the old colonial government, had for many years taxed the non-freemen, who were without representation in the government. Not until the shoe was on the other foot, did they claim the privileges of English law. It is interesting that the moderates, too, who controlled the provisional government and were members of Andros's council, did not at first object seriously to the loss of a representative assembly, as is clear from their acceptance of office, and that it was only when they found they could not dominate the council that they also raised the same cry. In other words, it was class, and not individual, representation that was such a precious thing to the colonists. While the theocracy was in control, the non-freemen desired a royal government, not that each individual might have his inalienable "right of an Englishman" to share in the government, but that he might be freed from the tyranny of the class in control, who had a monopoly of the power of government. The moderates, especially the non-free, formed a class whose interests were opposed to those of the theocrats, and it was for this reason that they desired to get into power. Although recognizing the expediency of continuing the representative assembly to which the Puritans were accustomed, as a source of strength to the government, they accepted office in Andros's council in spite of the fact that the request of the provisional government for a representative assembly had not been granted, because they expected the government to be administered in the interests of the aristocratic class to which they belonged.

It was only when the moderates discovered that they were not in control that they turned against the Andros administration and demanded the right of Englishmen to share in the government. It is, therefore, apparent that the Dominion experiment would have succeeded better had England maintained the representative assembly and taken advantage of the party strife to win the support of the moderates. In that case the cleavage would have been between the theocrats on one side and the moderates and England on the other. As it happened, however, England made the mistake of uniting both classes against the Dominion, because both clamored for a share in the government through a representative assembly.

Reports of the Essex revolt and of the Puritan attitude toward the local government act, which were sent to the Lords of Trade, so minimized the significance of this opposition that the lords looked upon the circumstance merely as an evidence of discontent on the part of the theocrats, because dispossessed of power. They were quite oblivious to the fact that the legislative feature of the new colonial policy was the rock on which that policy was in danger of being wrecked. To them, the experiment appeared to be successful. The superior authority of parliament was recognized and its acts were enforced. By means of instructions to the governor, the lords were able to obtain the passage of acts on matters needing reform, and all laws were under the control of the crown by means of the royal disallowance.[69] Andros's vigorous enforcement of the Dominion laws appeared to keep in check the colonial tendency to nullify unpopular legislation and to instil a spirit of respect for government.

[69] *Andros Tracts*, III, 72-73. In Andros's ''Answers to Instructions'' it is stated that up to the time of writing the king had not signified allowance or disallowance of any laws except the revenue act, of which he approved.

Nowhere is there to be found better evidence of the
different views that were held in England and the colonies during this century, regarding the relationship of
the colonies to the mother country, than in this clash over
the legislative power of Andros's council. The theocrats
considered the colonies independent political communities, with every right of self-government, bound to the
mother country only through the personal tie of the
king's royal charter, which granted the full rights of
Englishmen. With parliament, they had nothing to do,
for that body was on a par with their own legislative
assemblies. In England, the government looked upon the
colonies as dependent communities, subject to its rule,
except where special privileges had been granted in the
royal charters. To be sure, the "rights of Englishmen"
was a phrase found in all of the charters, yet it meant
only personal and individual privileges, not political. It
was to the corporation, not to the colonists, that the right
to govern by an assembly of its members was given, and
these corporations were looked upon as similar in character to the borough and other corporations in England.
The insistence by the mother country on the administration of the trade laws in American waters had forced
the colonists to recognize the right of parliament to legislate in matters of general commercial concern, but not
until the Dominion of New England was established did
she make it clear that legislation by the colonists, even in
local matters, was a privilege and not a right, a privilege
which the king could withdraw whenever he thought that
the colonists were using it unwisely. The first clash between these views came in the Essex county revolt. Putting down this revolt by force marked a temporary
triumph for the English point of view, and those in
authority at home, not unnaturally, assumed that for the
future the relations between the Dominion and England,

as far as legislation was concerned, had been clearly defined.

Though the king's position in the matter was legally justified, James and his advisers made a mistake of judgment when they failed to take into account the institutional development of fifty years in New England and the importance to the colonies of their own ways of thinking and doing. Having once accepted representative assemblies as a feature of government in the colonies, the British authorities acted most unwisely in withdrawing the privilege at so late a date, because in so doing, they gave an opportunity to the colonists to strike at a government which was hated for other and more potent reasons. It would have been better had the king preserved the representative assembly in the Dominion of New England, placing the right to vote on an adequate property qualification and providing an independent salary for the governor as a check to its growing power. Such a course might have assured there the success of the colonial policy.

CHAPTER V

ADMINISTRATION OF JUSTICE

It was as difficult for England to control the courts of the corporation colonies as it was to supervise their legislation. These colonies took the attitude that their charters gave them the liberty to develop their own judicial systems in any way that seemed best to them. Consequently they borrowed what they pleased from English legal custom, making modifications to fit the needs of frontier communities, and, in the case of Massachusetts and Connecticut particularly, to suit their theocratic ideas. By the latter part of the seventeenth century, each of the Puritan colonies had its own statute and common law governing judicial procedure. It is important, therefore, to trace the development of the judicial system there and to note the extent to which it diverged from that of England.[1]

The Puritans who came over to Massachusetts in the great migration evidently had, at the outset, no more idea of a political than of a religious break with the mother country. Just as they considered themselves still within the Church of England, so they thought of the colony as being a part of the realm of England and represented in parliament by the burgesses of East Greenwich, the manor to which the colonies were by charter

[1] Variations in legal practice were, of course, to be found in all of the colonies, but, owing to the theocratic character of the Puritan colonies, one finds in the latter a peculiar type of divergence.

attached.[2] As long as this conception of the political relationship survived, they could not well deny the authority
of parliamentary statutes and of the common law. On
the other hand, they felt the force of a higher law, the
law of God, as much more binding than that of England.
Since they thought of themselves as the chosen of God,
commanded by Him to found a theocracy in the New
World, they naturally felt that to fulfil their calling was
an obligation more important than their duty to the
mother country. They made a government, therefore,
which though conforming in most respects to the charter
requirements was in reality based upon the Old Testament and the Institutes of Calvin. Cases in court were
determined according to the law of the colony, but if no
law existed on the point at issue, then according to the
law of God.[3] At first, the variations from the English
judicial system were in matters of customary law only
and care was taken to keep the written law in conformity
with the law of England, according to charter stipulation.[4] Later, however, not even their written laws were
always in conformity with those of the mother country.[5]
Consequently, the whole legal system of the corporate
colonies, embracing statute law and common law alike,

[2] Winthrop, *Journal* (Original Narratives of Early American History),
II, 186.

[3] The General Court appointed a committee in 1636 to "make a draught
of lawes agreeable to the word of God, wch may be the ffundamentalls of
this comonwealth." *Mass. Col. Rec.*, I, 174-175. According to the Body
of Liberties (§1), completed in 1641, only capital cases were to be judged
according to the law of God when no other law existed on the point in
question. *Cf. Cal. State Pap. Col.*, 1675-1676, p. 464.

[4] Winthrop, *Journal*, I, 323-324.

[5] This statement is based on the charges which Randolph drew up against
the colony before the annulment of the charter, and on the revolutionary
pamphlet called "An Abstract of Some of the Printed Laws of New England Contrary to the Laws of England." *Andros Tracts*, III, 13-16. See
also *Cal. State Pap. Col.*, 1689-1692, §133.

developed a character of its own, differing in many respects from that of England.

The Massachusetts lawgivers were quite aware of this growing divergence from English law, but hoped that before England should call them to account for it, they would be strong enough to resist interference from outside. The defiant attitude of the Puritans during the early Restoration period is indicative of the fact that they were then more aware of their strength than in the early days of the colony and more certain of the righteousness of their independent position. But in the meantime parliament had changed its character; it was no longer Puritan and the bond of common interest was gone. The time had come, of which the magistrates had written in 1644, "If the parliament should hereafter be of a malignant spirit, etc., then if we have strength sufficient, we may make use of salus populi to withstand any authority from thence to our hurt."[6] Throughout this period, Massachusetts denied that the acts of parliament were in any way binding upon the colonies, unless re-enacted by the General Court;[7] she denied also that the colonists were subject to English common law, or that the king could hear appeals from colonial courts.[8] The other New England colonies took a similar, although less aggressive, stand. By repeated statements and actions, they showed that they considered themselves outside the English judicial system.

One must not forget that there were large numbers of people in Massachusetts, who were not free of the company and who enjoyed neither the rights of Englishmen nor those of colonists. They always favored the English point of view, and looked upon the modifications made

6 Winthrop, *Journal*, II, 186.

7 *Cal. State Pap. Col.*, 1675-1676, p. 407; 1685-1688, §2069; *Mass. Col. Rec.*, V, 200-201.

8 *Cal. State Pap. Col.*, 1661-1668, §1103; 1689-1692, §133.

in the charter requirements by the government of the
Puritan theocracy as unconstitutional and a subversion
of their liberties as Englishmen. Consequently, they admitted the jurisdiction, and claimed the benefits of English statute and common law.

The careful investigation of colonial affairs which was
entered upon by the Lords of Trade after 1675 brought
to light many irregularities in the law and practice of
the courts of New England, and made clear the need of
reform along the following lines: reorganization of the
courts in such a way that they would conform to English
legal practice; establishment of vice-admiralty courts for
the trial of breaches of the navigation acts similar to
those of England; establishment of a central court for
New England with original jurisdiction over intercolonial disputes;[9] and, finally, recognition by the colonial
governments of the rights of individuals to appeal from
the colonial to the king's courts. All these reforms were
rendered possible by the establishment of the Dominion
of New England.

Andros's commission outlined in detail the policy to
be followed in the administration of justice.[10] Governor
and council were to act as a supreme court, thus com-
bining in the same persons the highest judicial, legislative, and executive functions of government. They were to
have both original and appellate jurisdiction and to follow forms of procedure that were as nearly consonant
and agreeable to the laws and statutes of the kingdom
of England "as the present state and condicon of our

[9] Randolph had suggested the erection of a ''Great Council'' chosen out
of the ''chiefest and best of every colony,'' ''to be like the house of Lords
to heare all appeals from inferior Courts and to assigne places and persons
to try causes arising betwixt Colony and Colony, and Inhabitants of Different Colonyes.'' Toppan, *Randolph*, III, 57, 263; *Cal. State Pap. Col.*, 1685-
1688, §2069.

[10] *Pub*. Col. Soc. Mass., II, 47-50.

Subjects inhabiting within our said Territory and Dominion and the Circumstances of the place will admitt.''

Andros himself was empowered to establish, with the advice and consent of his council, such courts of justice as were necessary, and to appoint judges, justices of the peace, sheriffs, and all officers concerned in any way with the execution of the laws. He was also to erect one or more courts of admiralty ''for the hearing and determining of all marine and other causes and matters proper therein to be heard.''[11] As vice-admiral, he received from the king, who was at this time his own Lord High Admiral, a separate commission and instructions explaining in detail his duties in regard to admiralty matters.[12] Full power of pardon in capital and criminal cases (except wilful murder), as well as in matters of fines and forfeitures, was given to him and in all such cases he could grant reprieves until the king's pleasure were known.[13]

Thus instructed, Andros, upon his arrival in New England, established a judicial system which was conformable to English practice and custom. A law was passed in his council, embodying the principal features of the system, and to this law additions were made from time to time. Thereby were provided a supreme court of the governor and council, a superior court of common pleas, inferior courts of common pleas, courts of quarter sessions, probate courts, and a court of chancery.

The supreme court of the governor and council had original jurisdiction in civil and criminal causes of both a real and a personal nature, and appellate jurisdiction in cases of error from the lower courts where the amount involved exceeded the value of £100 sterling, the appellant

11 *Pub.* Col. Soc. Mass., II, 51.
12 *Ibid.*, 201-203, 370-372.
13 *Ibid.*, 49-50.

to give security to "answere such charges as shall be awarded in case the first Judgment be affirmed." From the governor and council cases exceeding the sum of £300 sterling could be taken to the king in council, provided the appeal were made within a fortnight after the decision and security were given by the appellant. The court was to be held twice a year at Boston or elsewhere, and oftener if the governor so desired.[14]

The superior court of common pleas could award judgment as fully as could the courts of king's bench, common pleas, and exchequer in England. It had original jurisdiction in all cases real, personal, or mixed, in pleas of the crown in all matters relating to the conservation of the peace, and in all civil causes or actions between his majesty and any of his subjects. The court had appellate jurisdiction in cases of error from the inferior court of common pleas, provided the appeal were brought within ten days. From the superior court, appeals could be taken to the governor and council in cases exceeding £100 sterling in value. The form of the proceedings and the judgment were to be as conformable as possible to the laws of England. The court was to consist of at least one councilor or such judge as the governor might appoint. Since this court was itinerant and held sessions in all the counties, it was a great improvement over its predecessor, the court of assistants, which had met only at Boston.[15]

The inferior court of common pleas, held in each county by an appointed judge and two or more justices of the peace, was to have jurisdiction in all civil cases not exceeding £10 sterling in value, where freeholds were not concerned, and in cases of misdemeanor and crime not extending to life, limb, or banishment. It was

14 *Laws of New Hampshire*, I, 193.
15 *Ibid.*, 192-193.

to sit at the same times and places as the quarter sessions, with the exception of the court in the county of Suffolk, the chief town of which was to be Boston. Since Boston was the centre of trade, and there was need of a "more Speedy dispatch of all Marratime and merchandizeing affaires," courts could be held there once in every two months and causes wherein freehold was not concerned, tried to the value of £20 with costs.[16] The quarter sessions courts in the counties were held by the justices of the peace, empowered to hear all matters relating to the conservation of the peace.[17]

Probate matters, which had formerly been handled by the county courts, were now taken care of by special courts set up for the purpose. In the counties of Suffolk and Middlesex, all wills relating to estates located there had to be proved at Boston, before the governor or such person as he should commission. In all other counties, because of the great inconvenience it would cause to bring witnesses to Boston from a distance, the inferior court of common pleas was empowered to examine witnesses to any will within their respective counties upon oath, and forward the certified will to the secretary's office at Boston. If the court were not in session, the judge with two justices of the peace could act in its place. The judges of the inferior courts in these remote counties were empowered to grant, in open court, probates of will or letters of administration to any persons where the estate in question did not exceed the value of £50. Appeal could be made to the governor and council within three months after the decision was made.[18]

The court of chancery established under the new system was a continuation of the one established in Massa-

16 *Laws of New Hampshire*, I, 191-192; Mass. Arch., vol. 126, pp. 245-246.
17 *Laws of New Hampshire*, I, 190-191.
18 *Ibid.*, 206-207; Mass. Arch., vol. 16, p. 428.

chusetts for the first time in 1685. It could hear all such matters of equity as were brought into the king's high court of chancery in England. It was to be held by the governor or such person as he should appoint as chancellor, assisted by five or more of the council, who should have the same power as masters of chancery in England. The court was to sit where and when the governor should decide. Appeals could be taken to the king in council under the conditions governing appeals from the court of the governor and council.[19]

The judicature act made no provision for special vice-admiralty courts, although Andros was empowered by his commission to establish them. Admiralty cases continued to be tried, as they had been under charter government, in the local courts,[20] and for the handling of the "Marratime and merchandizeing affaires" of Boston, the act arranged for more frequent meetings of the inferior court of common pleas of Suffolk. At the time this act was passed, the special admiralty court established in 1686 was still in existence, although one hears no more of it after the departure of Wharton, the judge, for England in July, 1687. Contrary to the practice in English vice-admiralty courts, where procedure according to the civil law was employed, cases in this court of 1686 were tried by a jury as in the common law courts.[21] Therefore it could have been no more effective in the trial of breaches of the acts of trade than were the ordinary courts, which was considered a sufficient reason for abandoning it. Why Andros did not introduce civil law procedure into the admiralty court instead of allowing

[19] *Laws of New Hampshire*, I, 193.

[20] *Cal. State Pap. Col.*, 1681-1685, §416. There must have been a variation in practice at different times, for Bradstreet, in his answers to the inquiries of the Lords of Trade in 1680, states that admiralty cases were tried "without a Jury, according to the See Laws."

[21] Sewall, *Letter Book*, I, 34; Mass. Arch., vol. 126, p. 32.

it to be crowded out by the common law courts is not easy to understand.

Trial by jury was guaranteed by the act of judicature in all cases arising in the courts of the Dominion. Jurors were chosen by the marshal, assisted by the justice of the peace, from among those possessing real or personal estate to the value of fifty marks.[22] This arrangement was contrary to the former laws of Massachusetts and Connecticut governing the choice of jurors, whereby they must be freeholders selected by the freemen. The change in the law was not fully understood throughout the Dominion and occasioned the frequent charge, which was brought against the Andros administration, of using picked and packed juries. Most of the jurors for the special oyer and terminer court held for the trial of the Essex county seditioners, were landless merchants and former non-freemen. This fact gave to the Puritans the impression that special care was taken to select men prejudiced against the prisoners on trial in order to bring certain conviction.

Dudley was appointed chief judge of the superior court, with a salary of £150, and Stoughton and Bulkley were made associate judges with salaries of £120 each.[23] The latter died about the time that New York was annexed, and John Palmer, a very able New York lawyer, who had served as councilor under Dongan and judge of the New York vice-admiralty court, was appointed in his place. Later he took the place of Dudley as chief judge.[24] The judges of the inferior courts received no salary, but were dependent entirely upon fees for remuneration. Dr. Bullivant was appointed attorney-gen-

[22] *Laws of New Hampshire*, I, 194; Amer. Antiq. Soc. *Proc.*, N. S., XIII, 464. A mark=13sh., 4d.

[23] *Ibid.*, 267, 472; *Cal. State Pap. Col.*, 1685-1688, §375; Mass. Arch., vol. 127, p. 33.

[24] Hutchinson, *Hist. of Mass.* (2d ed.), I, 371, note.

eral[25] under the first commission and James Graham of New York under the second.[26] Giles Masters was selected as king's attorney.[27]

An effort seems to have been made to choose men with the best legal equipment for these judicial positions, instead, as formerly, of allowing them to be held by orthodox church members, whose main qualifications were fear of God and a knowledge of biblical law. Unfortunately there was very little material of the right sort in the colony for this purpose. Randolph wrote Secretary of State Sunderland in March, 1687, shortly after the judicature act was passed, that among all those chosen out of the several colonies for councilors, there was no one who rightly understood the laws peculiar to the courts of England. For this reason, he advocated the sending of judges from England. Moreover, he foresaw that native judges would always be an obstacle to any attempt to introduce English land law in New England, because the judges themselves were likely to be interested parties. There was difficulty also in finding men equipped to serve as attorneys, there being only two at Boston during the first year of Andros's administration.[28]

A list of fees for all trials and issues at law was drawn up at the beginning of Dudley's administration and was temporarily continued under Andros. In the meantime a committee was appointed to make a settlement of all fees for courts, offices, and officers throughout the Dominion. The table which they drew up was strongly objected to in council, but was finally adopted. Though the fees were much larger than the people had been accustomed to pay, and larger than they really could

25 Amer. Antiq. Soc. *Proc.*, N. S., XIII, 267.

26 Mass. Arch., vol. 128, p. 271.

27 Amer. Antiq. Soc. *Proc.*, N. S., XIII, 267.

28 *Cal. State Pap. Col.*, 1685-1688, §1194; *Hutchinson Papers*, Prince Soc., II, 300; Mass. Arch., vol. 128, p. 223.

afford to pay, owing to the scarcity of money and the general hard times, they were no larger than those required in other colonies, where English ways and customs were practiced. Whether they were extortionate or not, according to the standards elsewhere, is not the point; the Puritans thought they were, and this belief must be taken into account in estimating the Puritan attitude toward them. This attitude is well shown in a "quaery" presented in a revolutionary pamphlet, "Whether those that Rob on the Road or in the night under the fear of Hanging are not honest Robbers in comparison of them that Rob in the capacity of Lawyers by making the Law itself but a Tool to manage the designs of Robbery?"[29]

In other and less important matters, changes were made which brought the ways of the colonies into closer conformity with English legal custom. In order to correct such irregularities of practice as came to light in the attempt to collect the first rates levied by the governor and council under the new revenue act,[30] Andros required all writs to be issued in his majesty's name throughout the Dominion.[31] Another change was made in the method of oath-taking, the English practice of touching the Bible replacing the New England custom of raising the hand. Many Puritans had scruples against the English method and were thereby incapacitated from serving on juries.

[29] *Andros Tracts*, I, 43-44, 136, 153; III, 21; Amer. Antiq. Soc. *Proc.*, N. S., XIII, 265, 266, 476-477; 4 Mass. Hist. Soc. *Col.*, V, 156-157. Before the table of fees was agreed upon, West seems to have taken heavy fees in executing the office of secretary and register. *Hutchinson Papers*, Prince Soc., II, 299.

[30] It will be remembered that some of the objectors opposed the rate because the writ was not issued in the name of the king, Usher, the treasurer, having used old blanks belonging to the former government. One of the early complaints against Massachusetts was that she did not issue writs in the king's name. 4 Mass. Hist. Soc. *Col.*, V, 165 ff.

[31] *Laws of New Hampshire*, I, 158, 247; Amer. Antiq. Soc. *Proc.*, N. S., XIII, 254.

Citing the concession made to Quakers concerning oath-taking, and the existence in Guernsey and Jersey of a custom similar to theirs, the Puritans accused the Andros administration of intentionally barring them from jury service by insistence on the English custom.[32] Still another unpopular change was made in the care of the poor, who had formerly been looked after by the inhabitants in town meeting and were now assigned to the justices of the peace "in such manner as by the laws and statutes of England is directed."[33] Marriages for the future were to be performed by ministers of the gospel and justices of the peace, and not by magistrates, as formerly, although both Dudley and Andros were instructed to confirm all marriages which had been performed according to former custom.[34]

The judicial system thus established did not greatly differ from that which had existed under the charter government. The General Court and the court of assistants, which had been replaced by the superior court of the councilors under Dudley, now gave way to the superior court of common pleas. The county courts, which were the courts of pleas and sessions of the peace under Dudley, became the courts of quarter sessions and inferior courts of common pleas. Probate matters, formerly han-

[32] *Andros Tracts*, I, 15, 46-47, 179-191; III, 198-199. Mather complained of this change in his petition to the king, August, 1688. *Cal. State Pap. Col.*, 1685-1688, §1878. There is at least one instance, noted in Sewall, *Diary*, I, 201, when a conscientious objector was excused from following the British custom, but there are also several cases of fining for refusal to swear according to law. *Ibid.*, pp. 202, 208, 210, 212.

[33] Amer. Antiq. Soc. *Proc.*, N. S., XIII, 486; *Cal. State Pap. Col.*, 1677-1680, §1360; *Andros Tracts*, I, 80; *Conn. Col. Rec.*, III, 300.

[34] *Cal. State Pap. Col.*, 1685-1688, §710. According to the colonial law, "no Person whatsoever in this jurisdiction shall joyn any persons together in marriage but the Magistrate, or such other as the General Court or Court of Assistants shall authorize in such place where no Magistrate is near." *Andros Tracts*, III, 15.

dled by the county courts, were taken care of in regular probate courts. Chancery jurisdiction, which until 1685 had been vested in the General Court, was granted to a special chancery court.[35] The court of the governor and council, in which the whole system centred, served the purpose of the intercolonial court for which there had been so much demand. In legal procedure, cases were tried according to the "lawes, Customes and statutes of the realme of England, and some peculiar locall prudentiall laws of the Country, not repugnant thereto."[36]

Although the new judicial system did not introduce any startling innovations in the structure of the law, it did clear away a host of practices which the colonists had brought into use in the process of adjusting English custom to the more primitive needs of the frontier and the idiosyncracies of a Puritan theocracy. Inevitably the Puritans resented some of these changes. For instance there was much dissatisfaction over the limited amount of power given to the inferior court of common pleas.[37] Hinckley of Plymouth wrote to Blathwayt urging that the king authorize a modification in the law, when it arrived for his inspection, whereby the inferior courts be given liberty to try any actions of debt or damage to the value of £20, as in Suffolk county, including cases of freehold of the same value. He claimed that otherwise the act of judicature was contrary to the laws of England, in requiring people to carry cases concerning land out of the county in which the lands lay, since the superior court of common pleas for both Plymouth and Barnstable county was held at Plymouth. He said, also, that the law, besides being illegal, brought great inconvenience and

[35] In 1685, Massachusetts passed an act authorizing the magistrates of each county court to act as a chancery court. *Mass. Col. Rec.*, V, 477.

[36] *Andros Tracts*, III, 21.

[37] Connecticut desired that the court of quarter sessions be given power to try any actions under the value of £30. *Conn. Col. Rec.*, III, 395.

hardship, for fees were greater in cases tried in the superior court of pleas, and writs had to be issued from the office of the secretary at Boston, thereby necessitating a trip which for the Plymouth inhabitants was expensive.[38] Whether or not Blathwayt made known the contents of this letter to the English authorities is not clear, but action was taken by the Dominion council in the autumn, partly in accordance with Hinckley's request. The power of the inferior court of common pleas was enlarged to hear all cases, personal and mixed, wherein title to land was not concerned, involving any sum or value whatsoever.[39]

Hinckley objected also to the provision of the law that dealt with probate matters.[40] The people of Plymouth found it a great hardship to be required to go to Boston for all cases involving more than £50. The long trip with the large fees often cost nearly as much as the property was worth.[41] Closely associated in their minds with this probate regulation was another requiring the keeping of all records of the former colonies in the secretary's office at Boston, where they would be more accessible to officers of the probate court, a measure which was quite necessary in order to correct the lax and careless methods of keeping the records to which colonial secretaries were

[38] 4 Mass. Hist. Soc. *Col.*, V, 158-159.

[39] Amer. Antiq. Soc. *Proc.*, N. S., XIII, 478, 490, note.

[40] Hinckley objected to the way the act was passed as well as to its contents, it having been adopted at weekly council, between the date of adjournment of the general legislative council, May 9, and the date set for its next meeting, June 22. 4 Mass. Hist. Soc. *Col.*, V, 157. This is true, but Andros was not guilty of a breach of instructions, for he could do business with a quorum of seven.

[41] Hinckley, in his letter to Blathwayt, complained that West had taken "35 shillings of a poor woman for the probate of her deceased husband's will, the inventory of whose whole estate amounted but to 52 or 53 pounds; and 40 shillings of another poor woman for letters of administration, whose husband died intestate." 4 Mass. Hist. Soc. *Col.*, V, 167-168, 176-177.

inclined. The Plymouth inhabitants, however, could see in this requirement only a design to "circumvent them of their lands," or to compel them to "take patents at dear rates."[42]

Many of the grievances against the courts arose in connection with the trial of the Essex county men for sedition. The charges of extortionate fees, unreasonable fines, packed juries, denial of *habeas corpus,* and the carrying of the accused out of his county were discussed at great length, while the offense of sedition was scarcely considered at all. In the opinion of those who were against the administration, the rebels were in the right of it, wholly justified in standing boldly for the privileges of Englishmen, when being taxed illegally. They thought the punishments were too severe for an offense which was merely an expression of opinion, entirely overlooking the fact that the rebels supported this expression of opinion with threats of disobedience.[43] It was really the first stand taken against the legality of the new government and its powers, and had it not been dealt with vigorously, it might have spread into a general insurrection. The colonists could not understand why such severe measures were taken and explained them as follows: "when our Oppressors have been a little out of Mony, 'twas by pretending some Offence to be enquired into and the most innocent of Men were continually put unto no small Expence to answer the Demands of the Officers, who must have money of them, or a Prison for them, tho none could accuse them of any Misdemeanour."[44]

The juries were, of course, made up of men from the party in power, since they were picked by the marshal and justice from a list of all property holders whose

[42] 4 Mass. Hist. Soc. *Col.,* V, 157-158, 177.

[43] Mass. Arch., vol. 107, p. 151 a; *Andros Tracts,* I, 14, 74, 144, 163; III, 195-196.

[44] *Andros Tracts,* I, 15.

estates, real and personal, were valued above a certain sum. It is probable that they were often men who had been treated none too well by the theocracy, and now enjoyed a certain satisfaction in the power which their jury duty gave them. They may have been prejudiced, but that they were purposely chosen to convict the accused is wholly improbable. The most frequent complaint was that they were not freeholders,[45] but according to the Dominion jury law, they did not have to be. It is possible that the law about jurors may not have been generally known, for it was published in the various towns only by sound of trumpet and beat of drum, a method of proclamation that even at best might leave many in ignorance.

To support the charge that the benefits of the *habeas corpus* law were denied the inhabitants, the case was cited of Samuel Appleton, who had been the most defiant of all the Essex insurrectioners.[46] It is true that he was imprisoned for a long time without trial, but he was arrested too late to be tried at the special court of oyer and terminer held in October and was unable to get the required bail. As for denying him *habeas corpus,* a perusal of the English Habeas Corpus Act passed in 1679 would, as Judge Palmer pointed out, convince ''any considering Man that it is particularly limitted to the Kingdom of England.''[47]

Complaint was made also of the illegality of trying, outside the county, cases which concerned inhabitants or land within the county.[48] On similar grounds, the Plymouth colonists, as we have seen, attacked the provisions made in the judicature act for cases concerning freehold when the value exceeded £10. Again, the method

[45] *Andros Tracts*, I, 74, 84-85, 112; III, 195-196.
[46] *Ibid.*, I, 15; III, 196.
[47] *Ibid.*, I, 46; *Cal. State Pap. Col.*, 1689-1692, §133.
[48] *Andros Tracts*, I, 144, 158; III, 197.

of the governor in bringing writs of intrusion against certain landowners was condemned as illegal.[49] But the most flagrant offense of the government was in trying the Essex rebels at a special court of oyer and terminer at Boston, instead of having them brought before the court of their county. The offenders considered this proceeding not only illegal but also unjust, for they were forced to incur the added expense of a long trip to Boston and were humiliated and embarrassed at the ordeal they had to undergo before the governor and council.[50]

Such innovations as were actually introduced by the new judicial system were objected to by the colonists on two grounds. First, that some of the changes were contrary to colonial law and legal custom, among which were the requirement that oaths must be taken on the Bible and the qualifications imposed in the selecting of jurors. Secondly, that some were contrary to the laws of England, such as the powers granted by the judicature act to the inferior court of common pleas, trial outside of the county of the accused, the appointment of James Sherlock as sheriff when he was not a freeholder, and the denial of *habeas corpus* to Samuel Appleton. These instances are significant as indicating the belief on the part of the Puritans that they could claim the benefits of any English law. Their position is inconsistent because, prior to the fall of the charter, they refused to recognize the statutes of parliament as in any way binding upon them. Their frequent answer to charges that they were breaking the navigation acts was that the laws of parliament were bounded by the four seas. They now insisted that by the charter clause "rights of Englishmen," they were entitled to the benefits of all English statutes and legal customs, whether the colonies were

49 *Andros Tracts*, I, 158, 164.
50 *Ibid.*, I, 14-15, 81-82, 144.

mentioned therein or not.[51] They laid claim to the benefits of Magna Carta and English statute law in their opposition to taxation without a representative assembly;[52] to the protection of English statute law in the case of Sherlock's serving as sheriff, insisting that his appointment was contrary to an act of the reign of Queen Elizabeth,[53] a statute passed before ever colonies existed; and, finally, to the privileges of the common law in many instances, among them the right of the accused to be tried within his own county.

The question of the legal relationship of the colonies to the mother country was frequently brought up during Andros's administration and in the revolutionary period that followed, yet there does not appear to have been at that time any clear-cut official definition of the status of a colony. Englishmen were too much occupied at home in determining the relative powers of king and parliament to concern themselves with the problem, and just as the relation of king and parliament was the great constitutional question of the seventeenth century, so the relation of mother country and the colonies was the equally great constitutional question of the eighteenth, each being accompanied by a revolution. Nevertheless, one finds at this time an occasional expression of opinion in regard to the matter. Evidently there were in England, as well as in America, two points of view concerning this relationship, one held by the parliamentary party, the other by the party supporting the royal prerogative. The attorney-general, representing the first, expressed his opinion, when consulted by the Lords of Trade as to

[51] An undated paper in the Hinckley collection defends the opposition to the rate on the ground of its being "contrary to rule of law in the statute of 25 Ed. I de Tallagio non concedendo." 4 Mass. Hist. Soc. *Col.*, V, 165.

[52] *Andros Tracts*, I, 14, 45, 82, 159.

[53] *Ibid.*, I, 74, 152.

the legality of establishing in the colonies a government without a representative assembly, that such a commission would be illegal.[54] In other words, he believed that Magna Carta and similar concessions formerly won from English kings were the common heritage of all Englishmen, whether they lived in England or in the colonies. John Palmer, an English-trained lawyer, who took up the defense of the Andros administration at the time of the revolution of 1689, in answer to the charges made by the revolutionists, represented the second point of view. He attempted to "lay down this as a certain Maxime, both consonant to Reason and the Laws of the Land, That those Kingdoms, Principalities, and Collonies, which are of the Dominion of the Crown of England, and not of Empire of the King of England, are subject to such Laws, Ordinances, and Forms of Government, as the Crown shall think fit to establish. New England, and all the Plantations are subject to the Dominion of the Crown of England, and not to the Empire of the King of England. Therefore the Crown of England may Rule and Govern them in such manner, as it shall think most fit.''[55] In order to support the legality of this position, he cited Wales and Ireland, and the usage of foreign nations in their plantations. Since the colonies were "subject to the Dominion of the Crown of England," he argued, their making their own laws was a privilege and not a right. Therefore the king could control their legislation as he saw fit, and although he might insist that their laws be conformable to those of England, English statutes and constitutional documents did not apply to them.[56]

[54] *Andros Tracts*, I, 125; *Cal. State Pap. Col.*, 1685-1688, §333.

[55] *Andros Tracts*, I, 35-42.

[56] It will be remembered that in the trial of the Ipswich objectors, they were told that the laws of England would not follow them to the end of the earth. Someone ironically remarked at the time that though the privi-

It is interesting to notice that by thus insisting on the full prerogative of the king to do with the colonies as he pleased, Palmer was denying to parliament the right to pass laws for the colonies. According to the first opinion, the colonies were incorporated into the realm, subject to its government in all its parts; according to the other, they were a part of the king's domain, subject only to his will. The claims of Palmer, who took the second point of view, are identical with those held by the colonists of Massachusetts before the fall of the charter, when they claimed that they were not under the jurisdiction of parliament, but bound only to the king by the compact of the charter.[57] The triumph of the parliamentary party in England in the revolution of 1688 was the triumph also of the parliamentary view of the relationship of the colonies to the mother country, and from that time forward, with increasing determination, parliament asserted its right of legislation over the colonies.

The colonists, on their part, considered that the king held his crown and all of his possessions by the will of the people expressed through the revolution, and thereafter, through parliament in England, and in the colonies through the assemblies which were on a par with parliament. These colonial representative bodies began to act toward the governor as parliament did toward the king, gradually throughout the eighteenth century encroaching upon his power, at the same time jealously guarding against any new assertion of royal authority over them. The Declaration of Independence was the logical out-

leges of the English law did not follow them, evidently the penalties did. *Andros Tracts*, I, 82.

[57] The General Court in answering the accusation that the colony ignored the navigation acts, took pains to show that although the laws of England were "bounded within the fower seas," they had re-enacted those laws as their own only because the king had signified to them his desire that they observe those acts. *Mass. Col. Rec.*, V, 200-201.

come of colonial application of the principle on which the revolution of 1688 was based, *salus populi est suprema lex.*[58]

[58] *Cal. State Pap. Col.*, 1689-1692, §§512, 548, pp. 177, 1384, 1420; 3 Mass. Hist. Soc. *Col.*, I, 100; VII, 23; *Andros Tracts*, I, 71-72; Hutchinson, *Hist. of Mass.*, I, 383; *Conn. Col. Rec.*, III, 460.

CHAPTER VI

LIBERTY OF CONSCIENCE

The policy of the Lords of Trade in regard to religious matters in the Dominion was clear and definite. They desired to destroy the Puritan theocracy and to introduce into New England liberty of conscience with special privileges for the Church of England.[1] Theocracy had been destroyed by the establishment of the provisional government without a representative assembly, but neither liberty of conscience nor encouragement of the Church of England had been much advanced before the arrival of Andros, though Dudley's commission stated as clearly as did that of Andros the policy which the committee wished to promote. Until those who were not Puritans should be freed from the burden of attending the Congregational church and paying for its support and were allowed to hold services of their own, their religious emancipation would not be complete.[2]

---

[1] The same religious purpose was shown early in the Restoration period, when the royal commissioners sent to New England were instructed to urge liberty of conscience, although they were to make it clear that there was no intention to alter the church government or "introduce any other forme of worshipp among them then what they have chosen: all our exception in that particular being that they doe in truth deny that liberty of conscience to each other, which is equally provided for and granted to every one of them by their charter." *New York Col. Docs.*, III, 58. One of the reasons for annulling the charter of Massachusetts had been that the Puritans there prosecuted and punished severely those who did not conform to the Congregational policy. *Andros Tracts*, III, 227.

[2] The penalty for not attending meeting was five shillings. *Ibid.*, 14; *Cal. State Pap. Col.*, 1661-1668, §1103, p. 345; Toppan, *Randolph*, IV, 87.

The number of people affected by the new religious policy was perhaps larger than one might suppose.[3] A comparison of the total population with the number of those admitted to the freedom of the company before the fall of the charter shows that only about one-fifth of the adult males were professing Congregationalists and shared in the privileges of church and state.[4] Undoubtedly a great many of the remaining four-fifths were in sympathy with the Puritan point of view, though there is reason to believe that a majority of them became in time very restless under the political influence of an intolerant group of elders and were out of sympathy with the minority rule. Many were Anglicans, Baptists, Quakers, Antinomians, and probably in a few cases Roman Catholics. None of these seems to have succeeded under the old charter government in holding services of

[3] Randolph wrote to the Archbishop of Canterbury, October 27, 1686, ''we have at present near four hundred persons who are daily frequenters of our Church, and as many more would come over to us. But some being Tradesmen, others of Mechanick Professions, are threatened by the Congregational Men to be Arrested by their Creditors, or to be turned out of their work, if they come to our Church.'' Andros Tracts, III, 206; Toppan, Randolph, IV, 106, 113, 131; Rhode Island Col. Rec., IV, 204.

[4] Randolph frequently insisted that the loyal party in Massachusetts was in the majority, and at one time asserted that as compared with the dissenting party, the church members were one to six. This was probably an exaggeration. Between 1660 and 1686 about 1,500 freemen were admitted, which was about one-fifth of the total adult male population, Andros having reported in 1690 that 7,364 men were enrolled in the militia in Massachusetts. The militia figures do not include the Maine and New Hampshire enrollments, while among the 1,500 were probably included the freemen elected from Maine throughout the whole period and from New Hampshire until 1679 when the royal government was established there. Toppan, Randolph, IV, 37; Cal. State Pap. Col., 1661-1668, §1103, p. 346; 1675-1676, p. 464; 1685-1688, §319; 1689-1692, §879; Hutchinson Papers, Prince Soc., II, 219. For lists of freemen, see Andrews, Lists of Freemen of Massachusetts Bay Colony, 1630-1691 (listed alphabetically), and Twenty-Ninth Report Boston Records, Miscellaneous Papers, pp. 133-163 (listed chronologically).

its own, unmolested, except the Baptists of Boston.[5] In the towns of Maine and probably in those of New Hampshire, the majority was Anglican. In Connecticut conditions were much the same as in Massachusetts, except that there were very many fewer adherents of other denominations,[6] while in Rhode Island liberty of conscience had legally existed since the granting of the charter in 1663. In that colony, therefore, the religious policy of the Dominion wrought no important change.

As is well known, under the charter government, the Congregational church in Massachusetts was supported by rates levied on all inhabitants, Puritans and non-Puritans alike, and by fines collected for non-attendance on worship. Similar laws existed in Connecticut and Plymouth. In spite of the fact that Dudley was instructed to allow liberty of conscience to all, no change was made in the laws governing church maintenance,

[5] The Friends had established a church in Boston in 1664, but were subject to constant persecution. A French Huguenot, ordained as an Anglican minister by the Bishop of London, and sent out to Carolina, went afterwards to Boston, where he met with every sort of opposition from the Congregationalists, particularly from Mather and Moody. *Report of the Boston Record Commissioners*, I, 6; *Cal. State Pap. Col.*, 1685-1688, §267.

That this persecution was not approved of by the majority, is suggested by the following statement, made in 1689 by one of the moderates: "The only thing (so far as I understand) which can with any truth be justly reflected on them as a fault, is that, in some matters relating to conscience and difference of opinion, they have been more rigid and severe than the primitive Christians or the gospel doth allow of. Yet this is to be said in their behalf, that things are reported worse than indeed they were; and that now many leading men, and the generality of the people, are of a more moderate temper. I know some that have a great interest there do abhor the spirit of presecution as much as any men in the world." 3 Mass. Hist. Soc. *Col.*, I, 97.

[6] The governor of Connecticut in "Answers to Queries" in 1680 reported as follows: "Our people in this Colony are, some strict Congregationall men, others more large Congregationall men, and some moderate Presbyterians, and take the Congregationall men of both sorts, they are the greatest part of people in the Colony. There are 4 or 5 Seven-day men, in our Colony, and about so many more Quakers." *Conn. Col. Rec.*, III, 299.

and they continued to be enforced. The coming of Andros brought no immediate relief, because he announced that all laws would be in operation until public proclamation was made of their repeal. The law which provided for the maintenance of ministers and schoolmasters was one of the first to be considered by the council, and occasioned great dissension in that body. The committee on codification tried to persuade the council to continue the act and to extend it to the rest of New England, but the Anglicans and Quakers in the council opposed it every time it was brought up. The non-Puritan cause was championed by Walter Clarke, a former governor of Rhode Island and a Quaker, who said that because the ministers of New England were as much dissenters from the Church of England as were the Quakers or any other sect, they should depend, as did the others, on the voluntary contributions of their hearers. On the other hand Hinckley, a former governor of Plymouth, insisted that because provision for the maintenance of a settled minister was one of the conditions on which townships had been granted in the Puritan colonies, no one of the inhabitants of the towns could escape this obligation. Clarke conceded this, but thought that the persons in any of the townships, who had not actually bound themselves to maintain a minister, should be left to their own devices and not be forced to pay against their wills. The Anglicans and Quakers won the day. The bill was not passed, the old law remaining in operation until the next council meeting only, after which it was to cease to be in force.[7]

But even before that time came, intervention from an unexpected quarter prevented the passage of a new act and stopped the operation of the old one, which was not due to expire until June 22, the date set for the next gen-

[7] Amer. Antiq. Soc. *Proc.*, N. S., XIII, 252-253, 257-258, 259; 4 Mass. Hist. Soc. *Col.*, V, 149; *Andros Tracts*, I, 139; Toppan, *Randolph*, IV, 163.

eral legislative meeting of the council. This event was the arrival of news of the king's Declaration of Indulgence, issued April 4, 1687, by which entire liberty of conscience was granted to all the king's subjects and all Dissenters were relieved of the penal laws and allowed the privilege of public worship. A test was made in Scituate where some Quakers refused to pay the ministers rates, claiming that the Declaration freed them from all obligation to do so. The constable, obeying the colonial law, seized their goods. They petitioned the governor and council for return of their property and on June 23, just after the opening of the council meeting, were granted their request on the grounds that the seizure had been made after the passage of the Declaration of Indulgence.[8] Thus liberty of conscience in the Dominion was established in full, for in the future, no church rates could be legally collected. All denominations were placed on the same level, and the system of support of church and ministers by voluntary contribution was introduced.[9]

One other effect of the Declaration of Indulgence is worthy of notice. The Puritans had already begun to fear that the Church of England might be established in the Dominion and all inhabitants taxed for its support. The Declaration having given them "hopes of deliverance from an approaching Persecution," the ministers of Boston appointed a day of thanksgiving to be celebrated

---

[8] Toppan, *Randolph*, IV, 167; *Conn. Col. Rec.*, III, 393; Sewall, *Diary*, I, 186. Although the Declaration was not published in the Dominion until August, news of it came from England much earlier, as is shown by the resolve of the governor and council, passed June 23, "That the said Wanton being a Quaker and attending other Worship than the Ministroy of the Towne and the Distresse made since his Majesty's gracious indulgence the same is not approved of, but the Goods Distrayned and now in the Constables hands as by his returne to be restored." Amer. Antiq. Soc. *Proc.*, N. S., XIII, 468, 469, 475; *Conn. Col. Rec.*, III, 393; Sewall, *Letter Book*, I, 55-57, note.

[9] *Andros Tracts*, I, 138; Mass. Arch., vol. 127, p. 55.

by each Puritan congregation. The Declaration having been published in Boston in August, 1687, the day set for the celebration came so soon after the Essex outbreak that Andros dared not give the ministers a chance to stir the people to revolt, as Wise had done at Ipswich. He therefore sent for them the night before and forbade the meetings.[10]

As for the second feature of the religious policy of the Dominion—encouragement of the Church of England,—little could be done immediately, because Andros had been instructed to introduce nothing new until he had first reported to the Lords of Trade on the state of the church in New England.[11] The lords evidently thought the failure of Dudley and his council to give encouragement to the Church of England had been a wise use of the discretionary power granted them in the king's commission and apparently they did not wish now that Andros should push the matter to the danger point. Though there must have been a number of Anglicans living in the Dominion, yet outside of Boston no demand for Church of England services seems to have been made. Even there, the congregation was very small. Consequently, the principal need for a church in that locality was for the use of the governor and those about him, Nicholson, Mason, Wharton, Randolph (and later, West and Palmer), and perhaps one or two others who were

10 Mass. Arch., vol. 128, pp. 142-143; *Andros Tracts,* III, 200-201. Andros's refusal to allow the meetings to take place was one of the grievances listed by Increase Mather in the ''Memorial of the Dissenters of New England,'' which he presented to King James in June, 1688. One would not, however, get any idea of Andros's political reasons for the action from the generalizations made in the Memorial, which reads as follows: ''For that they are not suffered to sett apart Days of Prayer and Thanksgiving: no, not even for the Blessing of your Gracious Declaration for Liberty of Conscience, Nor were the People there Encouraged to make humble Addresses of Thanks, but the Contrary.'' *Ibid.,* 137, note.

11 *Cal. State Pap. Col.,* 1685-1688, §680.

Anglicans, as well as most of the redcoats who came over with Andros. Some provision had to be made for the worship of these English officials, which would be suitable to the dignity of their position. The town-house, which served well enough for holding services during the Dudley administration, because the president and council were not officially identified with the Anglican church, was no longer a fitting place. Moreover, there must be adequate provision for the support of the minister. How far was Andros to go in the "encouragement of the Church of England," in the matter of minister's maintenance, and in the obtaining of a place of worship?

The small number of Anglicans made the support of the ministry a great burden to its members, yet there seemed to be no way in which the Andros administration could give them "special encouragement" in financial matters of this sort. Randolph's suggestion that the funds of the Society for Evangelizing the Indians be confiscated and used for paying a minister and building a church was out of the question.[12] Since at least three of the New England colonies were predominantly Congregational, the Lords of Trade were not willing to make Anglicanism the established religion by levying rates on the inhabitants according to the practice in Virginia, Maryland, and the Carolinas, for such procedure would be entirely out of keeping with James's policy of complete liberty of conscience to all. They preferred to leave the Anglicans, as well as all other denominations, free to support their church by voluntary contribution, even though such a policy imposed a heavy burden upon the few who identified themselves with the Church of England.

The few Anglicans in Boston could hardly have been expected, at the outset, to provide a place of worship, and

12 *Andros Tracts*, III, 206-207; Toppan, *Randolph*, IV, 90, 106, 131.

at the same time, bear the expense of maintaining services in it. Until they could build a church, they were allowed by Andros, acting under instructions, to hold services in one of the Congregational meeting-houses. On the day when he arrived at Boston, Andros spoke to the Congregational ministers about suitable accommodations for the purpose, and they immediately held a meeting to discuss the matter, but decided that they "could not with a good conscience consent" that one of the meeting-houses should be used for worship according to the Book of Common Prayer. The same evening a delegation of two of the ministers, Mather and Willard, called on the governor and "thoroughly discoursed his Excellency about the Meeting-Houses in great plainness, showing they could not consent."[13] Andros did not at that time press the matter further. Services were held, as formerly, in the town-house. Since this arrangement was not convenient at the Easter season, Andros gave notice to the members of the Third Church at Boston that he intended to hold services in their meeting-house, but without obstructing their use of it. He sent Randolph for the keys of the building, so that prayers could be said there on Wednesday, March 23. A delegation waited on the governor to remonstrate against its being put to any such use. This delegation exhibited extracts of deeds showing that the land and the meeting-house were both theirs, but Andros paid no attention to their objections. The sexton, who "had resolved to the contrary, was prevailed upon to Ring the Bell and open the door at the Governor's command."[14]

[13] Sewall, *Diary*, I, 162. There were three Congregational churches in Boston. James Allen was minister for the First Church from 1668 to 1710, Increase Mather of the Second, or Old North Church, from 1669 to 1723, and Samuel Willard for the Third, or Old South Church, from 1678 to 1707. Toppan, *Randolph*, I, 291, note.

[14] *Cal. State Pap. Col.*, 1685-1688; §1195; Sewall, *Diary*, I, 171.

Church of England services were held in the meeting-house on the following Sabbath at eleven and at four, but unfortunately, communion and an extra long sermon prevented the Congregational services from beginning at one-thirty, the scheduled time. The Puritans found this very irritating, and the Anglicans took pains to see that it did not happen again, although they continued to use the meeting-house.[15] Since its use occasioned no further actual inconvenience to the Congregationalists, Andros could see no harm in continuing the practice, but the Puritans considered it a desecration, and appointed a private fast for prayer that the burden might be lifted.[16] The arrangement was not a pleasant one for either party, so by the spring of 1688 the Anglicans began to plan for the building of a church of their own. Part of the money was raised by contribution, solicited throughout New England, but most of the expense was borne by the Anglicans themselves. Land was obtained near the centre of the town, and a small building erected which was called King's Chapel.[17]

The Puritans did not soon forget this Anglican appropriation of their meeting house, and treasured it up against Andros as one of the evidences of his arbitrary methods. Yet he only acted in accordance with his instructions and cannot be held responsible for the original idea. His fault lay in his manner, which was brusque and impatient. When the Puritans wrangled and argued over their rights, he frequently lost his temper and said things which made them accuse him of designs for their undoing.

The failure of the council to pass laws providing taxes

15 Sewall, *Diary*, I, 172; *Cal. State Pap. Col.*, 1685-1688, §1197.

16 Sewall, *Diary*, I, 176-177, 179-180, 216-219; Foote, *Annals of King's Chapel*, I, chaps. II, III.

17 3 Mass. Hist. Soc. *Col.*, I, 84; Sewall, *Diary*, I, 207, 210; *Andros Tracts*, III, 20-21.

for educational purposes brought a breakdown in the school system,[18] because after the expiration of the unconfirmed local laws, the chief means of maintenance for the teachers, who were in many places supported by rates, was gone. Moreover, the restriction that no one could teach without a license from the governor probably eliminated from the profession a number of Puritans of the stricter sort, and caused a scarcity of teachers.[19] In many places the schools ceased to function, while in others, the masters labored under great discouragements, owing to the uncertainty concerning their wages. To the Puritans this scarcity was most distressing, because it was a blow to education and a handicap to religion, for schools prepared for college the future ministers of the gospel and offered opportunity for bringing a religious influence to bear on the younger generation.

From an educational point of view the administration did nothing constructive during the brief period of its existence, although before its establishment Randolph frequently expressed a desire to supersede the Congregational school system by one that would be either non-denominational or strictly Anglican in character.[20] The chief drawback in this case, as in that of the support of an Anglican minister, was lack of funds, and Randolph had more than once advocated the use for this purpose of the money collected by the Society for Evangelizing the Indians, which he suspected was used by the Boston theocrats for "private or worse uses."[21] Schools under Anglican auspices Randolph thought necessary in order to strengthen the Anglican church and to develop in the

[18] *Andros Tracts*, I, 138; Mass. Hist. Soc. *Proc.*, 1871-1873, p. 110; 4 Mass. Hist. Soc. *Col.*, V, 149; *Conn. Col. Rec.*, III, 441-442.

[19] Amer. Antiq. Soc. *Proc.*, N. S., XIII, 467; Mass. Arch., vol. 127, p. 25; Mass. Hist. Soc. *Proc.*, 1871-1873, p. 110.

[20] Toppan, *Randolph*, IV, 90, 132.

[21] *Ibid.*, IV, 132.

youth a loyal attitude toward England. He and others advocated also the regulation of Harvard College because it was a training place for the ministers, who were the most seditious element in the Dominion.[22] The administration of the president and council, being Congregational but not theocratic in prejudice, was determined to forestall any radical change in the college, by a reorganization of its government. Before the fall of the charter, the governor and magistrates shared with the president of the college and the leading elders of the six adjacent towns, the administration of the affairs,[23] and under the reorganization, the president and council seem to have had much the same share in the administration that the governor and magistrates previously had, though the titles of the active officials were changed to those of rector and tutors. An attempt was made also to give the college greater security in the holding of its funds.[24] Andros introduced no change in the organization, but appointed Hubbard president after Mather had left for England.[25]

The disintegration of the church and school systems in the Puritan colonies was accompanied by a general laxity in moral and religious matters, a condition which was noticed by the stricter Puritans in Massachusetts during the period of the charter government, but which developed more rapidly as soon as the restraining influence of the theocracy was removed. Of course the new administration was blamed for this ungodliness. Drunkenness and street brawls were not uncommon, and English holiday customs, such as Maypole dancing and Shrove Tuesday pranks, were introduced. Dueling was

[22] Toppan, *Randolph*, IV, 109; VI, 245-246; *Cal. State Pap. Col.*, 1681-1685, §1320; *New England Hist. and Gen. Reg.*, XXXVII, 157.

[23] *Hutchinson Papers*, Prince Soc., II, 238-239.

[24] Toppan, *Randolph*, IV, 95-96; Goodrick, *Randolph*, VI, 245.

[25] 3 Mass. Hist. Soc. *Col.*, I, 83.

for the first time practiced in Boston, and "sword playing," says Samuel Sewall, was exhibited on a stage, "and
that immediately after the lecture, so that the Devil has
begun a Lecture in Boston on a Lecture day which was
set up for Christ."[26]

In conclusion, it may be said that the Dominion
achieved success in its religious policy, inasmuch as the
establishment of liberty of conscience brought New England in religious matters into line with the other English
colonies on the American Continent. Of them all, only
Massachusetts, Connecticut, and Plymouth had previously failed to practice religious toleration. The
Church of England founded in Boston represented the
preference of the English government for the church
which was the state church at home, but it foreshadowed
no intention of forcing Anglicanism on New England.
This is shown by the fact that although Andros was empowered to establish churches, no others than King's
Chapel were founded[27] and no effort was made to tax the
inhabitants for the support of the minister according to
the practice existing in the colonies where the Anglican
Church was the established church.

The theocratic governments of Massachusetts, Plymouth, and Connecticut had to be abolished before any con-

26 Sewall, *Diary*, I, 167, 173, 175-176, 178, 183; 2 Mass. Hist. Soc. *Proc.*,
XIII, 410-411. Among the propaganda material used after the revolution
by the theocrats in the campaign for support of the old charter government, there is a pamphlet accusing Andros of swearing, cursing, sabbath-
breaking, drunkenness, etc., and the query is put "Whether when a Governor has made his allowed Knot of Counsellors competently drunk at his
Bouts with them after midnight, they be not in a fine pickle to manage the
Government of this large Territory which no doubt now perishes for the
want of such Super-sober Counsellors." *Andros Tracts*, III, 194-195.

27 Originally it had been the intention to establish a few Anglican clergymen in other parts of the Dominion, but this intention was abandoned after
Andros came to understand religious conditions better. *Cal. State Pap. Col.*,
1685-1688, §1676.

sistent general colonial policy could be carried out in those colonies. The idea which the Puritans had of themselves as God's chosen people developed in them a peculiarly militant spirit of independence that made them defy any attempt on the part of the mother country to bring them into the colonial scheme. For this reason, the British government thought that the new religious policy was justified, but to the Puritans, it meant the failure of their divinely inspired mission and the end of everything for which they had sought refuge in the New World.

CHAPTER VII

TRADE

The founding of the Dominion of New England represents an attempt to regulate trade there in accordance with the interests of the British rather than of the New England commercial system. The British system was founded on the principle of protection and control by the mother country, the latter on that of free trade. In the two systems, there were certain overlapping areas of interest that were common to both. During the Restoration period, the English government had attempted to direct New England trade into the channels of the British system, while the Massachusetts authorities had resisted this attempt and with equal determination insisted that the colony was outside that system and not subject to its regulations. The moderates in control of the provisional government desired to effect a compromise between the two extremes in such a way as to preserve the necessary parts of both, but Andros, being totally unacquainted with New England commercial conditions, could only follow his instructions and demand a strict enforcement of the British navigation acts.

The British system required that all commodities to and from the colonies should be carried in English or colonial ships, a stipulation which gave a great impetus to colonial shipping and shipbuilding. Certain colonial products which England desired, were "enumerated" in the act of 1660, which required that these products be taken to England before they could be shipped elsewhere.

Such products were subject to an import duty at the English port and, after 1673, to an export duty at the colonial port of lading in all cases where bond was not given to carry the same directly to England. An additional impost was laid on sugar and tobacco in 1685, payable in England, not by the shipper at the port of entry but by the purchaser. Commodities of the growth and manufacture of Europe, except salt for the fisheries of New England and Newfoundland, wine of Madeira and the Azores, servants, horses, and provisions from Scotland and Ireland, could be imported into the colonies only by way of England, Wales, or Berwick-on-Tweed. It was the intention of the mercantilists that the Southern and Island colonies should take their products to England and bring back manufactured articles and provisions. The colonial goods thus brought to England would be put on the English market, and if unsold, might be reshipped with rebate of duties to foreign ports, along with British manufactures. From the Middle and Northern colonies, furs, lumber, and whale products were shipped, but there was little else from those parts that England wanted. None of these commodities had any place in the activities of the great mass of the people in New England, who lived either on small farms where they raised food products, or in the large towns. Since these colonies produced little that England wanted, they would have to maintain their economic existence by means of a more general interchange of products, supposedly within the British system, with the Southern and West India colonies, where foodstuffs and lumber could be sold and enumerated commodities taken in payment. In this way, the Northern colonies could provide themselves with hard money and additional raw materials available for the English trade.

In actual practice, however, New England trade

moved along quite different lines, and the British system, though well defined in theory, never found in this
part of the colonial world a willing ally or co-operator in
its plans. Left to themselves, the Southern and Island
colonies would undoubtedly have conformed easily and
naturally to the British requirements, but the New England and Middle Colonies, in the struggle for existence,
developed an elaborate network of trade routes and exchanges that lay partly or wholly outside the British
system and drew the sugar and tobacco colonies into the
orbit of the New England system.

The commerce of New England, as elaborated under
the leadership of Massachusetts, was based on the principle of free trade. Boston in the seventeenth century
became the centre of this commerce, the lines of which
radiated in all directions,—to the neighboring Northern
colonies, to the Southern continental colonies, to the West
Indies, to Newfoundland and Cape Breton, to the Wine
Islands, Spain, Portugal, and the Straits, to northern
Europe, and to the British Isles. For the products of
these places, Massachusetts paid with articles of her own
industry, with goods imported for purposes of re-exportation, and with money. She was dependent upon the
neighboring colonies for food, partly because her land
was too poor for extensive cultivation and partly because the coast towns were filled with many artificers
and workmen who were not agriculturists.[1] Beef, pork,

[1] Andros reported to the Lords of Trade that ''The Massachusetts
Collony, the most Considerable for number of Townes and Inhabitants
and well Scituated for Trade is One of the Smallest and poorest Tracts
of Land, and Produces least of any of the other Collonys for Exportation
Noe wheat haveing grown but blasted there in about Thirty Years past,
Nor have they of cattle or other Graine beyond their own Consumption,
but by reason of the great Number of Artificers, perticulerly in Boston,
shipwrights, smiths, etc., they build many ships and other Vessells.'' C. O.
5: 855, no. 90. An abstract of this report may be found in *Cal. State Pap.
Col.*, 1689-1692, §862.

and mutton were brought in from Plymouth, Rhode Island, and Connecticut, and wheat and other grain from Connecticut and New York.[2] Other articles which the Northern colonies had to offer were also in great demand in the colony. Masts, boards, and all sorts of lumber were brought from the Piscataqua River and other places in Maine and New Hampshire. Tar for use in shipbuilding was obtained in large quantities from Plymouth, Maine, and New Hampshire.[3] Whale oil was imported from Long Island, and whale fishing, which was developing at Cape Cod, promised a lucrative trade for the future.[4] Furs, too, were purchased at the northern ports or brought in from the frontiers. These commodities Massachusetts paid for with enumerated products from the South or the West Indies, with foreign and English goods, and with articles of home manufacture.[5] In Massachusetts and in Connecticut, considerable quantities of wool were made up into coarse clothing and bedding, and in some places good serges were woven. A coarse cloth like linen was also made "by the Mixture of Cotton and Flax."[6] Hats were manufactured from racoon fur, for the pro-

[2] *Cal. State Pap. Col.*, 1675-1676, §816; 1677-1680, §§1349, 1447; 1685-1688, §1160, p. 329, §1197; 1689-1692, §862; Toppan, *Randolph*, IV, 154; VI, 196; Gay MSS., State Papers, VI, 89.

[3] *Cal. State Pap. Col.*, 1689-1692, §§862, 884; C. O. 5: 855, no. 90.

[4] 4 Mass. Hist. Soc. *Col.*, V, 178; *Cal. State Pap. Col.*, 1661-1668, §1660; 1669-1674, §1145; 1665-1688, pp. 370-371; 1689-1692, §§862, 1691.

[5] Gay MSS., State Papers, VI, 119; *Cal. State Pap. Col.*, 1669-1674, §954; 1675-1676, §721; 1677-1680, §1360; 3 Mass. Hist. Soc. *Col.*, I, 98; *Hutchinson Papers*, Prince Soc., II, 239; Beer, *Old Colonial System*, pt. I, vol. II, 245-246. William Harris admitted to the secretary, before whom he was examined in London, that Rhode Island obtained linsey-woolseys and other coarse cloths from Massachusetts. Weeden, *Early Rhode Island*, pp. 114-115. By 1686, Connecticut and Rhode Island had, according to the report of the president and council, become quite dependent on Massachusetts for the clothing that they did not purchase from England. Gay MSS., State Papers, VI, 89.

[6] C. O. 5: 855, no. 90; *Cal. State Pap. Col.*, 1675-1676, §543; 1677-1680, §1360; 1685-1688, §§370-371; 1689-1692, §862.

tection of which industry, the exportation of racoon fur
was prohibited.[7] Hides and skins imported from the other
colonies were tanned, dressed, and worked for re-exportation.[8] Manufacturing, however, in comparison with
other economic interests of the colony, was at this time
a very insignificant industry. Such as it was, it had been
called into existence by Massachusetts's demand for articles with which to pay for her much-needed imports. The
great danger to the interests of the British woolen manu-
facturers lay in the possibility of its development in the
future.[9]

One of the earliest trading connections was with Virginia, to which colony convoys of merchant ships went
from the north every year. This was the trade which the
Dutch menaced by the recapture of New York in 1673.
Richard Wharton, writing of the seizure, off the Virginia
capes, of several vessels, urged that every effort be made
to restore New York to the duke, else this trade would
be ruined.[10] Ships went also to ports and landing places
in North Carolina, Maryland, Delaware, and Pennsylvania. From Virginia, Maryland, and Pennsylvania,

[7] *Mass. Col. Rec.,* V, 28.

[8] *Andros Tracts,* III, 15; C. O. 5: 855, no. 90.

[9] As early as 1661 the Council for Foreign Plantations was worried
about the interference of the colonies with British woolen manufactures.
They reported that the New Englanders had ''transported & increased
a Stocke of Sheepe to the number of neere one hundred thousand Sheepe,
whereby, not only, this Nation & the manufacture thereof are become less
necessary to them, but they are likely to be so stored with wool that the
Dutch, who Trade freely with them, may supply themselves from thence,
of such Wool as shall be necessary for them to mingle with their finer
Wools.'' Cited in Beer, *Old Colonial System,* pt. I, vol. II, 241. One of the
revolutionary pamphlets opposing restoration of charters asserted that ''If
these people be not prevented of their old way of Trade, they being so large
and fruitful a Country must necessarily in a short time destroy the trade
of England, by improving those Manufactures which the chief trade of
England depends on, and they do in some measure already effect it.'' *Andros
Tracts,* III, 8, 16.

[10] *Cal. State Pap. Col.,* 1669-1674, §§1144, 1145.

wheat and other grains were imported, but by far the most important commodity was tobacco, some of which was taken to Boston for local consumption, some was peddled to near-by ports, and some exported to England and the Continent.[11] These commodities from the Southern colonies were paid for with articles imported from the Continent and England, with home manufactures, and with lumber, fish, and provisions.[12]

The most extensive trade of New England was with the British West Indies. Even during the depressing days of the Andros administration, one hundred and thirty-six out of the two hundred and forty-nine vessels leaving ports of the Dominion in 1687, and one hundred and twenty-nine out of the two hundred and twenty-nine in 1688 went to the islands.[13] In this trade, refuse fish, lumber, horses, provisions, and European goods brought illegally to the islands were exchanged for sugar, molasses, cotton, rum, ginger, logwood, and Braziletto wood.[14] It was in this trade that the great competition with England existed, for New England threatened to draw to herself the entire traffic of the West Indies and the Southern colonies. England desired to furnish her West

[11] *Cal. State Pap. Col.*, 1669-1674, §1059.

[12] 3 Mass. Hist. Soc. *Col.*, I, 98; Crosby, *Early Coins*, p. 92; *Hutchinson Papers*, Prince Soc., II, 230-231.

[13] Mass. Arch., vol. 7, pp. 15-68; *Cal. State Pap. Col.*, 1661-1668, §1660.

[14] *Cal. State Pap. Col.*, 1669-1674, §1059; 1677-1680, §288; 1675-1676, §§543, 934, 953; 1685-1688, §1507; 3 Mass. Hist. Soc. *Col.*, I, 98; Weeden, *Early Rhode Island*, pp. 114-115; Osgood and Batchelder, *Salem*, p. 127; Toppan, *Randolph*, II, 303; *Hutchinson Papers*, Prince Soc., II, 230-231. There is a very interesting account of New England conditions, particularly those of Boston, written by a French Protestant refugee who came to America two years after the revocation of the Edict of Nantes in search of a place of refuge for ''his Comrades in the Faith.'' He writes that Boston carried on a great trade with the West Indies and gives much detail about the nature of the exchanges. *Report of a French Protestant Refugee in Boston* (1687), translated from the French by E. T. Fisher, p. 24.

India islands with manufactured articles and provisions, taking in return enumerated products for her own use and for sale in European markets. The Puritan traders, however, could sell their products, illicitly imported from Europe, in the West Indies more cheaply than the British merchants could sell theirs.[15] Again a conflict arose over foodstuffs, which were imported into the islands from Connecticut and Rhode Island, usually in Massachusetts ships.[16] England did not so much mind the competition in the provision trade, because it was not illegal, as she did being thwarted in the purchase of enumerated products and being crowded out of her markets for manufactures. Moreover, she suffered a loss in revenue, when neither the European articles illegally imported into the West Indies nor the enumerated articles illegally exported therefrom went to England and paid the customs as the law required. The West Indian trade is a good example of the competition and rivalry which arose between the British and the New England commercial systems, for New England was just as dependent upon the West Indian trade as was England. New England needed the markets for such goods as she had to dispose of, and she needed the enumerated products not only for consumption at home, but also for her lucrative illicit foreign trade and her trade with England.

[15] For references see below, note 30.

[16] Governor Bradstreet, in his answer to the queries sent him by the Lords of Trade in 1680, spoke of the decay of trade with the other British plantations in horses, boards, lumber, provisions, and fish, due to the clogging of those markets with similar commodities from England, Ireland, and other places. 3 Mass. Hist. Soc. *Col.*, VIII, 338. Governor Atkins of Barbados wrote Secretary Sir Joseph Williamson that the act of 1673 was a heavy burden on the West Indies, and he feared they would lose all commerce from New England and Ireland, whence they had all their provisions. *Cal. State Pap. Col.*, 1675-1676, §526. If what Atkins said was true, England was pretty well crowded out of the provision market in the West Indies as early as 1675.

A certain amount of trade existed between New England and the French Island colonies, but, owing to Colbert's policy of excluding foreigners from commerce there, it could not have been very great. French officials in the islands frequently reported that their foreign trade had been cut off, yet their letters often indirectly disclose the fact that it had not altogether ceased.[17] An exchange of products between the New England colonies and the French sugar islands was a natural commercial transaction and was therefore difficult to regulate. Each group needed the other badly. The French colonies from the first had been dependent upon the importation of foodstuffs, because the inhabitants occupied themselves entirely with the production of staples for export. Moreover as their crops increased, so did their need for markets. The French Continental colonies were intended to supplement the Island colonies by furnishing the latter with foodstuffs and with markets for the staples of the islands. In fact, however, they could not entirely feed themselves, and much less purchase the island staples, molasses and rum, in sufficient quantities to make the trade exchange worth while. On the other hand, the New England colonies were admirably equipped for trade relations with the French Island colonies, for they had a superabundance of foodstuffs and of Continental manufactured articles for sale. They, in turn, were suffering from a lack of the very things which the French islands wished to dispose of, for the British West Indies could no longer supply them with enough sugar, molasses, and rum, nor could they furnish sufficient markets for their increasing production of foodstuffs, live stock, and lumber.[18] The sugar refiners of the French West Indies were aware of the profit that might accrue from the de-

[17] Mims, *Colbert's West India Policy*, pp. 210-211, 214-215, 223.
[18] *Ibid.*, pp. 223-224.

velopment of a trade with New England, and knew of
the inability of the British West Indies to supply the
needs of the New England colonies. Through Patoulet,
the first intendant of the islands, they appealed to
Colbert in 1681 to permit the establishment of trade
"with the English colonies close to Boston," from which
"the king and the colonies would derive great profit."[19]
Colbert, however, refused to modify his policy of excluding foreign trade. Therefore, until the establishment of
the Dominion of New England, such trade as existed
between New England and the French Island colonies
was illegal, as far as French commercial policy was
concerned.[20]

Trade between the English and the French colonies,
although not specifically prohibited by the British navigation acts, was by official interpretation declared illegal.[21] In 1686 by the Treaty of Neutrality between England and France, each agreed to recognize the trade
regulations of the other.[22] Each was to allow the ships
of the other to enter the ports of its colonies for wood
and water or if driven by storm.[23] Under cover of this
clause, goods were illegally imported by the colonies of

[19] Mims, *Colbert's West India Policy*, p. 222.

[20] The governor of Petit Guavos wrote to Lieutenant-Governor Moles-
worth of Jamaica concerning the seizure by a French privateer of an
English ship, which had no passport or papers. He considered this certain
proof that the vessel had been trading with the French "which as you
know, is contrary to the orders of my King and yours." *Cal. State Pap.
Col.*, 1685-1688, §§111, 523, 558.

[21] *Acts, Privy Coun. Col.*, II, pp. 61, 88; *Cal. State Pap. Col.*, 1685-
1688, §§111, 1034.

[22] *Ibid.*, §1642.

[23] Complaint was made by the governor of Jamaica that the French
continually seized the ships of English subjects, when they came into
French ports in the West Indies to wood and water, and when driven
thither by stress of weather. Investigation showed that the French king
had given orders to confiscate all vessels anchoring in French ports. *Ibid,*
§558.

both countries. Similar agreements were entered into between England and Holland by the Treaty of Breda[24] and between England and Spain, whereby each recognized the commercial policies of the other. England, however, made one important concession to Spain, granting her the privilege of importing into the British West Indies a certain number of negroes, which were often badly needed on the plantations. Spanish ships abused this privilege when bringing in negroes, by often taking out enumerated products.[25]

The West Indian trade of New England, which was part of an important commercial cycle, cannot be studied by itself but must be examined in connection with the direct trade with Europe—a trade which furnished manufactured articles needed in the colonies, and markets for colonial enumerated commodities.[26] Fish in large quantities and lumber, especially pipe staves, were taken to Spain and the Straits, where they were sold for money or exchanged for fruits, oil, soap, wine, brandy, and salt.[27] The return trade, legally conducted, demanded

[24] *Cal. State Pap. Col.*, 1685-1688, §§1311, 1312. A complaint was made by captains of British ships that the Dutch carried products from the British colonies and imported into them Dutch goods and other products from the French Islands. *Ibid.*, §1288.

[25] C. O. 324: 4, pp. 142-143; *Acts, Privy Coun. Col.*, II, §182; *Cal. State Pap. Col.*, 1685-1688, §120.

[26] *Cal. State Pap. Col.*, 1669-1674, §1059; 1675-1676, §721. Most of the seizures made during the administration of the president and council were of ships illegally importing European goods. Toppan, *Randolph*, I, 294, note; 2 Mass. Hist. Soc. *Proc.*, XIII, 253, 271; Mass. Arch., vol. 126, pp. 53, 112, 115-116, 133, 134, 156, 164. In *Suffolk Deeds*, XIV, 110-111, is a deed of sale of the brigantine *Rebeccah*, condemned at the court of pleas for Suffolk, Oct., 1686. *Cal. State Pap. Col.*, 1685-1688, §925; Sewall, *Letter Book*, I, p. 34.

[27] *Cal. State Pap. Col.*, 1675-1676, §§543, 953; 1685-1688, §944-v; *Hutchinson Papers*, Prince Soc., II, 231; Crosby, *Early Coins*, p. 92. The French refugee does not mention salt as one of the articles bought in the trade with Spain and the Straits. He says, however, that the salt was brought from the island of Tortola. From this statement one might sup-

that the vessel stop at an English port on the way home
and pay the required duties. Since the bulk of the return
loadings was usually made up of salt, and European
products formed only a small part of the cargo, it was
deemed a great hardship by the colonists to have to go
to England and pay customs. Consequently, they frequently evaded the law and traded directly with the
Straits.[28] Enumerated commodities, together with provisions, lumber, and wool, both raw and manufactured,
were exported to France, Hamburg, Holland, and other
places in Europe, and from those places were imported
in return, "Not only Linnen but Woollen and all other
manufactures (which should be of the English growth)
Customs free; and this not only for their own consumption but also Supplying therewith most parts of the
world, particularly the English plantations which according to the Act of Navigation ought to be supplyed
from Old England."[29] This trade was disastrous to the
British commercial system in many ways. First, it hurt
British markets, for the Massachusetts traders could sell
the custom-free European products often as much as
fifty per cent cheaper than could the English merchants,
to the ruin of their plantations markets, while the carrying of the enumerated products to Europe spoiled the

pose that a large part of the cargo from the Straits, previously listed
as salt, was in reality wines and other things, which were brought directly
back to New England and that with the strict enforcement of the trade
regulations there was too much risk involved in bringing a cargo of
European goods disguised as salt, to make the importation of salt at all
worth while. *French Protestant Refugee*, p. 41.

[28] Osgood and Batchelder, *Salem*, p. 127; *Cal. State Pap. Col.*, 1675-
1676, §543; 1677-1680, §1017; 1685-1688, §944-v; Hanscom, *Heart of the
Puritan*, pp. 147-148.

[29] *Hutchinson Papers*, Prince Soc., II, 231; *Andros Tracts*, III, 4, 233;
Cal. State Pap. Col., 1669-1674, §§954, 1059; 1675-1676, §§543, 787, 898;
1677-1680, §§288, 1017, 1374; Toppan, *Randolph*, II, 303; III, 70-73,
323, 337; Goodrick, *Randolph*, VI, 143-144, 157.

markets there for the traders carrying goods legally
through England first.[30] In the second place, by the direct
trade, England lost thousands of pounds in customs
duties every year.[31] Furthermore, this trade was often
carried on by foreign ships, which brought the produce
of their country to colonial ports, thus cutting in on the
British carrying trade. Even when the goods were carried in colonial ships, the illegal commerce was a detriment to English navigation, for it allowed colonial ships
to monopolize a carrying trade in which the English ships
should have had a share.[32]

The Newfoundland trade was valuable to New England, because it furnished her with fish for trade to the
Straits and the British West Indies. It was also profitable because of the opportunity it offered for direct trade
with Europe. Newfoundland became "a magazine of all
sorts of goods brought thither directly from France,
Holland, Scotland, Ireland, and other places," and
"under Colour of a trade . . . for fish, great quantities of
Wine Brandy and other European goods" had been imported into New England. Likewise enumerated commodities were taken to Newfoundland and thence to
Europe.[33]

[30] *Andros Tracts*, III, 4; *Cal. State Pap. Col.*, 1675-1676, §§787, 898;
Goodrick, *Randolph*, VI, 143-144; *Hutchinson Papers*, Prince Soc., II, 231.

[31] Randolph claimed that England lost one hundred thousand pounds
yearly in customs revenue by this trade, but Bradstreet, though admitting
that an occasional vessel might slip out with tobacco for Europe, thought
that very little damage was done to England's customs revenue in that
way. 3 Mass. Hist. Soc. *Col.*, VIII, 331; *Cal. State Pap. Col.*, 1677-1680,
§1360.

[32] *Andros Tracts*, III, 4; *Hutchinson Papers*, Prince Soc., II, 232.

[33] Mass. Arch., vol. 126, p. 329; Toppan, *Randolph*, IV, 145; *Andros
Tracts*, III, 233-234; *Cal. State Pap. Col.*, 1685-1688, §§1097, 1507. Beer
says that the amount of New England trade in European goods imported
through Newfoundland has been greatly exaggerated. He bases his esti-
mates upon Randolph's accounts of Boston entries, which, for the period
May 18 to September 29, 1686, were only three. Beer, *Old Colonial System*,

The commercial status of Ireland and Scotland was that of foreign countries. Although the act of 1660 permitted the carrying of enumerated commodities to Irish ports, this direct trade was later forbidden.[34] With the exception of servants, horses, and provisions, the products of Ireland and Scotland could not be shipped directly to the colonies. In spite, however, of these restrictions, a considerable amount of direct trade with those countries existed. Sometimes the goods were brought in Scottish ships, but more often in those that were colonial.[35]

Trade between New England and the mother country was not extensive before 1700. Out of two hundred or more vessels leaving Massachusetts ports yearly, only about ten went to England.[36] These carried lumber, furs,

pt. I, vol. II, 223-226. It does not seem safe, however, to estimate the amount of illegal trade before 1686 by the legal trade which was carried on during a period when the navigation laws were fairly well enforced. After the revolution, when illegal commerce was again indulged in, Randolph reported that European products were again freely imported. *Cal. State Pap. Col.*, 1689-1692, §468-i.

34 *Ibid.*, §932.

35 *Andros Tracts*, III, 224-233; Goodrick, *Randolph*, VI, 100, 183; *Cal. State Pap. Col.*, 1675-1676, §953; *Hutchinson Papers*, Prince Soc., II, 231.

36 *Andros Tracts*, III, 4; *Hutchinson Papers*, Prince Soc., II, 231. The shipping list of Boston, from December, 1686, to April, 1689, in Mass. Arch., vol. 7, pp. 15-68, shows that for the year 1687 ten ships went to England, eight of which were Boston-owned, one was a Bristol vessel and the other of London; for the year 1688, twelve ships went to England, eight of which were Boston-owned, two were from London, one from Lyme, and one from Bideford. Further evidence that the trade between New England and England was at this time small in amount is shown by the applications for Mediterranean passes to ships outward bound from England in the period of warfare which followed the Andros administration. From May to the middle of August, 1689, forty ships applied, nineteen of which were bound to the West Indies, two to Virginia, one to Pennsylvania, thirteen to Newfoundland, and five to New England. In January, 1690, eighty applied, twenty-four of which were bound to the West Indies, forty-five to the southern colonies, six to the middle colonies, three to Newfoundland, and two to New England. *Acts, Privy Coun. Col.*,

whalebone, whale and fish oil, and enumerated products, which had been shipped into New England for re-exportation. They brought back manufactured articles.[37] Except for the need of some of these British goods, there was nothing attractive about the trade with the mother country. The act of 1673 made the carrying of enumerated products to England less profitable, because those goods, bought usually on a port-to-port cruise, had to pay the double plantations duties, that is, the export duty at the first port of lading and the import duty in England.[38] The new impost of 1685 upon sugar and tobacco brought added discouragement. Although the duty was intended to fall upon the consumer, the requirement that it be paid by the purchaser evidently made marketing of

II, p. 120. In September, 1690, the merchants of Virginia asked for convoy for sixty ships, those from the West Indies for sixty, and those from New England, for five. *Cal. State Pap. Col.*, 1689-1692, §§1049, 1052.

[37] *Hutchinson Papers*, Prince Soc., II, 231; 3 Mass. Hist. Soc. *Col.*, I, 98; VIII, 338; Osgood and Batchelder, *Salem*, p. 127. That New England was not at this time dependent on British manufactures is shown by the variety of articles imported from the Continent. The writer of the *French Protestant Refugee* (pp. 41-42) urged the prospective French immigrants to bring for sale "every kind of Merchandise," but especially "Cloth, blue Stuffs, white Stuff, printed Stuffs or East India Goods, Cables and Ship tackling, and Dutch Linen for sails." It is interesting to notice that even though the goods had to be shipped through England, he says that one could reckon on eighty to one hundred per cent profit, including the twenty-five per cent exchange on the money.

[38] *Cal. State Pap. Col.*, 1675-1676, §900. A letter from John Hull, treasurer of Massachusetts, to the colony's agents in London, in 1677, mentions the hardship of the double duties. Cited in Hanscom, *Heart of the Puritan*, pp. 147-148. Governor Bradstreet in his answers to the queries of the Lords of Trade in 1680, names the act of 1673 as one of the discouragements to trade. 3 Mass. Hist. Soc. *Col.*, VIII, 338. A memorial was sent to the king by the president and council in 1686, asking that all sugar shipped from any of the British West Indies to New England and from thence to England be given an abatement of the duties paid in the plantations, and that all tobacco shipped from New England to London have the penny in the pound abated. 2 Mass. Hist. Soc. *Proc.*, XIII, 245.

the goods more difficult.[39] Since New England could offer little that England cared to buy, the balance of trade was usually in favor of the mother country, a fact which necessitated paying the balance in money.[40] In the absence of a satisfactory staple of exchange for use in the English trade, Massachusetts might still have been able to purchase a considerable quantity of manufactured goods if there had been plenty of money, but of that there was a great scarcity. Consequently, she fell back upon the Continent for a supply of many of those things which might otherwise have been purchased in England.

The development of trade in Massachusetts was always handicapped by the scarcity of hard money.[41] In the beginning, the colonists used commodity-money, such as fish, fur, grain, etc., the prices of which were fixed by law, but with the increase of trade, foreign coins began to come in. Commerce was not greatly improved by this influx of Spanish and Dutch money, partly because some of it was poor and upset the standards of value, and partly because most of it was immediately drawn out of the colony again. Massachusetts finally found it necessary in 1652 to establish a mint of her own, the output of which was to be the sole circulating monetary currency. The law required that all foreign coins be melted down into the new silver coinage in the form of shillings, six pences, and three pences. This coinage gave a wel-

[39] *Statutes of the Realm*, VI, 1 James II, c. 4; C. O. 324: 4, pp. 145-148; *Cal. State Pap. Col.*, 1685-1688, §253. The act evidently brought great discouragement to the raisers of sugar and tobacco, for the planters of Barbados and Nevis complained bitterly concerning its effect on trade. *Cal. State Pap. Col.*, §§1380, 1661; 1689-1692, §§473, 1923. Randolph disapproved of the act and predicted that the New Englanders would "be ruined by these late new imposts upon Plantation Comodityes." Toppan, *Randolph*, IV, 49, 71-72; Goodrick, *Randolph*, VI, 235.

[40] Crosby, *Early Coins*, p. 92.

[41] Winthrop wrote in his journal, October, 1640, that the scarcity of money made a great change in all commerce. Winthrop, *Journal*, II, 17, 19.

come opportunity to disguise pirate money by melting
it down. To prevent the coins from being carried out of
the colony, the value was raised a third. The shilling,
although it passed as the equivalent of the English
shilling, was in reality worth only about nine pence,
farthing in sterling.[42]

Although the mintage of 1652 and following years
brought alleviation, it was not a complete success, for
the new coins began very early to leave the colony in
spite of the increased value, and foreign coins continued
to circulate because those of light weight were worth
more in trade than they would yield at the mint. To
remedy these evils, laws were passed forbidding the exportation of money and legalizing the use of Spanish
pieces of eight on which the New England standard of
value had been stamped.[43] As a result of this regulation,
foreign money soon drove out the heavier New England
coin. To prevent this, another law was passed in 1682,
rating both the foreign and the New England coin by
troy weight at six shillings, eight pence each, the former

[42] *Mass. Col. Rec.*, IV-1, 84; *New York Col. Docs.*, III, 582. In spite
of the way the act was worded, it is evident that the shilling never passed
for more than nine pence, for in the act proposed in 1654 to prevent the
exportation of coin, it is stated that there can be no profit to a man to
export it, ''but rather a fowerth part Losse Unlesse Such persons doe
oppresse & extort in the sale of their goods to make up the sajd losse.''
Mass. Col. Rec., IV-1, 198; *Cal. State Pap. Col.*, 1685-1688, §944-iv. This
is explained in the report of the commissioners of the mint, made in 1685,
''that to encourage the bringing of silver to the Mint, they promise that
there shall be but twopence in the shilling less in value than the English
shilling; but after the mint-master has coined the same, they order him
to pay the money out by weight, at threepence Troy weight for their
shilling, and proportionately for the other pieces, which threepence Troy is
about ninepence farthing sterling, and makes out the account to be 22½
percent, . . . besides the expense of coinage.'' *Cal. State Pap. Col.*, 1685-
1688, §944-iii.

[43] *Mass. Col. Rec.*, IV-1, 198; IV-2, 420-421; *Cal. State Pap. Col.*,
1685-1688, §944-iv.

to be marked according to its weight and fineness.[44] Besides the minting of coins, the prohibiting of coin exportation, and the regulating of pieces of eight, the colony tried other ways of providing money. Customs duties were established in 1668,[45] paper bills were used,[46] and attempts were made to establish a bank. None of these methods proved to be permanently effective.

Although Massachusetts by charter was not granted the right to coin money, no attention was paid by the British government to the mint until the Lords of Trade began to call Massachusetts to account for her many delinquencies.[47] While Randolph's "Representation of the Affairs of New England"[48] was under consideration, they ordered that "examination bee made whether by their Charter or by the right of making Laws they [the authorities in Massachusetts] are enabled Soe to doe."

[44] *Mass. Col. Rec.*, V, 351, 373.

[45] *Ibid.*, IV-2, 410. Marblehead, upon hearing that a customs duty was to be levied, petitioned the General Court that some other means be used for drawing in money and raising funds, urging that it would be a discouragement to trade and an irritation to the neighboring colonies. Moreover, the method might be "monopolized afterwards by such as may not be so acceptable to us." Cited in *Essex Institute Historical Collections*, LIV, 246. The levying of customs duties brought in a little hard money, as the court records show. *Mass. Col. Rec.*, IV-2, 464.

[46] The General Court, in answering the charges made against the colony in 1684, mentioned that "for some years Paper Bills passed for payment of debts, which were very subject to be lost, rent, or counterfeited, and other inconveniences." Mass. Arch., vol. 106, p. 223.

[47] The royal commissioners, sent to New England in the early Restoration period, had recommended that the mint at Boston be abolished, "for Coyning is a Royall prerogative." *Pub.* Col. Soc. Mass., I, 220, 221, 223.

[48] Randolph in his report to the Lords of Trade in 1676 had particularly called their attention to the mint at Boston, the coins of which he described in detail. "All the money," he wrote, "is stamped with these figures, 1652, that year being the aera of the commonwealth, wherein they erected themselves into a free state, enlarged their dominions, subjected the adjacent colonies under their obedience, and summoned deputies to sitt in the generall court, which year is still commemorated on their coin." *Hutchinson Papers*, Prince Soc., II, 213-214.

It was found that they were not, whereupon the agents were advised to sue for pardon for the colony's presumption in exercising an act of sovereignty and to ask for an additional charter containing the power to coin money and to regulate foreign coin.[49] The right was never granted because of the lords' decision to annul the Massachusetts charter. Since, however, the mint was not closed until 1684,[50] money conditions did not change a great deal until the establishment of the Dominion.

It is evident that the currency problem in Massachusetts involved something more complex than the mere coining of money. It involved a constant attention to the regulation of its standard of value as compared with that of the foreign coins which were constantly coming in. As trade developed, foreign money was increasingly needed, so that instead of restricting its importation, Massachusetts, in the latter part of the seventeenth century, made every effort to attract it. Although a certain amount came in each year through legitimate channels of trade, probably the most lucrative sources of supply were pirates and privateers.

Piracy was considered a necessary adjunct to the New England commercial system, because it brought into circulation hard money, needed for the trade with England, and silver plate used for coining money.[51] It also threw on the market quantities of cheap goods. Piracy attracted men of all classes by the opportunities it offered for acquiring wealth easily. There seemed to be no social stigma connected with it, for there were many retired pirates in all the colonies who were among the most

[49] Toppan, *Randolph*, II, 283; III, 159-160; *Pub*. Col. Soc. Mass., I, 221, 222, 224.

[50] Evidently no attempt to coin money was made after the annulling of the charter, for the memorial sent to the king in 1686 stated that the mint "hath long time discontinued." 2 Mass. Hist. Soc. *Proc.*, XIII, 244.

[51] *Andros Tracts*, III, 233-234.

esteemed citizens.[52] Perhaps the absence of any idea of its being a moral wrong was due to its very close connection with privateering. Many who held commissions allowing them to prey on the commerce of the enemy in times of war did not find it easy to give up the occupation in times of peace. These commissions were given out freely by the various colonial governors, because at a time when the West India islands were disputed by French, Spanish, and English, attacks on a rival's commerce were among the most effective means of asserting a nation's ownership.[53] Many of the governors looked upon piracy in this way. Thus, through desire for personal aggrandizement, love of aggressive adventure, and patriotism, men were attracted to piracy, which, prevalent enough anywhere at this time, became common practice in American waters. Because trade was so dependent upon it, colonial governments made no effort to suppress it.

A survey of all of the channels of trade connected with the New England commercial system shows that the most important routes were those to Europe and to the Brit-

[52] Goodrick, *Randolph*, VI, 275. Randolph wrote to Blathwayt in November, 1687, ''here had been severall South Sea men with plenty of money: They are instructed how to govern themselves and live undisturbed.'' *Ibid.*, 234-235. Again the next autumn, ''since my going to N: Yorke severall are come to this place and to N: London, have bought houses and lands are setled here bringing in 1000 or 1500 £ a man.'' *Ibid.*, 275. In a ''Plan of Union'' drawn up by a Virginian in 1701, the writer says ''without question New England Men pretend that they would not entertain Pyrates upon any account in the World, and yet it is observable that tho' they have long used those Parts none of them have been taken till of late.'' Carson, *History of the Constitution of the United States*, II, appendix, 458.

[53] Considerable complaint was made by the English in the West Indies that privateers pretending to have French commissions harassed English traders even in times of peace. They could easily indulge in this practice, because they were often not obliged to give security in their commission port as the treaties directed. *Cal. State Pap. Col.*, 1685-1688, §558.

ish West Indies. Unhampered by burdensome customs, the direct exchange of enumerated commodities for European products brought prosperity. It increased shipping and gave great impetus to shipbuilding, thus offering employment to the large numbers of workmen in the coast towns who found agriculture unprofitable. Into the midst of this prosperity came the British customs official. Through the medium of his reports, British statesmen began to see that the New England commercial system was crowding that of the mother country to the wall. The shipping privileges granted to the colonies by the navigation acts were helping to make possible the carrying on of illicit trade, and giving to New England the opportunity of monopolizing the carrying trade also, not only of the American colonies with each other, but that between England and her colonies as well. The purchase of enumerated products in the Southern and Island colonies for consumption in New England and for shipping directly to Europe deprived the mother country of her right to use those products for home consumption and spoiled her foreign markets. The direct importation of foreign manufactures not only supplied the wants of New England, but also encroached upon England's markets for her own manufactures in the Southern and Island colonies. Therefore, until 1686, the New England commercial system was thriving at the expense of the British. It is interesting to see how the Andros administration affected this encroachment.

Andros was sent to his post fully equipped with the necessary information concerning the British commercial system and the manner of interpreting its laws. He was given, as were all royal governors and collectors, a book of rates containing copies of the principal acts relating to plantation trade, together with instructions explaining them. These were supplemented from time

to time during his administration, by special circular
letters from the Lords of Trade, in which an attempt was
made to describe the colonial evasions and to show how
they could be prevented. It will be remembered that by
the act of 1663, no commodities of the growth or manufacture of Europe, except salt for the fisheries of New
England and Newfoundland, wines of Madeira and the
Azores, and servants, horses, and provisions from Scotland and Ireland, could be imported into the colonies
except by way of England, Wales, or Berwick-on-Tweed,
and in ships legally qualified. Colonial shippers and
others evaded this law by the use of forged coquets.
Andros's instructions required that no ships should
unlade in New England without a collector's warrant,
which would be issued only after a coquet, which had
been obtained from the collector of some English port,
had been given by the master of the ship to the naval
officer, showing an inventory of the goods, where laden,
the name of the master, and proof of legal navigation of
the ship.[54]

In order to enforce the enumeration clause of the act
of 1660, bonds were required at the port of sailing from
all ships entering colonial ports from England, Wales,
or Berwick-on-Tweed, that in case any enumerated commodities were loaded in the colonies they should be
brought back to the port of departure or some other port
in England, Wales, or Berwick-on-Tweed. Ships from
other places were to take bond at the port of lading in
the colonies to carry the goods to another colonial port
or to England, Wales, or Berwick-on-Tweed.[55]

A concise and careful explanation was also given of
the act of 1673 which had been passed to supplement the
enumeration clause of the act of 1660. The colonists in-

[54] C. O. 324: 4, pp. 160-162.
[55] *Ibid.*, pp. 151-166; 5: 904, pp. 330-332.

terpreted the latter to mean that after paying the plantation duty, and stopping at a colonial port, they were free to go directly to Europe if they pleased. The new act made it clear that no such liberty was intended, but that all enumerated commodities, if taken to some other of his majesty's plantations and not consumed there, must be taken directly to England, Wales, or Berwick-on-Tweed.[56] All vessels, except those trading coastwise from one port of the province to another, were required to make entry with the collector as well as the naval officer and give in their contents on oath. An attempt was made to check up the bonds taken out, by sending yearly or oftener to the commissioners of customs in England lists of all ships lading enumerated commodities.[57]

The machinery for administering the acts of trade in New England was already in existence, so there was little else for Andros to do but set it in motion. By a council act of March 8, 1687, Boston, Salem, Portsmouth, Pemaquid, Bristol, and Newport were named as ports of entry.[58] Officers in these ports were instructed to record all goods imported or exported, to take out bonds, to inspect bond certificates, and to send reports to the commissioners of customs in England. They were to be aided in the performance of their duty by H. M. S. *Rose* and the province sloop *Mary,* which were to ply up and down the coast or to go on special commissions in search of suspected vessels.[59]

[56] C. O. 324: 4, pp. 156-160.

[57] *Ibid.,* pp. 162-166.

[58] Amer. Antiq. Soc. *Proc.,* N. S., XIII, 248, note, 261-262. It is interesting to notice how often the reports which went to England, through Randolph as secretary, mention the fact that important measures were passed upon his representation.

[59] Mass. Arch., vol. 126, pp. 334, 335, 381, 408, 420; vol. 127, pp. 76-77, 83; vol. 128, pp. 140, 176, 209, 211, 245; vol. 129, p. 44; *Andros Tracts,* III, 75. Later another vessel, the *Speedwell,* a small ketch, was added. Amer. Antiq. Soc. *Proc.,* N. S., XIII, 467.

The attention of Andros was especially called to the need of putting an end to the direct trade with Europe, the suppression of piracy, and the making provision for a satisfactory medium of exchange. As regards the first, the shores of New England were so well policed that foreign vessels dared not show themselves in port, but a certain amount of direct trade with Europe was still carried on through Newfoundland, by colonial ships entering New England ports with forged coquets, falsely showing that the goods had been laden in England, Wales, or Berwick-on-Tweed. It was for this reason that the Lords of Trade sent to Andros an additional instruction, January, 1687, bidding him exercise great care in the inspection of all coquets. They ordered him to announce publicly that Newfoundland was not considered a plantation like the others, and that all European goods imported from thence would be seized under the act of 1663. In order to detect forged coquets, they bade him instruct all officers of the ports that no European goods could be unloaded until coquets had been shown to the collector of the customs or his deputy, and warrants issued thereupon, and then only in the presence of one or more officers appointed thereunto. And, finally, they ordered him to require all masters, before unlading, to leave with the naval officer the name of the ship and that of its master, proof that it was legally navigated, a complete inventory of its cargo, and the name of the port where its cargo was taken on.[60] Henceforth, it was difficult for vessels trading illicitly to slip through. One little brigantine, the *Swan,* while attempting to smuggle into Boston a few barrels of brandy and vinegar, was seized by Captain George and brought to trial for violating the act of 1663. The master, Haywood by name, was unable

[60] C. O. 5: 904, pp. 410-411; Toppan, *Randolph,* IV, 145-147; Mass. Arch., vol. 126, pp. 329-330; Osgood and Batchelder, *Salem,* p. 127.

to show a coquet that the goods had been shipped from England, Wales, or Berwick-on-Tweed. He claimed that he found the barrels floating on the water and took them on board, intending to report to the authorities on arrival. On pretense of innocence, he asked that the king's and the governor's share be returned to him. Circumstantial evidence was, however, too strong for him and he had to forfeit the ship and all its lading.[61]

All cases of condemnation during Andros's administration seem to have been for attempting to import illegally European products, usually wines or brandies, oils, and in a few cases, linen and woolen cloth.[62] Since Randolph, who was in a position to know, frequently reported to the Lords of Trade that the navigation laws were being strictly enforced, the small number of condemnations is evidently indicative of the fact that the seizures were few and that only the boldest traders dared to defy the law.[63]

This stoppage of direct commerce with Europe had the effect of curtailing the trade in enumerated commodities with the West Indies and the Southern colonies. Randolph wrote to Blathwayt in November, 1687, that "the Trade is not so quick as formerly. I feare the additionall Impost upon the Plantation Comodityes affects us, for our Trade to those parts does very much decay: and I know now nothing but hopps is with us a good commodity wee have two ships now ready to sayle halfe

[61] Mass. Arch., vol. 129, p. 288.

[62] Mass. Arch., vol. 126, pp. 282, 367, 380; vol. 128, p. 91; vol. 129, p. 121; Toppan, *Randolph*, IV, 164-165.

[63] Throughout Andros's administration, trial of breaches of the navigation acts seems to have been held in the ordinary courts. An unnamed vessel, condemned for importation of European goods, was tried at a county court held at Boston. The ship *Unity* was tried in the inferior court of common pleas. The ship *John* was tried in the superior court at Boston, October 25, 1687, and another vessel was condemned in the same court, July 30, 1688. Mass. Arch., vol. 126, p. 282; vol. 127, pp. 150, 250, 295, 299; vol. 129, p. 121.

loaden with them.''[64] Likewise, an officer of the customs
at Newport reported to Usher, the treasurer, that between February 16, 1687, and March 12, 1688, the amount
of foreign imports had been ''the Least that hath Bene
Imported heare this Many year, for wee have not had
one vessell directly from Barbados hear this year but
what hath com Round Som other way which hath not
onely Lessoned the Impost but made A greatt scarcity in
this place.''[65] Although there were other contributing
factors, the principal cause of this decrease was the lack
of articles of exchange, since the cutting off of the direct
trade with Europe had reduced the supply of manufactured goods. The impost of 1685 increased the price of
sugar and tobacco, while the scarcity of the labor supply,
owing to the difficulties of the Royal African Company,
restricted the output in the Southern and West Indian
colonies. These colonies did not in any case produce
enough of the enumerated commodities to supply both
England and the Northern colonies, and now that the
New England traders were unable to purchase these
commodities by underselling British merchants with the
cheaper, duty-free European goods, larger amounts were
shipped directly to England by the West Indian and
Southern planters. Captain Allen of H. M. S. *Quaker,*
who had been sent to aid in enforcing the navigation laws
in the south, wrote to the Lords of Trade in January,
1687, that he hoped a great deal of tobacco would reach
England during the year, for he had ''defeated the vessels of New York and New England.''[66]

This decline of trade with the West Indies and the
Southern colonies had no effect, strangely enough, on
New England's trade with the mother country. Cutting

[64] Goodrick, *Randolph,* VI, 235.
[65] Jeffries Family Papers, II, 100.
[66] *Cal. State Pap. Col.,* 1685-1688, §1507-i.

off the direct trade with Europe in manufactured articles might have been expected to arouse in New England
an increased demand for English goods, but it did not.
The shipping lists for the years 1687 and 1688 show that
each year only ten ships sailed for ports of the mother
country.[67] This was the usual number engaged in trade
in the years preceding and following the Andros period.
Reduction of the trade in enumerated products left New
England without a sufficient stock of articles of exchange
with which to purchase British goods. The result was
that such goods had to be bought with hard money, if
they were to be bought at all, thus drawing from other
channels of New England trade the little gold and silver
that was in circulation.[68] This scarcity of money was due
to the closing of the Boston mint in 1684, which reduced
the home supply, and to the suppression of piracy,
whence came the largest amount of foreign coin.

Scarcity of money made more necessary than ever
some immediate action in regard to the currency situation. The president and council had already petitioned
the king for the re-establishment of the mint, pointing
out that "having no staple commodities to pass current
in payments as in other Plantations—Trade for want of
money is much perplex'd and decayd."[69] Before the arrival of this memorial, the Lords of Trade had taken the
matter up with the Treasury Board, asking whether or
not it was desirable "to resettle the mint in Boston by
Andros's commission." The board referred the question
to the commissioners of the mint, who reported that the
mint at Boston should not be re-established unless the
silver coins be as fine as those minted in England. Their
opinion was that "the preservation of a fixed standard

[67] Mass. Arch., vol. 7, pp. 15-68.
[68] Goodrick, *Randolph*, VI, 236.
[69] 2 Mass. Hist. Soc. *Proc.*, XIII, 244.

in weight and fineness for the King's silver coinage in all his dominions is much for his security and advantage, and it cannot be altered in any colony without prejudice to the rest. The current coin will be withdrawn and prices will rise in proportion to the baser coin.'' A similar report had been sent in January, 1685,[70] and was consistent with the general policy of keeping the weight and fineness of the money to the English standard by opposing the establishment of mints in various parts of the British world.[71]

Andros, himself, favored the re-establishment of the mint. While his commission was under consideration, he presented to the Lords of Trade and the officers of the mint a paper expressing his views on the subject. He argued that money was the measure of value of goods and so could be artificially raised; that although the standard of English money had always been preserved in purity and fineness, the value and weight had often been changed according to the rate of silver and the increase of trade. Moreover, the Boston silver coin had been the accepted standard of value for years and the raising of it to the English standard ''would enrich the landlord & creditor but ruin the tenant and debtor, destroy the trade of the country and injure the King's Customs.'' Even if the mint were discontinued, he said, pieces of eight would have to be made current at the same rates as those proposed for the king's coin and this, from the English point of view, would be as great an inconvenience as the mint.[72]

[70] *Cal. State Pap. Col*, 1685-1688, §§762, 944-ii.

[71] *Cal. State Pap. Col.*, 1685-1688, §944-ii; Mass. Arch., vol. 100, p. 388; Crosby, *Early Coins*, pp. 88-89. The king had refused a patent in 1662 to Sir Thomas Vyner for coining money in Ireland, and again in 1679 to Lord Carlisle for a similar purpose in Jamaica. *Cal. State Pap. Col.*, 1677-1680, §§474, 779-i, 840, 841, 883, 903, 1030.

[72] *Cal. State Pap. Col.*, 1685-1688, §§929, 944-v.

The mint officers answered that while it was true that money was the measure of value of goods, goods could not be the measure of money. They agreed that the value of money had often been altered, but that that was no reason why the mint in one part of the king's dominions should not hold equal balance with the mint in another. Trade would in the future conform to the intrinsic value of the money and past debts could be discharged by regulation at the rate of fifteen shillings to the pound. They did not see that the regulation of pieces of eight was comparable to the establishment of a mint, for pieces of eight were but commodities like other merchandise, and the people should be left at liberty to barter one against the other.[73] The Lords of Trade, to whom this report was made, agreed with the commissioners of the mint that the Massachusetts mint should not be re-established, but recommended to the Privy Council that Andros be given power to regulate, by proclamation, the value of pieces of eight and other foreign coin. The order in council, which followed, shifted to Andros and his council the responsibility of determining the relative value of foreign coins in comparison with those of Massachusetts and England.[74]

Money was one of the first subjects considered by Andros's council. On February 23, 1687, Richard Wharton, representing the interests of the merchants, read a paper advocating raising the value of all money, but the coin of New England proportionately more than foreign coin. He recommended that the New England shilling should pass current for fourteen pence; the sixpence for seven; the threepence for four, and the twopence for

[73] *Cal. State Pap. Col.*, §§944, 944-vii.

[74] "To regulate pieces of eight and other foreign coin imported thither to such currant value as shall be found most requisite for his Majesty's subjects and the trade of his subjects here." *Laws of New Hampshire*, I, 172; *Cal. State Pap. Col.*, 1685-1688, §§909, 929, 944.

three. All Mexico, Pillar, Seville, and other pieces of eight, bullion, plate, or any manner of broken silver of sterling fineness should pass at seven shillings, sixpence per ounce, instead of being rated at the face value of the coin. Since sterling silver was rated at six shillings, eight pence per ounce, the troy weight value of all coins would thus be increased one-eighth, while the New England shilling would be worth one-sixth more than formerly. By these ratings, the New England shilling would be worth one shilling, twopence, face value (New England evaluation), but one shilling, one penny, two farthings by weight. Therefore the New England shilling would stay in circulation in the colony because its face value was slightly higher than its intrinsic value. Rating the lighter foreign coin by weight instead of by face value would prevent it from driving out the heavier New England coin, while raising its value, even though that was an intrinsic and not a token value, would tend to draw it into the colony.[75]

In the discussion which followed, great differences of opinion were expressed. One group was very anxious to have the value of money raised, because they thought to do so would make money plentiful and quicken trade. Another group opposed this on the ground that to raise the value of money would bring in only light money from the West Indies, which would wholly ''destroy the navigation of this Country for the lumber trade.'' Besides,

[75] Wharton's paper is entered in the Mass. Arch., vol. 100, pp. 162-163, under date, May 31, 1671, and in the Index is entitled ''Treasurer's Proposals.'' This is an error. Wharton was in no position to make such a proposal in 1671, as at that time he was not a freeman, and at no time was he treasurer. There is unmistakable evidence that the paper belongs to the period of Andros's administration, for it contains such expressions as ''bring into his Majesty's Dominion'' and ''for Support of his Government heer,'' which can refer only to a royal government. It also speaks of ''the money formerly Coyned in New England,'' thus placing the date of the paper at least after the vacation of the charter in 1684.

they said, if pieces of eight were brought in with the trade to the West Indies instead of molasses, rum, etc., there would be "no returns to be made from hence to England." The councilors representing agricultural interests were opposed to any change, arguing that the raising of money would help only the merchants, while the country inhabitants would be no better off, because they could not advance upon their goods. Andros at first favored raising the value of all money, but interpreting his instructions to apply only to foreign coins, in the end he "wholly declared against settling any value upon the New England money further than the intrinsic value."[76]

Before a decision concerning foreign coin was reached, Andros sought the advice of goldsmiths and merchants. The former declared that increasing the value of pieces of eight only, would bring them in plentifully, but that so doing would not better matters unless New England money were allowed to pass at the same value, because the latter would all leave the country before any money could be brought in to supply the immediate needs of trade.[77]

Merchants to whom Andros referred the question, favored continuing the New England money at the same rate as formerly, with strict regulations as to its exportation, but they thought that Spanish money ought to be raised, so that Mexico, Seville, and Pillar dollars should pass at six shillings, ten pence per ounce troy and all quarter pieces and reals, Mexico, etc., at five shillings, four pence per piece. Payment of contracts could then be required in current New England money or in Spanish money of Mexico, Seville, or Pillar at six shillings, ten pence per ounce troy.[78] When it became apparent to

[76] Amer. Antiq. Soc. *Proc.*, N. S., XIII, 252.

[77] Their answer was, of course, based on the theory that light money drives out the heavy. Amer. Antiq. Soc. *Proc.*, N. S., XIII, 254.

[78] *Ibid.*, 262-263.

Andros that the merchants wanted to consider money a commodity and not to make it current at a fixed price,[79] he accepted the advice of the goldsmiths. He ordered that all Seville, Pillar, and Mexico pieces of eight of seventeen and one-half pennyweight should pass in payment at six shillings a piece and that New England money should pass for value as formerly.[80] This rule made no change in the value of the foreign coin, which thenceforth was rated simply at a definite amount for each denomination instead of according to troy weight. The heavier coins were not affected at all, but those lighter in weight probably increased in circulation, because of the difficulty of giving them a definite value. This settlement of the currency question was very unsatisfactory, especially to the merchants, for, as Randolph wrote to John Povey, of the Plantation Office, Whitehall, regulating the rates of pieces of eight "does not answer the end, money grows very scarce and no trade to bring it in."[81] Not only was the scarcity of money increased by the slump in trade, but there was no hope of improving trade

[79] That is, place a value on the coin by its weight instead of making a definite price for each denomination of coin.

[80] Amer. Antiq. Soc. *Proc.*, N. S., XIII, 263. Through some error the copy of the order sent to England contains no reference to the New England coin. Amer. Antiq. Soc. *Proc.*, N. S., XIII, 262, note; *Laws of New Hampshire*, I, 197.

[81] Toppan, *Randolph*, IV, 163. Money conditions did not improve, for in August Sewall said that "times are extream difficult with us for procuring any coin." Sewall, *Letter Book*, I, 52. Randolph wrote to Blathwayt in November, "our money for want of goods to make returnes is sent to London." Goodrick, *Randolph*, VI, 236. In January, Randolph again wrote, "our money goes all away and shall have little or none to supply ordinary occasions." Of the other colonies, Plymouth and Connecticut also suffered from a scarcity of money. 4 Mass. Hist. Soc. *Col.*, V, 156-157, 174, 175; 6 Mass. Hist. Soc. *Col.*, V, 19. As will be shown later, it was this scarcity of money that made the fees charged for taking out new land patents seem so excessive. *Andros Tracts*, I, 143; III, 197; 4 Mass. Hist. Soc. *Col.*, V, 177-178.

conditions until a sufficient medium of currency was provided.

The money situation was made much worse by Andros's attempt to prevent piracy, because this attempt decreased the number of foreign coins coming in. The Lords of Trade made special efforts during the Dominion period to suppress piracy in American waters. In the Treaty of Neutrality of 1686, England had agreed with France that orders should be sent to the governors and other officers to proceed against all persons arming private men-of-war without a lawful commission, and that subjects of either king taking out commissions as privateers from any prince or state, with whom the other king was at war, should be punished as pirates. Instructions were accordingly sent by the Lords of Trade to the governors in America urging the passage of laws against pirates, and ordering them to act "with all vigor" against any such persons as might come into port.[82] The king issued a proclamation promising pardon to those who should, on certain conditions, surrender themselves to any of the plantations governments.[83] For the enforcement of these proclamations and orders, Sir Robert Holmes was sent to the West Indies in command of a squadron. He was empowered to seize pirates found

[82] C. O. 5: 904, p. 340; *Cal. State Pap. Col.*, 1685-1688, §1411.

[83] C. O. 324: 4, p. 239; *Cal. State Pap. Col.*, 1685-1688, §§1223, 1276, 1278. The proclamation was published in Boston, August 25, 1687. *Andros Tracts*, III, 73; *Cal. State Pap. Col.*, 1685-1688, §1413; Amer. Antiq. Soc. *Proc.*, N. S., XIII, 473-474. There was at least one surrender in New England, for a copy of the bond is in the Mass. Arch., vol. 127, p. 240. This bond was between Christopher Goff on the one hand and a Boston merchant and a surgeon on the other, and provided that if Goff went to England and received the king's pardon and otherwise fulfilled the terms of the bond, it should become void. In Bermuda, about seventy men from a Portuguese man-of-war submitted to the royal proclamation. *Cal. State Pap. Col.*, 1685-1688, §1772; 1689-1692, §45.

in those parts and to pardon all who surrendered within twelve months, if security for good behavior were given.[84]

In spite of all of these regulations, piracy was not suppressed as rapidly as was expected. In England this failure was attributed to the connivance of governors and others prominent in the colonies. Frequent information was received to the effect that "instead of a due Prosecution of Pirates that have been seized either upon the high Sea or upon Land, an unwarrantable practice has been Carryed on to bring them immediately to their Tryalls before any Evidence could be produced against them." By this and similar methods, the most notorious pirates were allowed to escape unpunished and to return to their former evil practices. To prevent this, the king notified all colonial governors that captured pirates should be kept in prison until he or Sir Robert Holmes should appoint the time and place of trial,[85] and as a further encouragement granted Sir Robert, by letters patent, all goods that he might take from pirates in the next three years.[86] On January 20, 1688, the king issued another proclamation for suppressing piracy and sent circulars to the governors ordering them to publish it and aid in its execution.[87]

Andros seems to have made every effort to stamp out the evil and, soon after his entrance into office, caused a law to be passed by his council providing for the trial of pirates.[88] He arranged for police protection by commissioning the captains of the frigate and sloop to cruise along the coast and by sending them on special missions

[84] *Cal. State Pap. Col.*, 1685-1688, §1411.

[85] This letter to Andros is dated October 13, 1687. C. O. 5: 904, pp. 365-366; *Cal. State Pap. Col.*, 1685-1688, §1463; *Laws of New Hampshire*, I, 173-174.

[86] *Cal. State Pap. Col.*, 1685-1688, §1508.

[87] *Ibid.*, §1602; C. O. 5: 904, pp. 378-380; *Laws of New Hampshire*, I, 179-181.

[88] *Laws of New Hampshire*, I, 195-196.

to particular places where pirates were thought to be in hiding.[89] A few arrests were made, but a condemnation rarely followed.[90] When the ketch *Sparrow* was caught in the summer of 1687, those arrested were immediately brought to trial and acquitted. Nicholas Page, a prominent Boston merchant whose reputation was none too good, was deeply concerned in this affair, but got off on the claim that he had ventured a cargo to the Southern colonies and the West Indies, the profits from which were in the bags of money found on the *Sparrow*.[91] A year later, Nicholson wrote from Boston that eight men were in prison there, suspected of being pirates. Not one of these men was convicted.[92] Despite these unsatisfactory results, there was a great decrease of piracy in New England waters during Andros's administration.[93] The measures taken by the king were effective in frightening many away from the business, so that what little piracy there was around New England was indulged in very cautiously.

The economic significance of this decrease in piracy lay in its effect on the money situation. At the very time when the old domestic source of hard money was cut off, the influx of foreign coins was decreased by the suppression of piracy. The process of readjustment to fit the new conditions was handicapped by the failure of Andros to appreciate the necessity of creating some arti-

[89] Mass. Arch., vol. 126, pp. 334-335, 381, 408; vol. 127, pp. 8, 76-77, 83; vol. 128, pp. 233, 287-288, 295; vol. 129, pp. 8, 11, 49-50.

[90] *Ibid.*, vol. 127, p. 62. Judging from a resolution of the governor and council in 1687, these piracy cases were tried in a special oyer and terminer court, whose members were appointed by the governor. Amer. Antiq. Soc. *Proc.*, N. S., XIII, 473-474.

[91] Mass. Arch., vol. 126, p. 416; vol. 127, pp. 4, 5, 6, 7, 9, 10, 11, 12, 13, 31, 32, 47, 188; Amer. Antiq. Soc. *Proc.*, N. S., XIII, 475; *Andros Tracts*, III, 73.

[92] *New York Col. Docs.*, III, 552-553.

[93] *Andros Tracts*, I, 41; *Cal. State Pap. Col.*, 1689-1692, §152.

ficial commercial attraction, which would draw money
into the colony. Without money and without staples,
Massachusetts could not easily recover from the depression in trade, and through trade alone could money and
a sufficient supply of staples be provided. New England's
economic hope for the future lay in the possibility of
creating or obtaining marketable staples. Failing in this,
the people would inevitably turn their energies to manufactures or to some doubtful channels of trade not here-
tofore specifically forbidden.

During the administration of Andros, for the first and
only time in the history of New England, from the reign
of Charles II to the American Revolution, the navigation
acts were strictly enforced.[94] What was the result? First
of all, viewing the effects from the standpoint of the
mother country, New England by artificial means was
forced to take her place in the mercantilist economic empire. By this means, she was so far shackled as to be able
no longer to interfere with England's control of colonial
enumerated products, or with colonial markets for British manufactured goods. England had not minded New
England's failure to furnish desired staples as much as
she had disliked New England's position as a competitor,
a commercial rival like Holland and France. The Dominion of New England brought an end to that rivalry.
In the second place, the effect on New England of the
strict enforcement of the British navigation acts was
deadly. Temporarily, at least, trade was completely
ruined. The closing of shops was a common occurrence
and many a merchant of former prominence went bank-
rupt.[95] The merchants in New England were unprepared

[94] *Andros Tracts*, I, 41; III, 21; *Cal. State Pap. Col.*, 1689-1692, §152.

[95] Goodrick, *Randolph*, VI, 235. In 1687, Randolph reported to Blathwayt
that "our shopkeepers break every day, and I beleive even in Boston
should the Merchants of England be earnest for their Debts not twenty
Shopps will long be open in Boston." *Ibid.*, 219. Richard Wharton, one

for this. In Massachusetts, many of them, as we have
seen, had grown weary of the tyranny of the old theocratic Puritan government and preferred a royal administration. They were Englishmen, proud of their birth-
right and desirous of a closer connection with the mother
country, economically as well as politically and socially,
but they had not expected that a royal government would
bring upon them so rigid an enforcement of the acts of
trade. In the past they had met and conversed with many
royal officials in the colonies, and knew that royal governors usually connived at a certain amount of illegal
trade, provided an outward show of obedience to the acts
was maintained. They had been glad to accept positions
in Andros's council, believing that in the future they and
others of the moderate party would be allowed to direct
the policy of the new government. Consequently, Andros's literal interpretation of his trade instructions
came as a severe blow to them and they saw, when too
late, that ruin stared them in the face. Only two lines of
action seemed open to them, either they must bring about
Andros's recall and have a man of the usual type of
royal governor put in his place, or they must adjust their
economic interests to fit the new conditions. At first they
chose the latter, and sought to save New England from
economic ruin by an increased output of staples. A number of them in Boston formed a company for mining
copper, in which they planned to invest the capital formerly used in mercantile adventures. They tried to persuade English capitalists also to take stock and applied
to King James for a charter of incorporation. The sudden
overthrow of Andros altered their plans and caused them
to enter upon the second line of action, for they saw that

of the wealthiest of the merchants and large landowners of Massachusetts,
died about the time of the revolution, leaving an estate so encumbered
with debt that his two daughters were forced to open a shop to make a
living. 3 Mass. Hist. Soc. *Col.,* VII, 199.

by joining the revolutionary movement, led by the Puritans, they could restore former trade conditions, a course which they distinctly preferred.[96]

These men might have taken up another interest and turned their attention to the manufacture of naval stores, an industry in which many prominent merchants of vision had long been interested, but before the fall of the Massachusetts charter it had not promised as certain and immediate a return as the pursuit of commerce. Now that their commerce was in danger of being destroyed, they were bound to take into serious consideration a staple with which nature had so abundantly endowed New England, and had they done so, persistently and on a large scale, it is likely that they would have made it profitable. Had the Dominion of New England survived, they would, without doubt, have found other staples also, for the New Englanders have always been an adaptable people. Forced by necessity to develop new industries or starve, they would in time have produced successfully the necessary articles of commerce. This very adaptability had brought into existence the New England commercial system, after the Puritan revolution in England had upset the trade relations of Massachusetts with the mother country, and even if they themselves had been wanting in sufficient interest to develop naval stores, a royal governor, who understood English and colonial economic conditions and was independent of local con-

[96] The writer of one of the revolutionary pamphlets believed that this plan for mining copper would furnish the New Englanders with a staple commodity, which might ''occasion reciprocal returns.'' *Andros Tracts*, III, 7-8. See also *Cal. State Pap. Col.*, 1685-1688, §§1629, 1809, 1839, 1840, 1850, 1855, 1859, 1863; 1689-1692, §2467; 3 Mass. Hist. Soc. *Col.*, I, 98; 6 Mass. Hist. Soc. *Col.*, V, 11-15; Toppan, *Randolph*, IV, 221. From time to time there seems to have been considerable interest in the development of mines in New England. Toppan, *Randolph*, IV, 4; Hanscom, *Heart of the Puritan*, p. 154; *Mass. Col. Rec.*, V, 383; *Cal. State Pap. Col.*, 1677-1680, §1349-i; 1685-1688, §901.

trol, could easily have directed their activities in the proper direction.[97]

The overthrow of the Dominion government restored the supremacy of the New England commercial system. Trade immediately sought its old channels. Direct trade with the European Continent was resumed, though never again recovering its former proportions as compared with trade in other directions. As commercial intercourse with the mother country increased, that with the Continent decreased. The emphasis in the seventeenth century was on the commercial cycle comprising New England, the Continent, and the British Islands and Southern colonies; that in the eighteenth century, except for a brief interregnum after the War of the Palatinate when an impetus was given to home manufactures, particularly woolen articles, by the difficulty of obtaining a sufficient supply from England and the Continent, the emphasis was on the cycle comprising New England, the foreign West Indies, and England. The mother country, greatly concerned over the menace of colonial manufacturing, passed the Woolens Act in 1699. As the trade with the foreign West Indies, which had taken great strides in the

[97] *Cal. State Pap. Col.*, 1669-1674, §§990, 1279; 1675-1676, §72; 1677-1680, §1360, p. 529; 1681-1685, §91; 1689-1692, §§1725, 1726, 1729, 1731; Toppan, *Randolph*, IV, 42, 93; Hanscom, *Heart of the Puritan*, p. 154; *New England Hist. and Gen. Reg.*, IX, 339. Andros reported that the northern parts of America could furnish any quantity of tar, pitch, and rosin, and that the ground was suitable for flax and hemp. A memorandum by ''Colonel Ledget'' claimed that all the shipping of England could be supplied from the American colonies, and that in New England there was ''great plenty of timber and trees which produce tar, which industry has no further improved than to satisfy the wants of the neighboring colonies and the West Indies.'' *Cal. State Pap. Cal.*, 1689-1692, §§1727, 1728. Col. Charles Lidgett was a New England merchant, who strongly advocated the production of naval stores by chartered companies, and some years later, at the request of the Board of Trade, drafted a charter suitable for such a purpose. Lord, *Industrial Experiments in the British Colonies of North America*, p. 20.

War of the Palatinate and Queen Anne's War, continued
to increase, England, alarmed by the complaints of the
British West Indies planters, passed the Molasses Act of
1733, an act which, by its very provisions, marked the
failure of the mercantilist policy. Other attempts also
were made to arrest New England's economic development along undesired lines. These measures were all
ineffective as far as New England was concerned, because it was impossible to control that region without
an independent royal governor. By the middle of the
eighteenth century, New England was too strong to be
easily controlled by force against her will. Yet had the
Dominion of New England survived, at least until New
England had taken her place in the economic empire, as
had the Island and Southern colonies, the imperial ties
would have been too strong to be broken when the dispute arose with the mother country. Had it been com-
mercially to New England's advantage to remain within
the empire, it is doubtful if she would ever have desired
political independence. It was the dominance of the New
England commercial system over that of Great Britain
that gave to New England, on the eve of the War of
Independence, the consciousness of economic independence, and with it, the desire for political independence.

CHAPTER VIII

THE LAND SYSTEM

In the colonial policy of the Restoration the colonies were looked at from two points of view: first as assets in building up the commerce of the kingdom and, secondly, as a legitimate source of profit to the king. Not for many years after their settlement did the latter realize that he had not derived from the colonies all the advantages that were legitimately his own by virtue of his prerogative. He could have asked quit-rents in the granting of all land and was entitled to one-third of the profits of forfeitures and fines, one-half of the treasure from wrecks, and other small perquisites. All these had been neglected down to 1660. But in that year and the years that followed, his attention was called to the opportunities which the colonies offered for a permanent and settled source of income, not only for the crown but also for the support of government in the colonies themselves. Such a fund would free a royal governor from the control of the assembly, by removing the necessity of depending on that body for funds. There are many indications during these years that the king was becoming interested in the financial possibilities of the colonies. In 1681 he declared in council that he would henceforth make no grant of quit-rents in any of the colonies, but would reserve them for the support of the respective governments there, according to his original intentions.[1] In 1680 he appointed

[1] This action was taken after the granting away of the quit-rents of Virginia to Arlington and Culpeper, against which there had been loud

William Blathwayt surveyor and auditor-general of his revenues in the plantations,[2] with instructions to collect the money and audit the accounts.[3] He let it be known that from this time forward quit-rents would be expected in all new grants of land.[4] In some, at least, of the charters granted after 1660, he demanded more than a mere nominal acknowledgment for the land.[5] Most important of all, in the great experiment of the Dominion, he sought to put the new policy into practice.

The omission from Andros's commission of all mention of a representative assembly made it necessary to raise the required revenue for support of government in other ways than by direct taxation. For this reason, the Lords of Trade accepted Randolph's suggestion that

complaint from the colony. The Lords of Trade disapproved of the grant and advised the king to make no more in Virginia or anywhere else. *Acts, Privy Coun. Col.*, II, §43, p. 22.

2 This officer was to have nothing to do with the revenue arising by the act of 1673, his duty being to audit the accounts of the king from fines, forfeitures, quit-rents, etc. He was to have his residence in England. William Blathwayt, the first to hold this office, was appointed under the great seal, May 19, 1680. He was empowered to choose deputies to serve on the place, auditing and forwarding the revenues to him. Randolph was made deputy for New England, excepting New Hampshire, October 15, 1681. Blathwayt's commission is printed in the *Mass. Col. Rec.*, V, 521-526, and his deputation to Randolph, *ibid.*, 526-529.

3 One of the charges against Massachusetts, in the period before the annulment of the charter, was that she refused to pay the king the fines and forfeitures which were due him and would not recognize Blathwayt's commission. Toppan, *Randolph*, III, 132, 214; *Cal. State Pap. Col.*, 1681-1685, §528.

4 The petitioners for grants in the Narragansett Country, both before and during the establishment of the Dominion, offered to pay the usual quit-rent of two shillings, six pence per hundred acres. *Cal. State Pap. Col.*, 1685-1688, §§91-i, 1695; *Acts, Privy Coun. Col.*, II, p. 79, §177.

5 In the Carolina charter of 1663, a yearly rent of twenty marks was reserved; in the New York grant, forty beaver skins; in the Mount Hope grant, seven beaver skins or fourteen marks. Thorpe, *Federal and State Constitutions*, III, 1638; V, 2745; 4 Mass. Hist. Soc. *Col.*, V, 32.

funds be provided by means of quit-rents.[6] They were aware that the introduction of such a feature into the revenue policy would bring a radical change in the land system and affect trade and they embarked upon it slowly and with caution, instructing Andros to reserve quit-rents only in the case of lands "yet undisposed of." In "other Lands Tenements and Hereditam'ts for which Our Royall Confirmation may be wanting," he was "to reserve Such acknowledgem'ts unto Us" for their confirmation as he might think "most equitable and conducing to Our Service."[7]

In adopting a revenue system based partly on quit-rents from land, the Lords of Trade committed themselves to a policy of land granting which demanded of the colonists recognition of their tenurial relationship to the king. The right of the king to introduce such a method of landholding in future grants was unquestioned, since he could give out his land under whatever conditions he chose. But whether or not he could demand quit-rents from holders of land granted by former proprietors was open to doubt. By a declaration in 1683, he had guaranteed to the inhabitants of Massachusetts their property rights, and it was largely this guarantee that won over the moderates to the support of the provisional govern-

[6] *Rhode Island Col. Recs.*, III, 207; Goodrick, *Randolph*, VI, 177, 179, 181, 219.

[7] *Laws of New Hampshire*, I, 159-160. In the royal commission, which was always made public, the land policy was sketched much more tactfully than in the instructions, which were for the governor's private perusal only. Andros was empowered, with the advice and consent of the council, to "agree with the Planters and Inhabitants of our said Territory and Dominion, Concerning such Lands, Tenements and Hereditaments as now are or heereafter shall be in our Power to dispose of and them to Grant unto any Person or Persons for such termes and under such moderate Quitt Rents Services and Acknowledgements to be thereupon Reserved Unto Us as shall be appointed by us." Therefore, to the colonists examining the commission, the policy as stated, would seem to apply only to grants of land previously undisposed of. *Ibid.*, 153.

ment and of Andros's administration. But when the Lords of Trade began working on the commission and instructions for the government of the Dominion, they saw the difficulty which the governor would meet in attempting, without question, to confirm all the old titles, many of which were defective and concerned land on which there were rival claims. They felt that a careful investigation should be made into the validity of these claims. Furthermore, they realized that free confirmation would signify to the Puritans the king's approval of the doctrine of absolute ownership of the soil which they had put into practice almost from the beginning. They thought it most unwise to permit the Puritans to hold this error because it could but give them a sense of security which would strengthen their attitude of independence toward the mother country.[8] The lords realized that they were handling a very delicate matter, one which could perhaps be dealt with more effectively by some one on the spot, and, therefore, they instructed Andros to obtain some sort of payment in return for confirmation, but left entirely to his discretion its character and amount.

The land policy, as outlined in the commission and instructions, disclosed a double purpose, the raising of revenue by quit-rents on all new grants and the settling of rival claims when confirming all old ones. At the same time the lords desired to bring uniformity into the tenure and method of granting land and to make all titles originate with the king. To understand the situation confront-

[8] It is interesting to notice that Governor Coney of Bermuda had in 1685 complained to the Lords of Trade of a similar independent attitude on the part of the Bermudians, which he ascribes to their holding their land without acknowledgment of outside authority. He therefore suggested as a remedy ''that if every Freeholder (as they term themselves) both in Town and Country doe pay a small quit-rent, according to the proportion they hold, it may bee one means to reduce them to obedience.'' Lefroy, *Memorials of the Bermudas*, II, 549, 558.

ing Andros it will be necessary to study briefly the various rival grants and tenures, which had already come into existence in New England.

Lands in New England were originally held of the king by the New England Council in free and common socage, as of the manor of East Greenwich, with a reservation of one-fifth of all the gold and silver ore.[9] As was the case with all grants to trading companies, no quit-rent was imposed. In its turn, the council sublet lands to "partners," that is, to its own members, and to private persons or associations.[10] In grants to partners, land was "to be holden of his said Majestie in the County of Kent in free and common Soccage and not in capite or by Knights Service"; one-fifth of all the gold and silver ore was to be reserved to the king "for all services dutyes and demands"; another fifth was to go to the New England Council; and an annual quit-rent was to be paid, if later demanded.[11] In grants to private persons, not of the council, land was to be held of that body, the grantee paying always one-fifth of the gold and silver to the king and one-fifth to the council, with the addition of a quit-rent, usually of twelve pence per hundred acres to be paid into the hands of the rent gatherer "at the feast of St. Michaell Tharchaungell."[12] Partners and non-members, who subgranted to tenants, usually imposed some

[9] *Farnham Papers*, 1603-1688, I, 34. (Documentary History of the State of Maine, VII.)

[10] *Ibid.*, 34, 62, 73.

[11] Examples of grants of this kind are the patents to Mason and Gorges for the land between the Merrimac and Sagadahoc Rivers (Maine), dated August 10/20, 1622, *ibid.*, 64-71; to John Mason, for the land between the Merrimac and the Piscataqua (New Hampshire), dated Nov. 7/17, 1629, Thorpe, *Federal and State Const.*, IV, 2433-2436; to Gorges and Mason for territory known as Laconia, Nov. 17/27, 1629, *Farnham Papers*, I, 98-107.

[12] *Ibid.*, pp. 120, 124, 140, 148, 151, 161, 164, 168.

sort of quit-rent, which, though rarely collected, was understood to be a real obligation resting on the land.

The first colony to make a successful settlement within the territory of the New England Council was Plymouth. By the first patent each associate, Pilgrim or other, was given one hundred acres at a quit-rent of two shillings each, to be collected after seven years.[13] But as private holdings did not begin in Plymouth for several years, no payment of quit-rents seems ever to have been made. When the lands were distributed, they bore no burden of quit-rent, and when the Bradford patent was obtained in 1630, the quit-rent had disappeared.[14] Although Mount Hope, which was added to Plymouth after King Philip's War, was held as a propriety of the king with an annual quit-rent of seven beaver skins or fourteen marks,[15] the lands of that region were given out, as were the first lands in the colony, without reservation of quit-rent. Throughout the history of the colony, the inhabitants held their lands without obligation of any sort.[16] Plymouth colony was, therefore, the first in New England to break away from the English land law.

Contrary to the usual custom of the New England Council in granting lands to non-members, the patent given to the Endicott associates, the forerunners of the Massachusetts Bay Company, contained no mention of quit-rents, although the double reservation of gold and silver ore was made.[17] On the other hand, the royal con-

---

13 *Farnham Papers*, I, pp. 46-53.

14 *Ibid.*, pp. 108-116.

15 4 Mass. Hist. Soc. *Col.*, V, 32. This quit-rent was actually paid from year to year, as is shown by Hinckley's apology to Blathwayt in 1682, for the apparent non-payment that year, due to the fact that the agent had paid the fourteen marks into the exchequer but had sent Blathwayt no order for the amount. *Ibid.*, p. 66.

16 *Ibid.*, pp. 168, 177, 179.

17 In the absence of this patent it is difficult to determine with accuracy regarding the reservation of the council's fifth of gold and silver. The royal

firmation of 1629 omits all reservation to the council, showing that the king was granting to the Massachusetts Bay Company, to be held directly of him, land which he had already granted to the council, and which the latter had granted to the Endicott associates. By the terms of the new charter, the Massachusetts Bay Company held directly of the king, without quit-rent, but with the customary reservation to the king of one-fifth of the gold and silver ore.[18] Because of the singular terms of the charter, Gorges, the president of the council, claimed that it had been surreptitiously obtained, and for the next ten years tried to bring about its annulment. Under his direction, the council divided its lands into eight parts, assigned to eight of its number, each of which was to constitute a separate propriety. The charter was surrendered in 1635 and a royal confirmation sought for each of the eight grants, making the grantee hold directly of the crown. The plan was to place a governor-general over the whole territory, thus giving governmental unity to the council's possessions in America. Grants legally made prior to this distribution were to be recognized by the new proprietors, upon the grantee's laying down his ''Jura regalia if he have any,'' and pay-

charter of 1629 repeats a part of this earlier patent, but makes no direct mention of such a reservation. The clauses relating to the king's fifth seem, however, to indicate that the double reservation had been purposely omitted from the royal patent,—''provided alwayes and his Majesties expresse Will and meaning was that only one Fifth parte of all the Gold and Silver Oar above menconed in the whole and no more should be answered reserved and payable unto Our said Royall Grandfather his Heires and Successors by colour or vertue of the said last menconed Letters Patents the doubel reservacons or recitalls aforesaid or any thing therein conteyned notwithstanding.''

There was at least one grant to others than partners, without this double reservation, the Muscongus patent to Thomas Leverett and John Beauchamp, March 23, 1630, later known as the Waldo patent. *Farnham Papers*, I, 125-128.

18 Thorpe, *Fed. and State Const.*, III, 1846-1860.

ing some acknowledgment. Thus opportunity would be
offered to examine doubtful patents, by which means the
Massachusettts charter could be called in question and
perhaps annulled.[19]

This plan was partly carried out. The division was
effected, leases were given to trustees,[20] the eight proprietors were enfeoffed, and the great patent was surrendered.[21] Investigation was begun into the circumstances
under which the grant to Massachusetts was made, with
the result that the charter was annulled, although there
was always a question as to how complete the legal
process was.[22] Gorges was appointed governor-general[23]
and received a charter for Maine,[24] to be held in free and
common socage, paying a quit-rent of a quarter of wheat
and certain other reservations. He was empowered to
grant land as he pleased, which he proceeded to do on
the usual manorial terms of a quit-rent.[25] His patent was,
however, the only one which passed the seals before
events in England drew the king's attention elsewhere,
and brought the council's plans to an abrupt halt.[26] The
surrender of its patent left the council without legal

[19] *Farnham Papers*, I, 183-188; 199-200.

[20] *Ibid.*, p. 188. An example of such lease is that of New Hampshire
to John Wollaston, April 18, 1635. Thorpe, IV, 2437.

[21] The eight proprietors held of the council or its successors ''per Gladium
Comitatus that is to say by findeinge foure able men conveniently armed
and arrayed for the warr to attend uppon the Governor of New England
for the publique service within ffourteene dayes after any warning given.''
Farnham Papers I, 183-188, 189-191; Thorpe, III, 1860-1861; IV, 2441-
2442.

[22] Toppan, *Randolph*, III, 3-5.

[23] *Cal. State Pap. Col.*, 1677-1680, p. 129.

[24] Thorpe, III, 1625-1637.

[25] *Farnham Papers*, I, 217; *York Deeds*, VIII, fol. 120.

[26] There is printed in the *Farnham Papers*, I, 205-208, a supposed royal
grant of New Hampshire to Mason, dated August 19/29, 1635, but it is
an error, for whatever steps were taken in that direction were never completed.

right to exist as a corporation, in spite of which fact it granted land as late as 1660.[27] Meanwhile many of the eight proprietors, seven of whom had no royal charters, proceeded to make grants, the legality of which was open to question.

In the meantime, the Massachusetts patentees followed the Plymouth custom of granting lands without tenurial obligation. As with other incorporated trading companies interested in colonization, the Massachusetts Bay Company at first held its lands in common, subject to division. When allotments were made, no quit-rents were reserved on the lands given to the adventurers or to the towns or proprietors for settlement.[28] Other lands, reserved for the support of government or for some public service, were granted under a quit-rent tenure. All islands of any importance along the coast were granted with rent payable to the General Court. Noddles Island (East Boston) was given to Samuel Maverick in 1633, on condition that he pay yearly "att the General Court, to the Govnr for the time being, either a fatt weather or a fatt hogg, or eleven shillings in money," reserving to Boston and Charlestown the right to fetch wood from the southern part of the island.[29] A year later, Long Island, Deer Island, and Hogg Island were all granted to Boston for the yearly rent of two pounds. In 1635, these, with Spectacle Island, were granted to the inhabitants of Boston to enjoy forever, paying a yearly rent of four shillings instead of three pounds, as formerly. Peddicks Island was given to the inhabitants of Charlestown and Thompson's Island to the inhabitants of Dorchester, both with a yearly rent of twelve pence. The Governor's Gar-

[27] *Cal. State Pap. Col.*, 1685-1688, §115.

[28] *Andros Tracts*, I, 142-143; *Suffolk Deeds*, I, xix.

[29] *Mass. Col. Rec.*, I, 104. This was actually paid, as was stated in 1683, by Samuel Shrimpton, into whose possession the island had come by purchase. Mass. Arch., vol. 16, p. 309.

den was rented at one-fifth of all the fruit growing there, though upon the request of John Winthrop, the reservation was changed to a hogshead of the best wine made from the products of the island. On July 5, 1631, the General Court ordered that all islands within the limits of the patent, viz., Conant's, Noddles, and Thompson's, together with all other islands within the limits, "shalbe appropriated to publique benefits & uses & to remaine in the power of the Gouvnr & Assistants (for the time being) to be lett and disposed of by them to helpe towards publique charges." Taylor's Island was granted to William Hutchinson in July, 1635, and Round and Grape Islands to the town of Weymouth in March, 1637. Besides the islands, the General Court seems to have reserved, here and there, farms which were not granted out in absolute ownership for settlement, but were leased under a quit-rent payment, these rents helping to swell the colony's exchequer.[30]

Although the towns generally distributed their lands without imposition of quit-rents, they too reserved some of them to be leased or sold under a quit-rent tenure, the money to go toward a permanent fund usually for some specific purpose. In Boston, the fund was dedicated to the use of a free school established there. A considerable piece of land near Bendall's Dock was used in this way.[31] Braintree, Charlestown, Salem, and Ipswich

[30] *Andros Tracts*, I, 142-144; *Mass. Col. Rec.*, I, 89, 104, 115, 139, 149, 189, 191; III, 292; IV-1, 444; V, 9, 413.

[31] *Boston Town Records*, 1634-1660, pp. 82, 92, 93, 94, 95, 97, 98, 125, 139, 140-141, 144; 1660-1701, pp. 149, 150. *Suffolk Deeds*, I, 116; II, 120-121; III, 454; VII, 169-170; *Mass. Col. Rec.*, IV-1, 444; Suffolk Files, Case 2416. That these rents were actually collected is shown by the frequent mention of rents in arrears, a good example being that found in the *Boston Town Records*, 1660-1701, p. 149, dated 1681, as follows: "Several beinge warned to appeare before said selectmen that were in arrears for rent due to the towne since Capt. Brattle was Treasurer and before apeared." Then follows a list of names.

each set aside large tracts for the use of schools. Lynn reserved Nahant Neck, allowing people to settle there as tenants of the town under payment of a small quit-rent. This fund seems have come into the treasury of the town to help pay its expenses.[32]

If only the Massachusetts Bay Company had taken care to grant its lands in accordance with charter provisions, the inhabitants of the colony need never have worried about the security of their titles or have had their tenures questioned. All patents should have been issued under the seal of the corporation, but in practice this was ignored.[33] Land was granted by the General Court either to individuals or to the proprietors of prospective townships in trust for future inhabitants of those towns.[34] The towns in turn, assuming the prerogatives of a corporation, granted the land to settlers. The grants of the General Court were usually made by order, and the use of the seal was neglected. Consequently, there were defects in the titles, sometimes because the titles lacked the provincial seal, sometimes because they came from the towns, which, not being corporations, had no right to grant lands. Later, the colony became aware of these irregularities, and attempted to correct them. A law was passed in 1685 stating that all grants of land previously made by the General Court or by any town in the jurisdiction, "were and are intended . . . to be an estate in fee simple, and are hereby confirmed to said persons and townships . . . forever." Should any person take

32 *Boston Town Records*, 1660-1671, pp. 99, 95; *Mass. Col. Rec.*, IV-1, 444; III, 202-203; Felt, *Annals of Salem*, I, 439; Suffolk Files, Case 2446; Mass. Arch., vol. 127, p. 174.

33 *Cal. State Pap. Col.*, 1689-1692, §181, p. 61. *Andros Tracts*, III, 21.

34 A good example of this kind of grant is that made by the General Court in 1683 to "Major Robert Thompson, Wm. Stoughton & Joseph Dudley, & such others as they shall associate to them," of a tract of land on condition that they settle on it, within four years, thirty families and "an able orthodox Minister." Mass. Arch., vol. 112, p. 341.

out an exemplification of any such grant of the court,
under the secretary's hand, and desire that the seal of
the province be affixed, the governor was ordered "in his
testimonial to insert that the sajd graunt of lands is confirmed by the Generall Court.'' This action was, however,
too late, the General Court having no legal authority to
pass laws after 1684.[35]

The Massachusetts land system was in vogue in Maine
and New Hampshire also, for Massachusetts had annexed
these provinces in 1652. After that date, lands there were
granted as in Massachusetts, though previous grants
from former proprietors, on which actual settlement had
been made, were recognized as valid. After the confirmation of the Gorges claims in 1677, Massachusetts bought
Maine and governed it as a propriety, of which the
Massachusetts Bay Company was territorial lord, and
thereafter the colony demanded the payment of all obligations formerly due to the proprietor.[36] Danforth, the
president appointed by the General Court, was instructed
to grant land in Maine under whatever quit-rent reservations he thought fit.[37] The result was that Maine possessed a variety of titles and confusion of tenures, due
to grants from the New England Council, occasionally
confirmed by Gorges, to grants by Gorges himself, to
grants by the General Court of Massachusetts in free
tenure, and to grants by that body, made after 1677, with
quit-rent reservations. In New Hampshire, there was
a similar confusion, except that titles derived from the

35 *Mass. Col. Rec.*, V, 470-471. By a Massachusetts law of 1657, confirmed and defined in 1672, a ''squatter's'' right to the land was recognized, if he had been in possession for five years, even though the land
had been previously granted to another person. *Mass. Col. Laws*, p. 124,
§1; p. 260, §5.

36 *Cal. State Pap. Col.*, 1681-1685, §528; Mass. Arch. vol. 126, p. 201;
Mass. Col. Rec., V, 326-327, 399; *Andros Tracts* I, 16.

37 Mass. Arch., vol. 126, p. 201.

proprietor were less secure than in Maine, owing to the fact that Mason himself never received a royal charter.

In the territory northeast of Maine, the County of Cornwall or Pemaquid, was to be found much the same confusion of titles and tenures as in Maine and New Hampshire. With New York and islands adjacent, this territory comprised the original propriety of the Earl of Stirling, whose claims, abandoned during the Puritan revolution, were revived during the Restoration, and bought by the Duke of York at the time of the conquest of New Netherland from the Dutch. Under the proprietary administration, and even before, settlers had squatted on the land without title, or with only such titles as were derived from the Indians. Some attempt seems to have been made under the duke's governors to introduce the English land law, and grants were made under a quit-rent tenure. A considerable amount of land was granted by Dongan at five shillings a hundred acres, but little care was taken in measuring and marking it, and rival claims constantly arose.[38] Settlements were made also by Puritans from Massachusetts, who pushed into this region and squatted there. The Massachusetts government, probably fearing trouble from the Indians should their lands be encroached upon against their will, and wishing to show a claim to the land superior to that of the Duke of York, sent commissioners into the region and forced the people to recognize the right of the Indians to the soil by paying them quit-rents.[39]

Connecticut, Rhode Island, and New Haven were settled without any legal right to the soil. The colonists either were squatters or bought titles from the Indians. But Connecticut, to which New Haven was added in 1664, received a charter from the king in 1662, and Rhode

[38] *Hutchinson Papers*, Prince Soc., II, 306.
[39] *Andros Tracts*, I, 51.

Island in 1663. In the beginning, these colonies adopted the "New England land system," already established in Massachusetts and Plymouth. The Connecticut Puritans were well aware that they had not been conforming to the requirements of the English land law, for when the General Court saw that the colony could not escape being added to the Dominion of New England, it ordered every township and individual to whom it had granted lands to take out patents for the same from the governor and company, and that the patents should be sealed with the company's seal and signed by the governor and secretary in the name of the General Court.[40]

Thus it came about that in the process of settling New England, great confusion arose in titles and tenures, resulting in conflicting claims. The encroachments of Massachusetts upon New Hampshire and Maine, and the subsequent interpretation of the charter boundaries as three miles north of the northernmost part of the Merrimac River, made a hopeless tangle of titles in that region. The granting of overlapping charters to Connecticut and Rhode Island brought to a head a long-standing dispute over the intervening territory,—the Narragansett Country,—which was also claimed by a descendant of one of the patentees of the New England Council. Between Massachusetts and Plymouth, Plymouth and Rhode Island, and Massachusetts and Connecticut, there were boundary disputes involving the titles of many inhabitants. Throughout the seventeenth century, confusion in grants caused litigation in all of the New England courts. When Randolph first came over, he reported the desirability of some intercolonial court with jurisdiction over land claims, and the necessity of some such court of claims with jurisdiction over all New England was one of the reasons advanced for a consolidated

40 *Conn. Col. Rec.*, III, 177.

royal government. There was the question, too, of illegal and invalid grants, due partly to the fact that the grantor sometimes had no right to the land he was conveying away and partly to his ignoring English legal custom in the form of the grant.

For the purpose then, of settling rival claims, correcting defective titles, and establishing a uniform tenure with due recognition of the king as ultimate owner of the soil, Andros was instructed to confirm all titles not obtained and held in the orthodox way. As the terms on which this was to be done were left to his discretion, he decided to impose the same quit-rent of two shillings, six pence for every hundred acres that was reserved in all new grants. He did not find it, however, an easy matter to persuade the people to take out new titles to lands already in their possession, and dared not announce his land policy by proclamation lest he frighten the people into a panic and perhaps precipitate a revolution. Therefore, he allowed the rumor to be started unofficially that all titles must be confirmed and left it to the councilors to inform the people in their respective localities that confirmation of title must be obtained. At the same time he asked the councilors to set the example by petitioning themselves for new titles.[41]

The new land policy divided the people of the various counties of the Dominion into two camps,—one composed of those who welcomed the opportunity to obtain security

[41] 4 Mass. Hist. Soc. *Col.*, V, 177-178. ''His excellency tryed all wayes to bring the people to quitt rents,'' wrote Randolph to Povey, May, 1687. Toppan, *Randolph*, IV, 162. In a pamphlet of 1691, entitled ''Revolution Justified,'' Andros was charged with asserting ''that now their Charter was gone, all their Lands were the Kings that themselves did Represent the King and that therefore Men that would have any Legal Title to their Lands must take Patents of them, on such Terms as they should see meet to impose.'' *Andros Tracts*, I, 73, 87. Dudley had his patents confirmed ''for his owne benifitt and for a good example to others.'' *Ibid.*, 160.

for their titles and readily sought confirmation, the other of those who looked upon the policy as a scheme to deprive them of their lands and for that reason refused to comply with the demand. A majority of the first class were non-Puritan inhabitants of Maine and New Hampshire, while the second was comprised largely of the theocrats of Massachusetts and Plymouth.

Of the one hundred and fifty or more applications for confirmation of title from the inhabitants of Maine, all show a genuine desire, on the part of the petitioners, to be relieved of anxiety as to the security of their holdings. These petitioners were of four classes: those whose grants conflicted with the grants made by other authorities; those who had a clear title to the land, but feared infringements on their property by new grants which might be made to others; those who knew their claims were poor; and those who had no titles but wanted a piece of land.[42]

Among the petitioners in the first class were many who had received grants from the New England Council or its patentees or had purchased such grants, and who had had their lands seized and subsequently regranted, either by the General Court of Massachusetts, after that colony had extended her jurisdiction there, or by Danforth, after the purchase of Maine.[43] Often the people living in the little frontier settlements were driven away by the Indians, and on their return found their land

[42] Mass. Arch., vol. 126, pp. 149, 201, 376, 401-402, 404, 413; vol. 127, pp. 2, 16, 17, 30, 35, 41, 45, 48, 56, 71, 110, 149, 195, 227, 237, 246, 248, 249, 254, 255, 256, 257, 258, 261, 263, 264, 301-302, 303; vol. 128, pp. 21, 22, 22a, 23, 25, 26. There are many more references of similar nature in these volumes.

[43] Robert Lawrence of Falmouth lost a piece of land when Danforth seized it and regranted it to Edward Tyng. During Andros's administration, the two claimants fell into a bitter dispute over the matter. Mass. Arch., vol. 126, pp. 401-402. Other cases may be found in volume 127, p. 71, and volume 128, p. 225.

occupied by those who had grants from the towns established by the General Court.[44] In the first class was one Robert Jordan, who obtained his land by purchase of an original grant and had made a small settlement at a great deal of labor and expense. When Massachusetts assumed control, Jordan denied her jurisdiction, and was arrested and sent to Boston. In the meantime, townships were set up, and one of his tenants, Robert Eliot, petitioned for a grant of the land on which he, Jordan, had lived. Jordan now sought redress from Andros, and prayed that Eliot be given only a life tenure, with reversion to himself.[45]

Many others, observing the experience of those whose lands were usurped, petitioned for the sake of security, recognizing that the best titles would be such as were obtained directly from the king, by a grant from his governor. Pendelton Fletcher held land in Saco which he had received of his grandfather, who bought it of Robert Jordan. The latter had purchased it of Richard Vines, who had received a grant from the New England Council. Nevertheless, Fletcher wrote, "I cannot think that thare be any titels of Lands that be farm and Substantiall onleas his Majesty do conforem them tharefore these considerations has cased me to make application to his Excelentcy the governor by way of patichan [petition] for warant of survay of my Land."[46]

There were many who knew that their titles would never stand in law. Some of these claimed by Indian grant only, others by town grant, later declared illegal, while still others, with no titles at all, were merely squatters, who hoped to hold the land because of length of possession and the improvements made upon it.[47] Finally,

[44] Mass. Arch., vol. 127, pp. 228-229, 270, 282.

[45] Ibid., vol. 128, p. 40.

[46] Ibid., vol. 129, pp. 77, 183; vol. 107, p. 55; vol. 126, p. 413; vol. 127, pp. 2, 16, 243, 245, 256, 301-302; vol. 128, pp. 23, 65.

[47] Ibid., vol. 126, p. 199; vol. 127, pp. 236a, 239, 254, 257, 278, 280;

there were a few holders of small tracts who wanted extensions, and a few landless men who saw an opportunity to become possessed of a property in their own right.[48]

It was a difficult task to settle the land question in Maine and at the same time to do justice to all. Andros took the greatest pains to find out the facts and circumstances before making any grants. In case of rival or doubtful claims, he referred the matter to Edward Tyng or Silvanus Davis for investigation.[49] Later these men were accused of prejudiced judgment and of being personally interested, but on the whole they seem to have been fair-minded. In all the petitions, the writers show themselves willing to accept a quit-rent tenure, although a few of them beg that the quit-rent be made as small as possible. Even Edward Tyng asked that the quit-rent settled by Danforth, when he entered Maine in 1679, be decreased, because the amount imposed was a hardship and a discouragement to settlement.[50]

In New Hampshire, while Cranfield was governor, an attempt was made to settle conflicting claims between Mason and the inhabitants. Cranfield was told that where there was a dispute he was to try to reconcile all differences, and if he could not do this he was to send the cases,

vol. 128, pp. 22a, 103, 109, 128, 137, 146, 174, 189, 200, 296; vol. 129, pp. 6, 66, 67, 69. One finds in the petitions such defects of title as are given in the following examples. Rev. George Burrough held land granted him by the town of Scarboro, but he prayed for confirmation because he held it "by no other right than a Town grant which is invalid." *Ibid.*, vol. 129, p. 111. Another held land "only by virtue of a town grant, which is little worth." *Ibid.*, p. 112. Timothy Woodbridge of Hartford petitioned for confirmation of an estate on the Saco River in Maine, admitting that he was aware of some defects in the lawful conveyance of the same. *Ibid.*, vol. 128, p. 277.

48 *Ibid.*, vol. 127, pp. 246, 258, 259; vol. 128, pp. 21, 26, 167, 246, 275, 277; vol. 129, pp. 71, 98, 99.

49 *Ibid.*, vol. 127, pp. 17, 56, 259, 261, 268, 273, 286; vol. 128, pp. 66, 125, 129, 167, 168, 174, 286; vol. 129, pp. 87-88.

50 *Ibid.*, vol. 126, p. 201.

fairly and impartially stated, together with his opinion, to England for the king's determination. Unfortunately he did not follow his instructions, but allowed titles of land to be decided in the courts. Many of the inhabitants, knowing of his instructions, would not recognize such procedure as valid, refused to appear to defend their titles, and lost their cases by default. Later during Andros's administration, executions on the judgments rendered in these courts began to be carried out. One man was levied upon and imprisoned and others feared lest the same should happen to them. As no writ of *scire facias* was issued, requiring the party proceeded against to show cause why the record should not be enforced,— as there should have been according to the council order of June 10, 1686,—this action seemed illegal. The inhabitants, therefore, petitioned Andros asking that the procedure be arrested, else they were "likely to be sore oppressed if not wholly ruined."[51] Because of many such bitter experiences concerning the security of their titles, the people of New Hampshire hated Mason and preferred to hold their lands of the king. The king, therefore, persuaded Mason to surrender his quit-rents to the crown, receiving in exchange an annual pension. Andros was then instructed to confirm all titles to land formerly held of Mason. Confirmation proceeded rapidly, because the people were only too glad to take advantage of this opportunity to free themselves from the tenurial relationship with Mason.[52]

Neither the advice to seek new patents nor the example of the councilors, who petitioned for a confirmation of their grants, influenced the theocrats of Massachusetts to accept the terms of the new land policy. Andros expected this and moved cautiously and sympathetically in

[51] Mass. Arch., vol. 127, p. 290.
[52] *Cal. State Pap. Col.*, 1681-1685, §1895; Toppan, *Randolph*, IV, 59.

the effort to win them to its support. He assumed that the mass of the people were ignorant of English legal custom and failed to appreciate the precariousness of the tenure on which they held their lands. He thought, and naturally, that the financial burden would not be heavy, for the people were accustomed to pay taxes on land, which, with several rates a year, probably exceeded what they would have had to pay in the way of quit-rents at two shillings, six pence on every hundred acres and only one annual country rate. Those who held large tracts of undeveloped land were required, by a Massachusetts law of 1682, to pay almost the identical amount, two shillings per hundred acres. Having therefore ascribed their opposition, not to financial hardship but to ignorance of the English land law, Andros attempted to educate them by explanations and discussions and a few test cases in court. A good example of his method of explanation is his discussion with a Boston woman, who testified after the revolution in 1689 that Andros, West, and several others came to her house and asked of whom she and her husband held their land.[53] When she replied that they bought it of John Parker, who obtained it of the Indians, West replied that Parker might as well have sold them all of Boston. Andros then explained that the land was the king's and they must take out patents or the land would be granted to others who would do so.

At Charlestown, Andros discussed land titles with Joseph Lynde. He asked Lynde what title he had to his lands. Lynde showed him the deeds, including one in particular of land for which he had been urged to take out a patent. Andros examined this deed, remarked that it was well worded and recorded according to New England custom, and inquired of Lynde whence the title was derived. Lynde answered that he had bought the land of

53 Mass. Arch., vol. 35, p. 186.

his father-in-law, to whom the town of Charlestown had granted it, the town possessing it by purchase from the Indians and by a grant of the General Court. Andros then told him that the title was of no value and he must patent the land if he would keep it.[54]

At Salem, where Andros stopped on his way home from the Indian wars in March, 1689, he had a talk with the Rev. Mr. Higginson.[55] He asked Higginson "Whether all the Lands in New England were not the King's?" Higginson, in reporting the conversation later, said that he was reluctant to express himself, since the matter was one of state and not of religion. Andros said that he wanted Higginson's opinion because he was a minister. Higginson then answered that, as he understood it, the lands belonged not to the king but to his subjects who, for more than sixty years, had had possession and use by twofold right: the right of occupation granted in the "Grand Charter in Genesis," whereby God gave the earth to the sons of Adam and Noah to be subdued and replenished; and the right of purchase from the Indians, who possessed the lands before England claimed them. Andros replied that the lands were the king's, who had granted certain of them to his subjects by a charter, the conditions of which had not been performed. Therefore, all the lands thus granted were forfeited to the king. The attorney-general, who was also present, spoke to the same effect, and one of them used the expression "Whereever an Englishman sets his foot, all that he hath is the King's." Higginson refused to be convinced, whereupon Andros in characteristic fashion lost his temper and said, "Either you are subjects or you are Rebels."

The idea that all land belonged to the king was par-

[54] *Andros Tracts*, I, 91, 152-153.
[55] *Ibid.*, pp. 88-90.

ticularly obnoxious when applied to the commons, which
Andros assumed had reverted to the king, with other
vacant lands, on the fall of the charter. He placed all
lands in one of two categories, granted or ungranted, and
since no titles existed showing individual or collective
ownership of the commons, he declared that they belonged in the category of ungranted lands. The inhabitants of the towns, however, could not understand how
the lands which had always belonged to them collectively,
and which had been used by them in common, could be
otherwise than their own. One of the first cases bearing
on this point was that of a grant made to Charles Lidgett
of a piece of the Charlestown commons lying near his
farm at Mystic. A summons was sent to Charlestown
ordering any one to appear who could show reason why
the land should not be so granted. The town sent a written answer, stating that the land was not vacant, but
had been actually improved for fifty years. In spite of
this, a patent was given to Lidgett, who successfully sued
for possession. The inhabitants of the town thought they
had been robbed, and when the surveying was finished
some of them pulled up the stakes. For this action, they
were arrested, imprisoned, and fined.[56]

In October, 1687, Randolph petitioned for Nahant
Neck, which belonged to the town of Lynn. The council
issued an order instructing the constables of the town to
give notice to any having claims to appear before the
governor and council on March 7. The proprietors of
Nahant and the inhabitants of Lynn presented their case
in writing. They stated that the land was first purchased

[56] *Andros Tracts*, I, 16, 49-50, 51, 153; C. O. 5: 855, no. 90. Lidgett's
petition aroused the people of Charlestown to a sense of their danger,
and many appealed at once for confirmation. Mass. Arch., vol. 126, pp.
395, 403; vol. 127, pp. 11, 34, 37; vol. 128, p. 224; vol. 129, p. 82; Amer.
Antiq. Soc. *Proc.*, N. S. XIII, 471.

from the Indians and afterwards confirmed to the town of Lynn by the General Court; that the right to dispose of it was placed in the hands of the freemen who granted it to inhabitants "to plant & build on and possess"; that these inhabitants were tributaries or tenants and were required to pay a yearly rent to the town during their lives, but could not bequeath their right to their heirs; that the proprietors among whom the land had been divided for planting purposes, afterward by agreement converted what remained into a pasture; and, finally, that if the pasture land were alienated, the inhabitants of Lynn would be impoverished, since they lived "not upon Traffique & trading as many Seaport townes doe, whoe have greater advantages, But upon Husbandry & raising such stocks of cattle & sheep as they are Capable and as their outlands will afford." Randolph replied that it did not appear by whom or at what rent the lands petitioned for were disposed of, nor even that the town of Lynn had ever been incorporated, and if this were true then the town was not invested with the power of disposing of land, the so-called "freemen" being "free" only of the colony and not of the town, because Lynn was "equall to a village in England & no otherwise." The inhabitants then petitioned Andros for permission to hold a town meeting in order to discuss what was best to do, but he refused, fearing another outbreak like that in Essex county. A general consensus of opinion was, however, obtained in some other way than in town meeting, and the request was made that Nahant be divided and granted to them as individuals on a quit-rent tenure. The final settlement was made on this basis, and the people retained possession of their lands, but the seeds of hatred for the "foreign government," which would take from them their means of livelihood, were sown and throve, to bear fruit at the time of the revolution against Andros a year and a half later.[57]

Randolph also petitioned for a grant of vacant land containing about seven hundred acres, lying between Spy Pond and Saunders Brook near Watertown. The inhabitants of both Cambridge and Watertown, having claims, were warned to appear before the governor and council on Wednesday, March 7, and show why the said land should not be granted. The method of delivering the warrant was a great shock to the Puritans, for it was sent from Boston to Cambridge by boat on a Sabbath morning, and posted on the door of the meeting-house. The inhabitants of Cambridge wrote in answer that the land was neither vacant nor unappropriated, but had been granted by the king to the Massachusetts Bay Company and by them to the town, which had caused it to be distributed among the inhabitants; that Watertown's share had been "improved in common" and each man's right lawfully settled to him for more than forty years; and that it furnished firewood, lumber, and pasture, without which about eighty families would be ruined.[58]

Randolph answered that if the inhabitants of Cambridge could show a royal grant of the land to the Massachusetts Bay Company, and another from the company to the inhabitants of the town, and could prove that the town was legally qualified to receive it, he would withdraw his request. In reply, Cambridge did not attempt to meet the legal argument in any way, but contented itself with saying, "Yor Excellency have not required of us to show or demonstrate that the formallity of the Law have been in all Circumstances thereof exactly observed nor doe wee judge it can rationally be expected from a

57 Amer. Antiq. Soc. *Proc.*, N. S., XIII, 491; Toppan, *Randolph*, IV, 171; Mass. Arch., vol. 127, pp. 172, 173, 173a, 174, 176, 178.

58 Amer. Antiq. Soc. *Proc.*, N. S., XIII, 492; Mass. Arch., vol. 128, pp. 7, 85, 111-112.

people circumstanced as the first Planters were, by whome those matters were acted in the Infancy of those Plantations, They not haveing Council in the Law to repaire unto, nor would the imergencies that then inevitably happened admitt thereof." They claimed security for their title by Charles II's declaration when the *quo warranto* was issued, as well as by James II's Declaration of Indulgence. As this reply was not considered satisfactory the Cambridge petitioners were again notified to appear before the governor and council to make a "full answer." Samuel Andrews and others, purporting to act for the proprietors, appeared and made answer, but so ineffectually that the decision went against them. They then petitioned the king, on behalf of the inhabitants of Cambridge, for relief, but before an answer could arrive, the revolution had taken place.[59]

Randolph petitioned three times for land in Rhode Island: once for vacant land near Portsmouth; once for about two hundred and fifty acres at Newport; and the third time on behalf of Henry, Earl of Clarendon, for one thousand acres in Portsmouth and Newport.[60] Nothing else that he did was more severely condemned by the Puritans than this attempt to acquire land at the expense of the colonists. He seemed to them to be the prince of beggars, seeking to exploit New England for his personal profit. Other members of the council also made themselves unpopular by petitioning for grants of land: John Usher asked for and received Long Island in Casco Bay;[61] Jonathan Tyng petitioned for vacant lands near Concord, possessed by the Indians who agreed to leave;[62]

[59] Mass. Arch., vol. 128, pp. 112, 115, 197, 281, 298, 299, 300; Amer. Antiq. Soc. *Proc.*, N. S., XIII, 496.

[60] Mass. Arch., vol. 129, pp. 106, 109.

[61] *Ibid.*, vol. 127, p. 30; Amer. Antiq. Soc. *Proc.*, N. S., XIII, 474; *Andros Tracts*, I, 98.

[62] *Andros Tracts*, I, 495; Mass. Arch., vol. 129, p. 22.

Nathaniel Clark petitioned for Clark's Island, which was claimed by Plymouth, and received the island; although the people of Plymouth signified their willingness to bear the expense of a suit and signed a paper to that effect, "for which they were termed factious," the signers being sent to Boston for trial, where expensive delays and what seemed like unreasonable charges only added to the prevailing discontent.[63]

Although Andros was successful in spreading information about the new land policy and in making known the legal basis for it, he was utterly unsuccessful in persuading the Puritan theocrats to accept it. Those of the second generation, most of whom had been born in New England, knew little from personal experience of the English land law and could not be convinced that a grant from the crown was always necessary for the legal establishment of a title. It was of far more importance to them that the land be obtained from the Indians by "fair Contract or just Conquest." Therefore when Andros found that his efforts met only with scepticism, distrust, and defiance, he decided to bring the matter sharply to an issue by a few test cases in court, where the question might be decided according to the land law of England. He caused writs of intrusion to be issued against five of the wealthiest landowners of the Dominion, Samuel Sewall and Samuel Shrimpton of Boston, Joseph Lynde and James Russell of Charlestown, and one other, an inhabitant of Rhode Island. The writs were served in the summer of 1688. Sewall, Russell, and Lynde decided not to stand suit and petitioned for confirmation of their lands. The others refused to yield and their cases were tried in October in the superior court of pleas, judgment being given against them. Shrimpton appealed his case

[63] Mass. Arch., vol. 127, p. 298; *Andros Tracts,* I, 50-51; *Cal. State Pap. Col.,* 1685-1688, §1868.

on a writ of error to the governor and council, but his appeal had not been determined when the government fell.[64]

In the cases of Sewall, Russell, and Lynde the issue was far from settled by the apparent submission of the three men. Sewall appealed to Increase Mather, who was in England at the time, to find out "if persons are thus compelled to take patents." He wrote also to Richard Wharton and Eliakim Hutchinson, who were likewise in England, asking them to do what they could and promising a contribution of fifty pounds toward the costs of any action they might deem it wise to take. Sewall's attitude was due partly to public spirit and partly to personal concern. "The generality of People," he wrote Mather, "are very averse from complying with any thing that may alter the Tenure of their Lands, and look upon me very sorrowfully that I have given way."[65] At the same time, he shared with the other large landowners a dislike of the fees that would have to be paid in taking out patents for so many pieces of land. Some time previous to the serving of the writs, Joseph Lynde had applied for a patent for his whole estate, comprised of several scattered holdings. The patent was refused him on the ground that he must have a new patent for each piece of land, wherever located,[66] a rule which if literally carried out would have involved a very great expense in fees. When the next summer the writs of intrusion were issued, they were directed not at the whole estate of each

[64] Mass. Arch., vol. 129, pp. 83, 101, 228-234; C. O. 5: 855, no. 90; *Andros Tracts*, I, 49, 91, 152-153; *Cal. State Pap. Col.*, 1685-1688, §1868.

[65] Sewall, *Diary*, I, 219, 220-221, 231, note. Sewall wrote Mather, "I had cast myself on the sea to come for England before petitioning, but knew not how to get away from my friends." Not satisfied with the way things were proceeding, he left for England shortly after this, to join with those already there seeking redress. *Ibid.*, 229, note.

[66] *Andros Tracts*, I, 91.

man but at one piece of property only. Therefore, Sewall, Russell, and Lynde, in deciding not to stand suit but to apply for patents, limited their request in each case to the one piece of land against which the writ had been issued. This limitation, as well as a further appeal to England against the enforcement of the rules of English land law in the colony, brought to naught Andros's attempt to settle the land policy by the use of writs of intrusion.

During Andros's administration, there seem to have been about two hundred applications for patents in the whole Dominion, including petitions for new grants of land.[67] Slightly over one hundred warrants were given to surveyors authorizing them to lay out lands petitioned for,[68] but not over twenty of these ever passed the seals.[69] Of the petitions, about fifty were from Massachusetts, ten from Plymouth, seven from the Narragansett Country, twelve from Rhode Island and four from Connecticut, the rest being from Maine and New Hampshire. The small number of actual grants in proportion to the applications was due to Andros's careful investigation of each claim, to delays in surveying, and to Andros's inability to consider many of the applications, because of his sudden departure to Albany to see about Indian affairs.[70]

It is difficult to tell how general the opposition to the land policy was at this time. Judging from the available material, there seems to have been very little outside of

[67] These are to be found in the Mass. Arch., vols. 126, 127, 128, 129.

[68] There is a small volume in the public archives department of the state house at Boston entitled ''Sir Edmund Andros's Land Warrants, 1687-1688,'' containing the warrants to the surveyors to lay out certain tracts of land petitioned for. This volume contains no orders for surveys east of Casco Bay.

[69] *Andros Tracts*, III, 21.

[70] Sewall, *Diary*, I, 229, note; Mass. Arch., vol. 35, p. 186. The matter was usually referred to the councilors residing where the land lay. C. O. 5: 855, no. 90.

Massachusetts and Plymouth. In Maine and New Hampshire, where the people were accustomed to tenures by quit-rents, there is no evidence that any opposition existed. Connecticut, having used greater care than Massachusetts in granting her lands according to recognized legal form, was able to preserve her free tenure for all to whom land had already been given. Since neither the question of the commons nor of defective titles seems to have arisen there, Connecticut had no cause for complaint in those particulars. Little is known about the effect of the land policy in Rhode Island, although the fact that one of the writs of intrusion was issued against a wealthy landowner of that county shows that the same insecurity of title must have prevailed there as existed in Massachusetts. To all appearances, the Rhode Island inhabitants did not resist the land policy; instead they ignored it.

Plymouth naturally felt keenly the burden of the policy. Her people were poor and the land was almost worthless, so any additional burdens upon the land were bound to be intolerable. Furthermore, the Plymouth associates had never been actually incorporated and had no right to grant land, therefore their descendants had ample reason to worry about the insecurity of their titles.[71]

Massachusetts had the same cause for alarm, since she had been equally careless in the distributing of her lands. It is difficult to tell how large a proportion of titles in that colony were defective. Randolph says that not over ten landholders in the whole colony could show good, clear titles.[72] This statement is probably exaggerated,

[71] 4 Mass. Hist. Soc. *Col.*, V, 168, 177-179.

[72] In his "Report of His Administration" (1690), sent to the Lords of Trade after the revolution, Andros said that the late corporation had not "passed or conveyed any pursuant to the directions in their Charters." *Andros Tracts*, III, 21. One of the moderates writing at the time of the revolution, in an answer to a Puritan account of that event, said that he

although it is not difficult to believe that the number was small. Except in the case of the common lands, there is not much evidence, even for Massachusetts, to show that Andros met with serious opposition in the carrying out of his land policy. Practically all our information on this subject is derived from the *Andros Tracts,* which was propaganda material carefully gathered after the revolution for use in the campaign against the re-establishment of the Dominion government. Knowing the Puritans of old, one is inclined to believe that except in cases where their property was actually in danger of confiscation, they were following out their old policy of procrastination, believing that after God had sufficiently punished them for their sins He would restore their charter government. Increase Mather went to England in the summer of 1688 to petition for a modification of the colonial policy, and until they actually heard from him that there was no hope, they would continue to resist Andros's attempt to force confirmation of title upon them.

It is difficult to understand why the Puritans objected so strongly to the introduction of quit-rents. There seems to be no adequate constitutional or legal explanation. They could not argue that the new land policy was illegal, for it merely required that the rules of English law be applied in cases where land had been granted contrary to that law. They could point to nothing in their charter that authorized them to establish a new land law, for that document required that their laws be conformable to those of England. Though they contended

had "heard from men well skilled in such matters that there often were mistakes and omissions in granting the titles of lands for want of observing the directions in our charter, and I am forced to regard the power granted by the King to ascertain as certain estates, and mend defective titles to be [an] act of special grace." *Cal. State Pap. Col.,* 1689-1692, §181.

that the charter stipulation applied only to written law
and not to custom, they could not prove their point
legally and they knew it. Their strongest argument was
that the new land policy was a violation of the royal
promise, made to them in the Declaration of 1683 and
in the Declaration of Indulgence of 1687, that their rights
of property would be guaranteed to them. It was on this
basis that they sought redress in England.[73]

Perhaps the best explanation lies here. During the
period of virtual independence from 1652 to 1660, the
extreme Puritans evolved the theory, expressed very
clearly by Higginson in his discussion with Andros, that
God was the only overlord whose claims they need recognize, and that all land was His, and was by Him granted
to His people under the terms of the "Great Charter in
Genesis." According to this theory, the Indians had a
right to the soil they possessed, and title from them was
sufficient. Again, according to this theory, the legal basis
for landholding was not the law of England, but the law
of God, and titles based on long possession of an unoccu-
pied and unclaimed soil or on purchase or conquest from
the Indians, gave the holder sufficient security. This
theory did not explain how the New England land system
came into existence. It was merely a theory shaped by
the Puritans to defend conditions which had arisen since
the first division of their lands. To explain the origin of
the system we must look for causes that were economic
rather than political or religious.

The Puritans did not, on principle, object to quit-rents.
They themselves collected such rents from lands reserved
for public use, although such land was comparatively
small in amount. Again, when Massachusetts bought
Maine, the government, in its capacity as lord proprie-

[73] *Andros Tracts*, I, 15-16; Mass. Arch., vol. 128, pp. 115, 297, 300;
Sewall, *Letter Book*, I, 53, note.

tor, sent Danforth, the deputy governor, there as president, with power to grant land under whatever reservations of quit-rent he thought fit, and appointed an officer at the same time to take charge of the rents that were paid.[74]

Had the Puritans objected to a quit-rent tenure, the General Court would, without doubt, have placed itself somewhere on record as opposed to it. The Body of Liberties of 1641 did not forbid, as is commonly believed, the use of quit-rents. The law reads, ''All our lands and heritages shall be free from all fines and licenses upon Alienations and from all hariotts, wardships, Liveries, Primerseisins, yeare day and wast, Escheates, and forfeitures, upon the deaths of parents or Ancestors, be they naturall, casuall or Juditiall.'' No mention is made in this law of quit-rents nor can they be included in any of the above categories.[75] It is interesting to notice that this law is similar to one passed by the parliament of the kingdom in 1646, of the Protectorate in 1656, and of the Restoration in 1660, in which aids, fines for license to alienate, purveyance, pre-emption and the like were abolished, while quit-rents were expressly retained.[76]

Again, when Massachusetts was facing the loss of her charter, the magistrates, believing that the king desired some acknowledgment of the colony's dependence on the crown, as a check to her growing independence, proposed, at a meeting of the General Court, to pay him an annual quit-rent. The deputies would not agree to this suggestion, but as they would not have agreed to any suggestion made by the magistrates looking to a compromise with the king, their attitude cannot be construed as indi-

[74] Mass. Arch., vol. 126, p. 201; *Mass. Col. Rec.*, V, 326-327, 399; *Cal. State Pap. Col.*, 1681-1685, §528.

[75] *Col. Laws of Mass.* (1887), p. 88, §1.

[76] Firth and Rait, *Acts and Ordinances of the Interregnum*, 1642-1660, I, 833; II, 1043; 12 Car. II, c. 24, secs. I, V, VI.

cating opposition to quit-rents as such. Certainly, the magistrates, who were the leading men of the colony, could have had no objection to such payments.[77]

Many of the moderate Puritans held land outside of the colony on a quit-rent tenure. Fitz-John Winthrop held Gardiners Island (under the jurisdiction of the Duke of York) on the annual payment of a lamb.[78] He and his brother Wait, with a number of other Puritans comprising the Atherton Company, petitioned for a tract of land in the Narragansett Country to be held on the payment of a quit-rent, the land to be sublet on the same terms.[79] Another company, partly made up of Puritans, applied for a royal grant of lands in Maine, also to be held on a quit-rent tenure. In 1688, William Stoughton, one of the most conservative of the moderate Puritans, bought Hogg Island in Casco Bay of Vines Ellacott and his wife for the use of the "Governor & company of the corporation in London for Propagation of the Gospel to the Indians in New England and other places adjacent in America," paying to the king annually, forever, ten shillings.[80]

In the charges brought against Andros after the revolution by the "Five Councilors," an attempt was made to explain the land policy of the Massachusetts Bay Company. In the pamphlet which they wrote a splendid opportunity was given to present the moral and religious objections to quit-rents, had there been such and had a system of quit-rents been at variance with the principles of the Puritans. Instead, one finds in the pamphlet noth-

[77] Mass. Arch., vol. 106, pp. 220, 220a, 222-224, 238, 239a, 240, 241a.
[78] 6 Mass. Hist. Soc. Col., III, 460, 461, 462-463, 463-464. Connecticut coveted this island and seems to have been not unwilling, if possession could be obtained, to continue the quit-rent tenure under which it was held of the Duke of York. Ibid., 461.
[79] Cal. State Pap. Col., 1685-1688, §91-i; Mass. Arch., vol. 126, p. 158.
[80] York Deeds, VIII, fol. 217.

ing more than the conventional argument based on economic grounds. The original patentees, so the councilors maintained, granted the land "without any charge to the Planters as in the Settlement of so large a Countrey was thought to be most agreeable: And so much of a publick spirit and design were those Noble Gentlemen [the patentees] that (though well they might) they settled not one single Penny of service or acknowledgment to themselves and Heirs of any of their Grants, a thing so self-denying and worthy that few Instances can be given of the like."[81] The New England system was based on practical necessity, and neither principle nor political theory was responsible for the practice of free land grants adopted by the company at the outset, the lands being distributed in such a way and under such terms as to further settlement as much as possible.

Finally, it is to be noted that among the other trading companies promoting settlements in America those of Virginia and Bermuda followed a similar plan, although they were not of Puritan origin, while the Providence Company, which was Puritan in origin, membership, and purpose, distributed lands to its settlers in Old Providence Island at a fee-farm rent to be paid yearly in tobacco, cotton, and other staple commodities.[82] The failure on the part of the Massachusetts Bay Company to require quit-rents of those to whom lands were granted in the early history of the colony was not due to the Puritan character of its members or to any objection that they may have had to quit-rents as such. It was due

[81] *Andros Tracts,* I, 142-144.

[82] *Records of the Virginia Company,* I, 75; Brown, *The First Republic in America,* pp. 318-319. A copy of the first deed of sale recorded in Bermuda makes no mention of a quit-rent. Lefroy, *Memorials of the Bermudas,* I, 23, 88, 90; II, 549, 558. See above, note 8, where reference is made to Governor Coney's suggestion that quit-rents be introduced into Bermuda. For the conditions on which land was held in Old Providence Island see *Cal. State Pap. Col.,* 1574-1660, pp. 228, 237, 264.

to the fact that the company was a corporation and not a feudal proprietor and was granting lands on as favorable terms as possible, not to individuals for personal advantage but to groups of settlers, generally organized as Christian communities, who were to arrange the final terms on which the land should be divided among themselves. These settlers in the towns that they founded apportioned the lands with the highest regard for the principles of equality and mutual advantage and were as careful as was the company to impose upon their fellows no unnecessary burdens in the way of tenurial rents. When no hardship was involved Massachusetts could introduce a quit-rent without any scruples as to principle. She granted in this way lands for public use, accepted quit-rents from the lands which she acquired in Maine, never put herself on record as opposed to quit-rents in any legal action or otherwise, allowed members of the colony to hold by a quit-rent tenure, even proposed in 1681 to pay a quit-rent to the king, and, finally, in the exposition by the five councilors of the land policy of the colony, made no objection whatever to the payment of quit-rents.

In studying the Puritan attitude toward quit-rents, we notice a gradual divergence of opinion on the subject between the theocrats and the moderates, a divergence that appears in the attitude of the two parties toward all questions involved in the relations of the colony with the mother country. In 1641, when the Body of Liberties was adopted, Massachusetts still considered herself a part of England, and the General Court evidently did not believe that the omission of quit-rents had anything to do with the colony's tenurial relationship to the king. But after 1652, when the colony declared its independence of the mother country, the theory expressed by Higginson at the time of Andros began to take form. Still later, in the Restoration period, the moderate party arose and, refusing to follow the lead of the theocracy, favored the establishment of closer relations with England. The members of this party among the magistrates saw the wisdom of recognizing the colony's tenurial obligations to the king, and tried, in 1681, to win the theocrats to their position. But the latter refused to make any concessions, even though, at this very time, they were playing the part of lord proprietor toward the holders of lands in Maine and were exacting from the colony's tenants there payments similar in kind to those that the king was demanding of them. The point at issue between the parties was not one of principle, touching the use of quit-rents, but rather one of wisdom, touching the colony's tenurial relations with the crown. That such relations legally existed the theocrats strenuously denied, because to do otherwise might involve them in obligations which would limit seriously their independence as a commonwealth and obstruct their service to God and the church.

Such an explanation does not, however, account for the opposition raised by the moderates themselves to the policy which Andros sought to enforce. Their objections were based on purely financial grounds. They would gladly have taken out patents in the king's name had not the expense of doing so been greater than they could bear. Money at the time was very scarce,[83] and the

---

[83] In the revolutionary pamphlet "Quaeries," the question is asked "Whether it were possible for all the money and Movables in New England to have paid the prices that must have been enacted for the Patents, which we are now obliged to take for our Own Lands, even as they are stated in the Fees of the Secretaries Office?" *Andros Tracts*, I, 16; III, 197. The Plymouth inhabitants, in their petition to the king about land titles, claimed that "it being rationally supposed by sundry observing men, that all the money left in this Colony will not Suffice to pay the one half of the charge for warrants surveying and patents, if every man must be forced thereto." 4 Mass. Hist. Soc. *Col.*, V, 177-178.

amounts that have been recorded of fees actually paid
are very large. Richard Smith was reported to have paid
fifty pounds for the confirming of titles to an estate worth
only about four times that sum.[84] If that figure is correct, and other large landowners were called upon to pay
similar amounts, we can understand why the moderates
cried out against the policy. The merchants, too, as well
as the landowners, expressed their disapproval. The
insecurity of titles depreciated the value of land, which,
when precariously held, was much less useful as security
for credit. Since trade at this time was a matter largely
of credit and exchanges, owing to the scarcity of specie,
the merchants found themselves embarrassed in the running of their business enterprises. Furthermore, the
withdrawal of so much money from trade at a time when
it was sadly needed to meet the new conditions, caused
great concern to commercial interests generally.[85] Even
the moderates,—landowners, merchants, and others,—
sympathetic though they were with much that the Dominion represented, could not approve of a policy that
was injuring the prosperity of the colony.

In conclusion, we are probably safe in assuming that
the opposition of the Puritans of Massachusetts and
Plymouth to Andros's land policy was due primarily to
two factors: the economic hardship involved, because of
the payment of large fees for new patents, at a time when
money was scarce; and the change in the form of land
tenure, which would be a constant reminder to the theocrats of the overthrow of their government and the im-

[84] *Andros Tracts*, I, 98.

[85] Sewall, *Diary*, I, 251. In a letter to Thomas Papillon, written in
April, 1689, Sewall uses this argument, evidently intending therewith to
influence the English merchants and to win the support of the House of
Commons for the bill restoring corporations to their ancient rights and
privileges, which was designed to apply to New England and other plantations.

position of what seemed like a foreign rule. Had Andros understood trade conditions and Puritan psychology better, he would have confirmed, by order and without fees, all old titles which, upon their registration in the secretary's office, showed no conflict of claims.[86] Such a procedure would have appeased the moderates and probably somewhat mollified the theocrats, who would not have minded so much holding their land of the king, if they had not been constantly reminded of it by having to pay quit-rents. Such opposition as might have arisen would probably have waned with the passage of time and finally died out had the Dominion survived. This settlement would, to be sure, have meant an abandonment by the king of his plan of using quit-rents as a source of revenue, but, on the other hand, it would have made possible the establishment in New England of the English land law and so have aided in the process of royalizing the colonies there and of securing a recognition of the king's ultimate ownership of the soil. Such a result might have served to bind New England more closely to the mother country in the eighteenth century.

[86] Such a settlement would probably have met with the approval of those among the Puritans who favored the Andros government. One of them, who wrote ''An Answer to the Account of the Revolution at Boston'' and whose opinion has already been quoted on the subject of the land policy, after saying that he thought it ''an act of special grace'' on the part of the king to correct defective titles, added ''But I would gladly see the same procured on easy terms as might be done here, so I would not have my countrymen spoil a sheep for a half-penny worth of tar.'' *Cal. State Pap. Col.*, 1689-1692, §181.

CHAPTER IX

DEFENSE

At the end of the seventeenth century, England's leadership in the commercial and colonial world was threatened by the ambitions of Louis XIV, who desired to found not only a great colonial empire but also a "Universal Monarchy."[1] This ambition was an inheritance from the Reformation struggle, because of which France had become the most powerful Catholic country of Europe. It was not religion alone, however, which prompted him to fulfil his ambitions, but even more the desire for power and for commercial expansion. Both in the Old World and the New, England was the most formidable obstacle which obstructed his plans. On the North American continent, the conquest of New Netherland and the activities of the Hudson's Bay Company gave to England the opportunity of drawing into her control the fur trade of the American Continent, the most lucrative of all the enterprises in which the French continental colonies were engaged. Her colonists were likewise encroaching upon what France considered her fisheries preserves. In the West Indies, each nation watched with a jealous eye the expanding interests of the other, and contested that expansion at every point, each desiring to control the sugar trade of the world. This rivalry was intensified by the commercial relations

[1] Hampden, "State of the Nation" (1692), printed in Hansard, *Parliamentary History of England*, V, appendix, lxviii-lxix.

which existed between England's northern continental colonies and the thriving island possessions of France. The crowding of the French and English colonies into the valley of the St. Lawrence especially, aroused fears that a great life-and-death struggle was about to take place and each of necessity adopted a policy of preparedness, building forts and negotiating with the Indians, but always at the same time using great caution not to antagonize the other unnecessarily and thus bring on war prematurely.[2]

In the struggle, thus inevitably approaching, the French had two important advantages over the English —centralization of political and military administration and a remarkable ability for getting on with the Indians. England's resources were limited to a long fringe of coast colonies, disunited, having very little connection with the mother country, and possessed of almost no power of military defense. They had no standing military forces of their own, depending upon the citizen militia which trained a few times a year and, in time of need, was called into service by request for volunteers or by impressment.[3] Military equipment—arms, ammunition, and stores of all kinds—was always inadequate, and forts were few in number and usually in a state of bad repair. The colonies were quite oblivious to the necessity of mutual military co-operation and indifferent toward appeals from their neighbors for aid. The Puritans especially were little interested in problems of defense, because faith in God's protection was substi-

[2] *Cal. State Pap. Col.*, 1681-1685, §1863; 1685-1688, §§1178, 1493, 1518, 1538, 2157, 2178; 1689-1692, §§89, 152, 155.

[3] *Mass. Col. Laws*, pp. 73, 111; *Conn. Col. Rec.*, I, 94; *Plymouth Col. Laws*, pp. 44, 179, 215. Usually the government first issued a call for volunteers and, if that did not bring enough recruits, it ordered a press. *Plymouth Col. Laws*, p. 44; *Cal. State Pap. Col.*, 1689-1692, §§310, 800, 906.

tuted for the building of expensive forts and the training of skilled soldiers. They ascribed military defeat to God's displeasure with them for their sins rather than to their own unpreparedness and strategic errors.[4]

Moreover, the Puritans had no uniform Indian policy, for each colony dealt with the Indians as it pleased, without regard to the others. Occasionally a royal governor arose, like Dongan of New York, who understood the importance of Indian diplomacy, but elsewhere, particularly in the New England colonies, the leaders had no appreciation of its significance. To the Puritans, Indians were of two kinds, the friendly and the unfriendly; the former to be converted and encouraged to live in the settlements or to serve on the frontier as protection against the unfriendly Indians and to serve as purveyors of furs which were paid for in rum and military stores; the latter to be carefully watched and treated severely if occasion demanded. Even those with whom the Puritans were on good terms often resented the extreme rigor with which the latter executed the colony's laws. One of the charges against Massachusetts, at the time of the annulment of the charter, was that the Puritans antagonized the Indians by selling rum to them at a great profit and then punishing them for the sin of intemperance.[5] It is no wonder that the Indians usually preferred the God of the French Roman Catholics to the Calvinistic Deity of the Puritans. Dongan, appreciating this fact, sent a few

[4] *Cal. State Pap. Col.*, 1689-1692, §906. Cotton Mather, in his essay on "Frontiers Well-Defended," asserted, "It is remarkable to see that when the Unchurched Villages have been so many of them, *utterly broken up*, in the *War*, that has been upon us, those that have had *Churches* regularly formed in them, have generally been under a more *sensible Protection* of Heaven." He adds later, "Sirs, a Church-State well-form'd may fortify you wonderfully!" Cited in Turner, *The Frontier in American History*, p. 64. See also *Andros Tracts*, I, 15, note.

[5] *Cal. State Pap. Col.*, 1675-1676, §721; Toppan, *Randolph*, III, 12.

English priests among them and promised to send more.[6]
Randolph suggested that Massachusetts do the same
thing, as a means of drawing the Indians away from
the French, but such an idea was revolting to the Puritan mind. In social as well as religious relations also,
the French had the advantage with the Indians. The easy-
going, pleasure-loving Frenchmen, who treated the
Indians as brothers, made a more favorable impression
upon them than did the stern, uncompromising Puritans,
who maintained an attitude of moral uprightness and
were unscrupulous in trade. The French, when necessary, could become Indians with the Indians, but the
English always sought to make the Indians into Englishmen.

The one great asset of the English in this rivalry was
the alliance with the Five Nations, who had been from
the first antagonistic toward the French. Located as they
were in western New York, they were like a dam stopping the flow of the beaver trade toward Canada and
diverting it through Albany and the Susquehanna south-
ward into the hands of the English. If the French were
to control the beaver trade of North America, they must
either win over or destroy the Five Nations. For this
reason, they were continually sending priests among
them and encroaching upon their territory and that of
the English with forts and garrisons. The governors in
Canada were deaf to English protests and refused to
withdraw, because they realized how powerless the English were to carry out their demands by force. British
officials in America urged consolidation as the only thing
that would command the respect of the French and
strengthen the confidence of the Five Nations.[7]

[6] *Cal. State Pap. Col.*, 1685-1688, §§2151, 1429-i, ii, 1432.

[7] *Ibid.*, 1681-1685, §1863; 1685-1688, §1429-i; 1689-1692, §152; Toppan,
Randolph, III, 334-335. Because the French asked permission to send
missionaries among the English Indians, Dongan accused them of making

Such consolidation it was the object of the Dominion of New England to effect. By drawing together the northern colonies into a single government, the Lords of Trade hoped to unify all available military forces and resources and provide a single head whose military policy could be easily controlled. They realized that there was even more need of consolidating the second group of colonies with New York as the nucleus, if the Five Nations were to be protected and French encroachments on the southern side of Lake Ontario were to be stopped. Neither in men nor in money was New York strong enough to bear the burden of defense alone. It was partly for this reason that Dongan suggested adding Connecticut, Rhode Island, the Jerseys, and the northern part of Pennsylvania to New York, for such a union would bring the needed centralization of defense and trade, add men and revenue, and make possible the control of the beaver trade with Albany as an English centre.

The appointment in 1686 of Andros as captain-general of all the military forces within the territory stretching from the St. Croix to the Hudson, and in 1688 to the Delaware, was the most formidable act of preparedness that the English could have performed. From a military point of view, its importance can hardly be overestimated, for it brought centralization of command which made possible a comprehensive military campaign, gave opportunity for the fortification of the weakest spots on the frontier at the common expense, and prepared the way for the adoption of a uniform Indian policy, according to which the Indians of the north and east would be able to deal with one powerful governor instead of with a number of more or less inefficient executives.

Andros, upon his arrival, found military affairs in

"religion a stalking-horse to establish their claims." *Cal. State Pap. Col.*, 1685-1688, §1638.

an almost hopeless condition. He brought with him double arms for the two companies of grenadiers, "viz. Fuzees and snalhance Musketts, Byonetts, etc., 100 Barrells of Powder and other Stores," but could discover no stores of arms or powder within the territory, except "about 50 Old Match Locks at Boston and some few old Arms & Necessarys for Great Guns at Castle Island with about a Barrell of Powder & a few Cartridges." Thinking that the missing equipment must be in private hands, he issued a proclamation on December 30, 1686, commanding all persons who had any of the great guns, small arms, or other munitions of war belonging to the government to give account of them in writing at once, and followed up this proclamation by an order in council for all arms and equipment wherever found to be brought to the treasurer.[8]

He found fortifications also in poor condition. The most important coast defense was a stone "castle," situated on an island in Massachusetts Bay about three or four miles from Boston, and commanding the channel by which ships approached the town. It was equipped with thirty guns and garrisoned with a small force of men, which was augmented in time of war. Boston was further protected by a small brick fort at the south end, mounted with twelve guns, but not garrisoned. On the north side of the town, commanding the river as far as Charlestown, was a platform made of stones and turf, mounted with two small guns, also ungarrisoned. Elsewhere there were a few scattered forts, but for the most part, out of repair, poorly equipped, and insufficiently manned.[9]

Andros immediately set about the task of rectifying

[8] C. O. 5: 855, no. 90; Mass. Arch., vol. 126, pp. 184, 185; Amer. Antiq. Soc. Proc., N. S., XIII, 264-265.

[9] Hutchinson Papers, Prince Soc., II, 221; 3 Mass. Hist. Soc. Col., VIII, 333-334; Cal. State Pap. Col., 1685-1688, §§1195, 1197; Amer. Antiq. Soc. Proc., N. S., XIII, 476.

these conditions. He first turned his attention to the needs of Boston itself and because the fort at Castle Island was too small to lodge a garrison and too far away from the town to be effective, he built new fortifications at Fort Hill, which commanded the town and all avenues of approach by sea and land, and as there was a good channel close to the shore near the fort, he had warehouses and a dry dock built for ease in bringing supplies.[10]

He strengthened the frontier by building a fort at New Dartmouth, a redoubt on the Damoriscotta River, four forts on the Kennebec River, at Sagadahoc, Newtown, Fort Anne, and Pejobscot, respectively, one at Falmouth on Casco Bay, one on the Saco River, one at Kennebunk, and one at Wells, and repaired the fort at Pemaquid. At the time of the Indian trouble in 1688, he garrisoned these forts partly with English troops and partly with militia. He stationed English forces also on the upper Merrimac, and on the Connecticut, and instructed them to co-operate with the militia of those regions. For purposes of communication and for the provisioning of these new forts in time of war, he caused a ketch to be purchased and men to be detailed for the service by land.[11]

The total muster roll of the militia of the Dominion included 13,279 men, to which about two thousand more were added after the annexation of New York. There were seven regiments of foot and twelve troops of horse in Massachusetts, three regiments of foot in Plymouth, four regiments of foot and one troop of horse in Connecticut, two regiments of foot in Rhode Island (including the Narragansett Country), one regiment of foot in New

[10] Amer. Antiq. Soc. *Proc.*, N. S., XIII, 241, 246, 472; *Andros Tracts*, I, 72; III, 72; Mass. Arch., vol. 126, p. 281; vol. 127, pp. 61, 77; *Cal. State Pap. Col.*, 1685-1688, §§1534, 1536.

[11] 3 Mass. Hist. Soc. *Col.*, I, 85; Amer. Antiq. Soc. *Proc.*, N. S., XIII, 472; Mass. Arch., vol. 126, pp. 371-372; vol. 127, pp. 55, 267; *Cal. State Pap. Col.*, 1689-1692, §912.

Hampshire, one in Maine, and one in Cornwall.[12] Besides the militia, Andros had a small standing force of two companies of British regulars at Boston, to serve as his bodyguard and as the mainstay of the colonial army in time of war. This force was at first supported from funds appropriated for the establishment in England, all surplus money accruing through the difference of exchange between English and New England money to be used for the salary of a chaplain, an armorer, and a gunner, but the intention was that later the companies should be supported out of the Dominion treasury, as soon as a satisfactory revenue system had been adopted. After the annexation of New York, the two independent companies of regulars already there were added to the Dominion troops. According to his instructions, Andros could lead these forces against the Indians, but he could not declare war or advance against any other enemy.[13]

While Andros was thus putting the Dominion into a state of defense, the French menace was becoming more threatening. By the treaty of neutrality between Louis XIV and James II, signed November 10, 1686, each sovereign agreed to desist from hostilities and to recognize each other's claims to colonial possessions, whether or not there was war in Europe. This treaty settled nothing on the New York frontier, however, because the position of the Five Nations was not defined. In 1684, through the efforts of the governors of New York and Virginia,

[12] *Cal. State Pap. Col.*, 1689-1692, §879. By order of March, 1688, all men above sixteen years of age were required to serve, except members of the council, justices of the peace, court officers, ministers, president, officers, and students of Harvard College, schoolmasters, physicians, etc. *Amer. Antiq. Soc. Proc.*, N. S., XIII, 494. The figures given in the text, which are from Andros's report, do not include the men in the regiments of Maine and New Hampshire.

[13] C. O. 1: 59, no. 37; Mass. Arch., vol. 126, p. 344; vol. 127, pp. 70, 179; Toppan, *Randolph*, IV, 122-123; *Cal. State Pap. Col.*, 1685-1688, §§832, 1080.

the Five Nations had acknowledged themselves English subjects, under the government of the Duke of York, but the French refused to recognize this new relationship. Therefore, the French did not consider it a breach of the treaty to attack the Iroquois. With Louis's consent, the governor of New France sent out an expedition which fell upon the Senecas above Albany. Although considerable damage was done to crops and villages, the attack was repulsed.[14]

Fearing that this affront might bring on war between France and England, Dongan immediately sent Judge John Palmer to England to report the circumstances attending this invasion of the king's territory. He also asked permission to build forts on the frontier to be garrisoned by four or five hundred men from England and Ireland, and further requested that Connecticut and the Jerseys be added to New York in order that New York might be better supported with men and funds in the war that he feared was approaching.[15] Before Palmer left, Dongan thoroughly investigated the circumstances of the French attack, inquiring of the chiefs of the Senecas, Cayugas, Onandagas, Oneidas, and Maquas whether they had first given any provocation. They answered that they had not, and that the only reason they knew for the attack was their having given their lands and their allegiance to the king of England. They begged the English to aid them and not allow them to be destroyed when the French gave support to their enemies in America, for they realized that the French would do anything to get control of the fur trade. Dongan urged the chiefs to "make a chain" with the more distant Indians who were friendly to the French and draw the

[14] *New York Col. Docs.*, III, 347; Mass. Arch., vol. 127, p. 62; *Cal. State Pap. Col.*, 1685-1688, §§1123, 1348, 1416, 1421, 1424, 1427, 1428, 1429.

[15] *Cal. State Pap. Col.*, 1685-1688, §§1429, 1429-iii, 1479, 1494.

trade of the latter to Albany, and he promised, while awaiting orders from England, to supply them with arms and ammunition, though he could not at the time give them military aid.[16]

In order to guard against a surprise attack, he took two hundred men to Albany to add to the garrison already there, and planned to stay for the winter. He strengthened his forces by calling to his aid five or six hundred Iroquois Indians, who were stationed near Albany and Schenectady,[17] because persistent rumors of French plans for new fortifications, of great preparations in Canada to invade the Five Nations, and of the belligerent attitude of the new governor of Canada, convinced him that the English should if possible take the offensive.[18] At this juncture, he heard of the union of Connecticut with New England, and immediately urged that New York also be added. Then he began his preparations for attack. He appealed to Andros for aid, asking him to have in readiness one hundred redcoats with fifty horse and two hundred of the "youngest and lustiest" of the militia, well armed for immediate service, and requesting that if, when his request was received, Connecticut had been added to New England, then he should send from that colony an additional two hundred foot soldiers and fifty horse.[19]

Before further trouble arose, Dongan received a letter from the king authorizing him to attack the French if they persisted in invading English territory and annoying the Five Nations, and empowering him to build whatever forts and batteries he thought necessary and to call

[16] Mass. Arch., vol. 127, p. 62; *Cal. State Pap. Col.*, 1685-1688, §§1123, 1377, 1378, 1428, 2151.

[17] *Cal. State Pap. Col.*, 1685-1688, §§1432, 1433.

[18] *Ibid.*, §§1413, 1427-i; Mass. Arch., vol. 127, p. 62.

[19] Mass. Arch., vol. 127, p. 62; Amer. Antiq. Soc. *Proc.*, N. S., XIII, 487; *Cal. State Pap. Col.*, 1685-1688, §§1432, 1479, 1548-i.

upon the neighboring colonies for aid. At the same time, Andros was separately instructed by the king to give Dongan whatever assistance he required.[20]

While these preparations for war were going on, France and England each appointed a joint commission to arbitrate the points in dispute. The points included French encroachments on the territory of the Hudson's Bay Company, English aggressions in Dominica, the rival claims of both nations to the island of St. Lucia, and jurisdiction over the Iroquois Indians. Neither side would make any concessions, so no agreement was reached other than that boundaries should be definitely settled and for a year,—between January, 1688, and January, 1689,—all acts of hostility should cease. King James authorized the commissioners to treat concerning boundaries and wrote to all of the governors asking for exact information concerning the limits of the colonies.[21]

The winter proved to be a comparatively quiet one. The French gave no sufficient cause for attack, so Dongan merely held his forces in readiness for immediate action. Andros took advantage of the breathing spell to train the militia of the Dominion and to improve the equipment, knowing that troops would be needed on other frontiers if an outbreak occurred in New York. As outbreaks were to be expected on the exposed Maine frontier, he took particular pains to anticipate them by placing that region in a state of defense. He ordered Captain George to cruise along the eastern coast and up the Penobscot River, getting all the information he could regarding the Baron de St. Castine, a Frenchman who

[20] *Cal. State Pap. Col.*, 1685-1688, §§1506, 1505, 1548-ii; *New York Col. Docs.*, III, 503.

[21] *New York Col. Docs.*, III, 505; Amer. Antiq. Soc. *Proc.*, N. S., XIII, 466; *Cal. State Pap. Col.*, 1685-1688, §§1178, 1180, 1491, 1493, 1504, 1518, 1543, 1550, 1600, 1642, 1681, 1826; 1689-1692, §152.

had been given permission to reside there, and instructing him, in case he met with any persons not allowed to be in that territory, to order them to depart or to apply at Pemaquid for permission to remain. A month later he issued an order forbidding persons without a license to settle or trade in the eastern part of the territory west of the St. Croix River. Finding a personal tour necessary, he visited Pemaquid and the principal settlements as far as the Penobscot, sending a few men on to the St. Croix. At the Penobscot he found a small trading house which belonged to Castine, whom he had reason to suspect was selling arms and supplies to the Indians and trying to draw them over to the French. After waiting several days and still finding nobody at the trading house, he entered it forcibly. Arms, powder, shot, and other supplies were found, which he ordered taken to the fort at Pemaquid. That the Indians might not be alarmed by tales which Castine would probably tell, Andros gave immediate notice to the chief sachem of those parts that the supplies would be turned over, upon application, to whomsoever was concerned, but that neither Castine nor any others, except Indians, would be allowed to remain there without permission. Andros left the sachem and his Indians well disposed.[22]

While trouble was thus brewing on the frontiers, New York and the Jerseys were added to the Dominion, making it possible to bring all of the latter's formidable supplies of men and money to the support of the New York frontier. Albany became the centre of action. Andros, with all the resources of his large, centralized territory behind him, reiterated Dongan's demand made upon the governor-general of Canada that the French withdraw

[22] *Cal. State Pap. Col.*, 1685-1688, §§1684, 1745, 1825, 1901; Mass. Arch., vol. 128, pp. 140-141; C. O. 5: 855, no. 90; *New York Col. Docs.*, III, 571.

the garrison and forces settled at Oniagra in the Senecas's country. The French complied at once.[23]

Having been specially instructed to provide for the protection of the Iroquois, Andros held a conference at Albany immediately upon his assumption of the government of New York and the Jerseys. He found the Indians friendly, ready to recognize the authority of his office, and willing to accept his guidance in their relations with the French and hostile Indians. He endeavored to impress upon them the necessity of keeping the truce with France, but at the same time cautioned them to allow no encroachments upon their territory. They agreed, and went away "very well satisfied and Pleased." After that Andros visited the River Indians and others in those parts, "who shewed the like Demonstration of theyr satisfaction and good Inclination to the Government in every respect."[24]

While Andros was still at Albany, an incident occurred which, but for his skilful management, might have precipitated war. Five Indians were murdered at Spectacle Pond near Springfield and, soon after, six Christian Indians at Northfield—all of them apparently by eleven straggling Indians to the northward, who were friendly to the French. He at once sent an express to the governor of Canada, demanding that the murderers be forthwith seized and sent to him, and he then dispatched an order to Major Gold, who had charge of the militia in those parts, to apprehend the murderers or any strange Indians detected prowling about, and to offer all the protection possible to Indian subjects. Returning to Boston by land, he stopped at Springfield and Northfield to quiet the Indians there and assure them of his protection.

---

[23] *Andros Tracts*, III, 20; C. O. 5: 855, no. 90.
[24] C. O. 5: 855, no. 90; *Andros Tracts*, III, 19-20; *Cal. State Pap. Col.*, 1685-1688, §§1895, 1901.

Thanks to his care and vigorous action, the incident passed without any serious results. Later, he received an answer from the governor of Canada saying that the murderers had fled to the woods, but that they would be apprehended as soon as possible.[25]

Similar depredations took place at Saco, but were of more serious consequence because the councilors at Boston, who were administering the government in Andros's absence, failed to handle the affair as skilfully as Andros would have done. Captain Blackman, in charge of the forces at Saco, seized twenty Indians suspected of the depredations and sent them to Boston. This action alarmed their relatives and friends, who captured several English at Casco Bay, intending to hold them for exchange. Stoughton, one of the councilors, entered into negotiation with the Indians and arranged with them a place and a time for exchanging and freeing of captives, but unfortunately, through a misunderstanding, the Indians arrived after the English had left. They sent an English captive and two Indians in a canoe with a flag of truce to an English house which was garrisoned near by. Although the Englishman leaped on shore and delivered a letter which signified the intention of the Indians to return the captives and make reparation for the damage they had done, the captain in charge was suspicious, and would not admit them to the house. Many of the Indians then tried landing at a place opposite and attempted to seize some Englishmen there. The latter resisted and in the skirmish several were killed. The Indians escaped into the woods and later committed other depredations. The French had taken advantage of the situation to stir them up against the English, and

25 *Cal. State Pap. Col.*, 1685-1688, §§1868, 1901; 1689-1692, §152; Sewall, *Diary*, I, 223, 224; *Andros Tracts*, III, 86; Mass. Arch., vol. 129, pp. 137, 241, 243.

Castine, especially, who had been incensed at the raid on his house, tried to incite them to attack and, according to many reports circulating at the time, promised them supplies to use against the English.[26]

News of the Casco Bay incident reached Andros while he was still at Albany. He immediately wrote to Colonel Tyng at Great Island and severely upbraided him for exceeding his instructions, in which he had been cautioned to be careful and steady in doing his duty, but not to make war. Instead of that, "By Yor seizing and disturbing the Indians you have alarmed all your parts and put them in a posture of war." He gave orders, if the Indians had not already been returned, to let all of them go except the criminals.[27]

Meanwhile the councilors at Boston were receiving letters from Stoughton, Hinckes, Colonel Tyng, and others, who were in the eastern parts, telling of the restlessness of the Indians, asking for aid in forces and provisions, and saying that a panic had seized the people on the frontier and that many of the more exposed parts were deserted. A "press" was agreed to, and a force immediately mobilized. A sloop carrying forty men with stores and provisions was sent "to assist in the resettlement of North Yarmouth and to comfort the people in the other parts." Upon receipt of news that two or three Indians had been seen skulking about along the frontier, orders were dispatched to the outlying towns of Dedham, Medfield, Wrenham, and Mendon to send eight or ten armed horsemen every day, to scout in search of Indians and to kill any who refused to submit themselves. This action was reported to Andros at New York. Joshua Pipon, commander at Pemaquid, in a letter full of condescension, recommended to Andros greater severity in dealing

[26] Mass. Arch., vol. 129, pp. 165, 166, 251-252, 262; C. O. 5: 855, no. 90.
[27] Andros Tracts, III, 87; Mass. Arch., vol. 129, pp. 194-195.

with the Indians, implying that he was inexperienced
and too much inclined to leniency.[28]

There was nothing lenient about Andros's letters to
the councilors and the officers on the frontier, for they
left no doubt of the definiteness of his Indian policy, or of
his expectation of implicit obedience from them all. His
letter to the councilors at Boston was answered by Dudley, the acting head of the government, who replied in a
humble but aggrieved tone, assuring his superior in office
that "what was done by the Gentlemen here was what
we truly thought your Excellencey would Expect of us
that the province might not be lost in your absence but
by the little help sent they might be able to preserve
themselves until your Excellency's command arrive."
Andros hastened to Boston, and immediately upon his
arrival sent to the frontier the two companies of regulars
together with several vessels, for the defense of the coast
settlements and the fisheries, and issued a proclamation
commanding that all of the king's subjects who had been
taken lately by the Indians be released and calling on
all Indians concerned in the murder of any Englishmen
to surrender. All other Indians, he announced, would
receive protection wherever they desired to settle.[29]

A few days later, news came of the burning of New
Dartmouth and Newtown and of other Indian outrages,
whereupon Andros decided to adopt more stringent
measures. He caused an order in council to be issued
providing for the dispatch to the frontier of a force of
four or five hundred men, from the several regiments of
militia under the command of Major General Winthrop.
Three hundred of these he called out and dispatched at
once. Winthrop was ill and declined the service, where-

[28] Mass. Arch., vol. 129, pp. 167, 168, 172-173, 178-179, 188, 190, 217,
219; Sewall, *Diary*, I, 225.

[29] Mass. Arch., vol. 129, pp. 238, 239; *Cal. State Pap. Col.*, 1685-1688,
§§1901, 1917.

upon Andros, by the advice of the council, resolved to command the forces himself. He led them northward, distributed them among the eleven newly garrisoned forts, which had been built at exposed points on the frontier, and arranged that supplies should be provided by means of armed vessels, constantly plying along the coast. When the time was ripe, he attacked the Indians unexpectedly, destroying their habitations, provisions, and canoes, before the ''least harm or mischief was done by them.'' The Indians, in desperate straits, began to sue for peace. Seeing that the worst was over, Andros established his forces in garrisons in command of British officers from his small standing army of regulars, and then hastened back to Boston.[30]

When the revolution broke out in England against James II, French officials were convinced that the opportunity had come for capturing New York and thus, by a bold stroke, ''securing Canada, firmly establishing the Religion, Trade and the King's authority throughout all North America,'' and safeguarding permanently the possessions of France in the New World.[31] In their turn, English officials were urging the capture of Canada, without which the ''English Collonies will never be at rest or safe.''[32] Thus news of the declaration of war between the two countries in April, 1689, found each colonial contestant ready to spring at the other's throat. At this critical moment, when the French were about to attempt the invasion of the English colonies and an Indian war was imminent, occurred the uprising in Boston, which overthrew the government of Andros and brought to an

[30] *Andros Tracts*, I, 55; 3 Mass. Hist. Soc. *Col.*, I, 85; Mass. Arch., vol. 129, p. 353; Sewall, *Diary*, I, 234-235.

[31] *New York Col. Docs.*, IX, 404-408; *Cal. State Pap. Col.*, 1689-1692, §89.

[32] *New York Col. Docs.*, III, 611-612; *Cal. State Pap. Col.*, 1689-1692, §1.

end the Dominion of New England. Andros and many of his chief military officers were seized and imprisoned, while those actually in command of troops on the frontier were removed from their posts. The forces were withdrawn, the frontier exposed, and the formidable check which the great Dominion offered to French and Indian aggression disappeared overnight, and the enemy were given, suddenly and almost by accident, the rare opportunity of taking the offensive under most advantageous circumstances. But for this disaster, the combined English and colonial forces, under the able leadership of Andros, might have invaded Canada successfully and crippled the power of France in America, thereby striking a blow that would have altered to no small extent the relations of the two countries in the century that followed.

The Dominion of New England fulfilled the expectations of the Lords of Trade as a solution of the colonial problem of defense. It had the desired effect upon the French and hostile Indians, for it checked their encroachments upon the English settlements in northern America. It strengthened the confidence of the Five Nations in the English and made the alliance more secure. It added to the prestige and efficiency of the New England colonies and brought credit to Andros, whose military policy was the strongest feature of his administration. By his diplomatic dealings with the Indians and the French, his garrisoning of strategic points, and his vigorous warfare, he made New England formidable to its enemies, an opponent worthy of their consideration and respect.[33]

The Puritan revolution in New England brought to an end the only effectual system of defense that England ever had for the colonies in America. Never again could any group of colonies, north or south, be brought to the

33 *Andros Tracts*, I, 42; Sewall, *Letter Book*, I, 114-115.

point of effectual co-operation in any enterprise directed against the common enemy, unless that enemy were at their very doors. It is true that in each of the four French and Indian wars to follow, New England attempted to strike a spectacular blow at the French by an invasion of Canada, but the expeditions were always so poorly organized and equipped and the forces so poorly trained that they usually failed to accomplish anything and were always accompanied with a tremendous waste of life and money. Except for these sporadic ventures, the frontiers were so exposed and the colonies so little prepared for attack that there was always the danger of a successful French invasion in spite of the superior numbers of the English. Time after time, in the eighteenth century, England tried either to unite the colonies for military purposes or to get them to do so themselves, but without success. They recognized their need of union for defense, but, as Franklin said in 1754, "Every Body cries, a Union is absolutely necessary, but when they come to the Manner and Form of the Union, their weak Noddles are perfectly distracted." Had a well-planned invasion of English North America been directed by the French against the New York frontier centring at Albany, New York might easily have been conquered at almost any time in the eighteenth century, before her neighbors could have mustered troops to send to her aid. The capture of New York would doubtless have meant the eventual loss of the other English seaboard colonies. To protect her own interests in America, England should have organized her colonies more effectively for defense, a process well begun under the Dominion of New England, but unfortunately abandoned after its downfall.

CHAPTER X

REVOLUTION

The theocrats could not believe that the Dominion government would be permanent, nor that the theocracy had been destroyed forever. They had not revolted when Andros was inaugurated, because they thought God intended them to suffer in order that they might be purified of their sins. Three years of a foreign administration had been a heavy punishment, but during that time, they had made great efforts at reformation, which they hoped God would reward by mitigating their punishment, perhaps even by restoring their charter. Consequently, in the spring of 1688, after Andros's attempts to regulate land titles, Increase Mather felt himself called upon to undertake the mission of appealing to King James in person.[1]

Arrived in London, he joined Hutchinson and Nowell, two men who had evidently been serving as agents for the colony since the loss of the charter, in an attempt to

[1] 2 Mass. Hist. Soc. *Proc.*, XIII, 333; *Cal. State Pap. Col.*, 1689-1692, §261; *Andros Tracts*, I, 18. Cotton Mather, in *Parentator*, says that his father wrote in his diary in 1687, "I fought unto God in Secret with Tears that He would send Reviving News out of England: and I could not but Believe that He will do so." *Andros Tracts*, III, 125, 126-127. Shortly after this, "Superior Gentlemen in the oppressed Country" suggested that Mather go to England to see if with the help of some prominent Dissenters there, he might not be able to obtain some relief for the colony. Mather attempted to "discern the Mind of God" in regard to the matter, by leaving the decision to his congregation. They unanimously agreed that he should go. *Ibid.*, III, 126-127; Sewall, *Diary*, I, 197.

modify the worst features of the Dominion government. They presented to the king a petition asking for changes in regard to legislation and taxation, administration of justice, land policy, and religion.[2] Realizing that more could be gained by compromise than by a plea for a restoration of the charter,[3] they asked also that the colony be granted a representative assembly, the members of which should be chosen by the freeholders, promising in return to supply a fixed sum of five thousand pounds for the support of the government, beyond which amount no money should be raised without the consent of the governor, council, and representatives of the people in general assembly, and no laws be passed except by that body. They did not ask that the colony be allowed to elect the governor, but they wanted, for the better administration of justice, local probate courts and a "court of equity for all considerable causes." With reference to the land policy, they made two requests: that old titles be confirmed; and that the rights of common, formerly belonging to the landholders of the towns, be recognized, each town having the authority to settle all regulations in regard to such matters. Concerning religion, they desired liberty of conscience, each denomination to support itself independently. Thus they hoped to guarantee to the Puritans security against Andros's use of their meeting-house for the Anglican service and against the possibility of his demanding a general tax for its sup-

[2] Hutchinson, *Hist. of Mass.*, I, 367-368; 4 Mass. Hist. Soc. *Col.*, VIII, 712.

[3] Cotton Mather says that his father, upon the king's request that he put all the grievances in writing, prepared a "Memorial of Grievances" and a petition for the redress of them, "in several Proposed Instances." Although "he could not now propose the Restoration of the Condemned & Vacated Charter," he "did Propose (what the King himself had Instructed him to call) a Magna Charta for an everlasting Liberty of Conscience to the Churches." *Andros Tracts*, III, 137-139; 4 Mass. Hist. Soc. *Col.*, VIII, 712.

port. Having heard rumors to the effect that the college
at Cambridge was to be taken over and given to the
Anglicans, the agents begged that it "be confirmed to
those that erected it."[4]

The Lords of Trade, to whom the petition was referred,
struck out the parts concerning an assembly, liberty of
conscience, and Cambridge College, and sent it with their
report to the attorney-general.[5] Mather and his associates, upon being informed of the action of the committee,
presented another petition in which they asked that
"untill his Majesty shall be graciously pleased to grant
an Assembly, the council should consist of such persons
as shall be considerable proprietors of lands within his
Majesty's dominions, and that the counties being continued as at present, each county may have one, at least,
of such of the inhabitants of the same to be member
thereof. And that no acts may pass for law but such as
have or shall be voted by the manifest consent of the
major part of the council."[6] This request, like that for a
representative assembly, met with the disapproval of
the Lords of Trade. The agents then sent still another
petition asking only "for liberty of conscience and of
property, and for a charter confirming the government
of Cambridge College as originally established."[7] The

[4] This petition, found in *Cal. State Pap. Col.*, 1685-1688, §1860, is like
the one printed in the *Andros Tracts*, III, 138, and in Hutchinson, *Hist.
of Mass.*, I, 368, except that in the last two, the paragraph suggesting the
fixed sum of £5,000 is omitted. The manuscript in the Mass. Arch., vol.
106, p. 369, from which these copies appear to have been taken, is probably
an expurgated copy made by Mather, of the official one presented to the
Lords of Trade.

[5] *Cal. State Pap. Col.*, 1685-1688, §1860. Mather asserted that the Lords
of Trade at first agreed upon a report in which an assembly was mentioned,
but that Lord Sunderland "struck out that clause with his own hand"
before the report was presented. *Andros Tracts*, II, 10; Hutchinson, *Hist.
of Mass.*, I, 367.

[6] Hutchinson, *Hist. of Mass.*, I, 369; *Andros Tracts*, III, 143, note.

[7] *Cal. State Pap. Col.*, 1685-1688, §§1878, 1878-i. This is an abbreviated

king declared his willingness to grant this last petition by charter under the great seal.[8] Before he could carry out his promise, two events made further action unnecessary. In October James II was forced to publish his proclamation for "restoring corporations to their ancient charters, liberties rights and franchises," and although he did not mention colonial corporations therein, the agents took advantage of the somewhat ambiguous wording of the document and interpreted it to include the colonies.[9] At about the same time, the Lords of Trade received from Sir Thomas Powys, the attorney-general, whose favor the agents had in some way obtained, a report that the Massachusetts charter had been illegally annulled. The lords therefore promised the agents a charter "with larger powers," and ordered the attorney-general to examine Andros's commission and instructions, for the purpose of making them conform to the old charter provisions until the new charter could be prepared. This was the limit of progress made when the Revolution of 1688 occurred.[10]

To the Puritans, the overthrow of King James came as the answer to their prayers for deliverance. The agents immediately petitioned the new monarchs for the restoration of all the former governments in New England, asserting that inasmuch as the charters of the four New England colonies had been taken away by "illegal and arbitrary proceedings," and the commission which had

text of the petition in Mass. Arch., vol. 11, p. 44, and in *Andros Tracts*, III, 136, note.

[8] *Cal. State Pap. Col.*, 1685-1688, §1879.

[9] *Ibid.*, §1913. On October 18, the day after the publication of the proclamation, Richard Wharton wrote to Governor Hinckley telling him about it, and expressing his opinion "that Revolution seems to be hastening on, out of which New England may, I hope, find deliverance." 4 Mass. Hist. Soc. *Col.*, VIII, 713.

[10] *Cal. State Pap. Col.*, 1689-1692, §152.

been given to Andros, permitting him to make laws "without the consent of the people by their representatives," had terminated "by the devolution of the Crown upon your Majesty," the colonies should be restored "to their ancient privileges," and the governors and magistrates who held office in 1686 be permitted to resume their offices. The Lords of Trade, to whom, as usual, the petition was referred, were instructed to investigate the "allegations contained therein" and to report their opinion as to the best method of procedure.[11] Since the investigation would take considerable time, the lords, acting "upon the application of Sr. William Phips and Mr. Mather," did not dispatch to New England a copy of the general instruction, which they were sending to the governors of the colonies, ordering them to proclaim William and Mary and to continue in office all Protestant civil and military officers, but stopped it and ordered it "not to be sent."[12]

On February 20 the Lords of Trade took into consideration the petition of Mather and Phips and called them in to explain it. When the agents complained of a flaw in the *scire facias,* the lords, who were new appointees, asked the attorney-general to attend the next meeting with a record of the judgment upon which the charter had been annulled. The attorney-general showed that the court had made no error in the proceeding, and

[11] Gay MSS., Phips Papers, I, 17, 18. The petition printed in *Andros Tracts,* III, 149, note, and taken from Mass. Arch., vol. 129, p. 317, is probably an original draft of the one actually presented. Mr. Prince thinks, however, that it is a letter, sent after the presentation of the petition, to stop the king's circular letter to New England confirming all officers in office. If this were the case, the letter would doubtless have been mentioned in the *Calendar of State Papers.* The petition which was presented is recorded in Gay MSS., Phips Papers, I, 17, and a calendar of it is in *Cal. State Pap. Col.,* 1689-1692, §18.

[12] *Andros Tracts,* III, 149; *Cal. State Pap. Col.,* 1689-1692, §§8, 17, 19, 20, 21, 22; C. O. 5: 905, pp. 41-42.

that the charter had been revoked because its provisions
had been violated. The colony in its government had
deviated from English law and legal tradition and by its
breaches of the navigation acts had impaired the king's
revenue. The Lords of Trade, satisfied that the proceedings against the charter had been legal and just and convinced by the recent invasion of New England that union
was necessary, strongly recommended to the king in
council that the Dominion be continued. They wished,
however, to make some administrative changes. They
advised the recall of Andros, and in his place, the
appointment of a provisional governor, who should be
instructed not to raise money by council vote only. In
the meantime, provision should be made for a permanent
establishment which should "preserve the Rights &
privileges of the people of New England & yet reserve
such a dependence on the Crown of England as shall be
thought requisite." The king accepted this report and
referred it back to the Lords of Trade, with instructions
to prepare the draft of a charter for New England on the
basis recommended. Instead of the appointment of a provisional governor, he ordered that the government be in-
trusted temporarily to two commissioners, one of whom
should be nominated by the merchants and planters then
in England.[13]

This action of the king was not quite what Mather had
expected, and certainly not what he desired. He wanted
an immediate restoration of the old charter and the re-
instatement of the former magistrates, and he wanted
also an additional grant of power, "without which the
Old Charter would not answer the Occasions and Necessi-
ties of the People."[14] Finding that he could not persuade

[13] *Cal. State Pap. Col.*, 1689-1692, §§25, 28, 37; Gay MSS., Phips Papers,
I, 19-20, 21, 22; *Acts, Privy Coun. Col.*, II, pp. 124-125, §278.

[14] Mass. Arch., vol. 129, p. 317; *Andros Tracts*, III, 152-153.

the king, against the advice of the Lords of Trade, to restore the charter, he turned for help to the parliamentary party, and as a result of "most Indefatigable Applications unto the Principal Men in that Convention Parliament," he succeeded in getting mention of plantations charters in the bill for restoration of corporation charters which was at that time before the House of Commons.[15]

While waiting for the passage of the corporation bill, Mather schemed to force from William a provisional settlement of government, which would be satisfactory to the Puritans. He objected to the continuation of the Dominion, because the moderates, who were in power, would thus be able to oppose the campaign of the Puritans among members of parliament for a share in charter restorations. Moreover, in case the corporation bill failed to pass, the best chance of winning a liberal charter from the king would be by trying to identify the old theocratic party with the revolutionary movement in England, at the same time making it appear that the Dominion government stood for James. If the Dominion government were left as it was, except for the recall of Andros and the appointment of a commission, there would be no opportunity to make it appear disloyal to William. Furthermore, if it were continued temporarily, the Lords of Trade might be able to persuade the king to continue it permanently. If, instead, the theocracy were actually in control of the provisional government, a change back to the Dominion was less likely. Evidence points to the conclusion that Mather suddenly decided upon a bold step, the suggestion to the theocratic leaders at Boston that they overthrow the Andros government in the name of King William, thereby placing the new sovereigns

15 *Andros Tracts,* III, 153; 4 Mass. Hist. Soc. *Col.,* V, 211.

under obligation to them for having saved New England from supporting James.[16]

Conditions in New England were ripe for an outbreak. The people were in general discontented with Andros's administration, and they had been led to believe, even before the arrival of news of William's invasion of England, that their charters were about to be restored. On January 10th, Mather's letter arrived, telling of Powys's report that the charter of Massachusetts had been illegally annulled, and advising the Puritan leaders of that colony to "prepare the minds of the people for a change." The leaders, interpreting his injunction literally, suggested revolt, but cautious counsel voted the occasion premature.[17] At about the same time, the Plym-

---

[16] *Andros Tracts*, I, 71-72; II, 206; III, 226; 3 Mass. Hist. Soc. *Col.*, I, 100; Hutchinson, *Hist. of Mass.*, I, 380; note, 381; *Cal. State Pap. Col.*, 1689-1692, §§152, 285. Randolph maintained that "the revolt here was pushed on by the Agent in England, Mr. Mather, who sent a letter to Mr. Bradstreet encouraging him to go cheerfully to so acceptable a piece of service to all good people." *Cal. State Pap. Col.*, 1689-1692, §407. That some sort of encouragement to revolt came from England is to be suspected by the air of assurance in a revolutionary pamphlet, in the "query," "Whether common cursing and Swearing and sabbath breaking be not admirable qualities in a Governor, and such as may make any New-Englanders dote upon him, or endeavour his re-establishment, when we have all the assurance in the world that we shall be commended by the Authority of England for our deposing him?" *Andros Tracts*, III, 194. Gershom Bulkeley in his *Will and Doom* asserts that the theocrats of Connecticut in 1689 received "encouragement by letter from England, to take their Charter Government again, telling them, they were a company of *hens* if they did not do it." *Conn. Col. Rec.*, III, 456. See also *ibid.*, 465, note.

[17] *Andros Tracts*, II, 210; III, 226. Caleb Moody of Newbury declared after the revolution that sometime in January, 1689, Joseph Baylie of Newbury gave him a paper which he, Baylie, had picked up on the highway, entitled, "New England alarmed to rise and be armed, let not Papist you Charme I meane you no harme." The purport of the paper, according to Moody, was to warn the people of the danger from Andros's having pressed about one thousand soldiers into service on the frontier, lest he betray them to the French. Andros considered the paper seditious and arrested Moody. Mass. Arch., vol. 35, p. 167.

outh Puritans were stirred by Wharton's letter from London to ex-Governor Hinckley concerning the king's proclamation restoring corporations.[18] In Connecticut, the same spirit of restlessness, due to expectations there also of a return to charter government, existed throughout the spring.[19] In March, Andros, who was at Pemaquid, received word through Lieutenant Governor Nicholson at New York, of William's invasion of England, whereupon he hastened to Boston to be in readiness should trouble arise there.[20] The news of the invasion was unofficially made public in Boston, on the arrival of John Winslow from Nevis, April 4, bringing a copy of William's "Declaration from the Hague," reprints of which were soon widely circulated.[21] Report of the celebration of the proclamation in Barbados was also spread, thereby calling attention to Andros's not having ordered a similar celebration at Boston. The fact that Andros had issued James's proclamation concerning vigilance against a Dutch invasion but had not proclaimed William and Mary, and that he had imprisoned Winslow for bringing the news of the success of William's invasion

[18] See above note 9.

[19] John Allyn wrote Wait Winthrop that there were rumors ''that things will be as sometime they have bin by reason of a proclamation made by his Matie October last that restores charters.'' 6 Mass. Hist. Soc. *Col.*, V, 19. Bulkeley further declares in his *Will and Doom*, that rumors were current in the winter of 1688 of ''a plot on foot in Connecticut as well as other parts of the countrey, to make insurrection and subvert the Government.'' He suggests that the Connecticut theocrats were in collusion with those of Massachusetts favoring insurrection, citing as evidence, ''J. W. [John Winthrop?] his going to Boston on the same account so near about the time of Sir Edmund Andros, his apprehension; for he came to Boston the very day that Sir Edmund was apprehended; his siding with the transaction, taking advice there, and busy promoting of the Revolution here after he came back.'' *Conn. Col. Rec.*, III, 455.

[20] *Cal. State Pap. Col.*, 1689-1692, §2732; *New York Col. Docs.*, III, 591, 660, 723.

[21] *Andros Tracts*, I, 9; II, 209; III, 145, note.

served to arouse suspicion in the minds of the credulous Puritans that he would support King James and turn New England over to the French.[22] These suspicions were increased by the growing fear that he had instigated the Indian War against them and had transported large numbers of militiamen to service on the frontier, under the command of "Popish" officers, in order that he might the more easily carry out his plans for their betrayal.[23]

Winslow's news stirred the people of Massachusetts into a frenzy of excitement which was fed by mingled hope and fear—hope that news would arrive announcing the restoration of the charters and fear lest, before the news came, Andros might surrender the Dominion to Louis XIV.[24] So certain were they that their charter

[22] *Andros Tracts*, I, 18-19, 72, 73, 75-76, note, 79, 118, 119; *Cal. State Pap. Col.*, 1685-1688, §1910; 1689-1692, §§5, 180. That this fear was genuine with a part of the Puritans at least, there is no doubt, for it was a natural fear, considering the compromising position in which Andros was placed. There was the same panic of fear in St. Kitts and in Maryland, that the Catholic officers might turn their colonies over to King James. *Cal. State Pap. Col.*, 1689-1692, §§193, 194. The Puritans even circulated the rumor among the Five Nations that Andros intended to destroy them and that he was in league with France. *Ibid.*, §2741. When the revolution later spread to New York, this fear of Andros was carried with it, and given by the rebels as the cause of the outbreak. "We were prepared to wait in patience," ran the address of the New York militia to the king and queen, "but invited by your royal declaration we resolved to secure ourselves to save us from betrayal to a foreign enemy. We have therefore secured the fort though we should not have presumed to do so but for our dread of being betrayed by Sir Edmund Andros." *Ibid.*, §221.

[23] *Ibid.*, §261-i; *Andros Tracts*, I, 17, 73, 118, 150-151; II, 207.

[24] Andros was aware of the tension, for he wrote to Brockholes at Pemaquid, on April 16, "there is a general buzzing among the people, great with expectation of their old charters or they know not what." Hutchinson, *Hist. of Mass.*, I, 372. Randolph reported to the Lords of Trade that "Upon the eighteenth of Aprill last, the people of this country being prepossessed with strange fears and jealousyes against Sir Edmund Andros Govr and some of the members of the Council, took armes." *Andros Tracts*, III, 225. The instructions of the General Court to the agents in 1690 bear out this evidence. They read, "The just and amazing fears this people were surprized with upon the notice they had of the late King

would be restored by William, that they began again to entertain the idea of revolution, an idea which was apparently planted in their minds by Cotton Mather at his father's instigation. At this critical time, when only a spark was needed to light the conflagration of revolt, report came that a company of soldiers, who were in service on the Maine frontier, had mutinied and started for Boston.[25] Immediately some of the "more sensible Gentlemen" met to consider how they could prevent the arrival of the mob of soldiers from precipitating a bloody revolt. These gentlemen had for weeks past exerted their influence against revolution, and had tried to point out to those who agitated for it that it would be much better to await orders from England than to anticipate by force the governmental settlement, which would probably be made for them anyway. They now consulted with Mather, but whether for the purpose of dissuading him from further agitation or not, it is difficult to say. At least they agreed with him that in case the soldiers started trouble, they would first make every attempt to "extinguish desire for revolt," but if the mob succeeded in stirring the people to an outbreak, they would then appear and try to assume the leadership, in order to prevent the mob from doing that which might bring down very severe punishment upon the colony. They arranged for the preparation of a "declaration" of the reasons for revolt, in

James' being in France, lest Sir Edmund Andros (whose Governor and Confidant he was) should betray them into the power of the French King, other circumstances concurring to strengthen these fears." *Ibid.*, 59. Another contemporary pamphlet expresses the same idea, "New England is the key of America. If the French King had got that into his possession he would soon have been master of America, and this in probability would have been done this summer, if the New-Englanders about Boston perceiving what designs were carrying on, had not risen as one man, and seized Sir Edmund and on those few ill men who Andros joined with him in his tyranny." 3 Mass. Hist. Soc. *Col.*, I, 100.

25 Mass. Arch., vol. 129, pp. 368, 369-370; *Andros Tracts*, III, 145, note.

imitation of the English revolution, intending thereby to make the uprising, should it take place, appear, not as a local insurrection, but as a part of the English movement for the overthrow of James.[26]

The troops from the frontier must have arrived late on April 17, for early the next morning before the officers of the law, whom Andros had ordered to assist in marching them back to their posts, were able to apprehend them, their friends called out the Boston and Charlestown militia to aid in an insurrection against the government. By ten o'clock, the rapidly increasing militia army numbered about one thousand men. The first act of hostility was the seizure of Captain George of H. M. S. *Rose,* in order to prevent him from interfering with their plans.[27] When they began to capture other Dominion officers, the "gentlemen" who had agreed as to the method of procedure in case of revolt, seeing that the time for action had come, repaired to the town-house where they read the previously prepared declaration and decided upon their course of action. The fact that the tone of the declaration was inconsistent with the expressed attitude of the "gentlemen" toward an uprising, leads one to think that at least two different points of view regarding the revolt were represented by those present at the town-house,—that of the moderates, desiring only to direct the movement which they had been

[26] *Andros Tracts,* III, 145, note; Hutchinson, *Hist. of Mass.,* I, 380-381, note. Palmer in his "Impartial Account" says that the Puritans simply made "use of this juncture of Affairs and Their Majesties' names to cloak their Design whilst their Service was never intended." *Andros Tracts,* I, 25.

[27] There are several accounts of the revolution: Andros's report of it in *Cal. State Pap. Col.,* 1689-1692, §901; Randolph's in *ibid.,* §152; Captain George's, *ibid.,* §196; one supposedly by Riggs, Andros's servant, *ibid.,* §261; Byfield's (pro-revolutionary), *ibid.,* §96, and in *Andros Tracts,* I, 1-8; and an anonymous letter to the governor of Plymouth, quoted in Hutchinson, *Hist. of Mass.,* I, 376-379.

powerless to prevent, and that of the theocrats, welcoming it as the successful result of their propaganda. It is significant that on the very day of the outbreak, Cotton Mather was to have been taken into custody for preaching sedition.[28]

In the meantime, the mob attacked the fort, where Andros in anticipation of trouble had taken quarters. When he came out to inquire the meaning of the gathering, he was presented with a paper from the town-house group asking him to surrender the government and fortifications, in order to prevent bloodshed, and to come to the town-house to advise them how they might appease the people. He refused to surrender, but upon the advice of the gentlemen with him, went to the town-house. He found there assembled a coalition of various cliques and interests: five of the magistrates of 1686, among whom were the former governor, deputy governor, and secretary; five Dominion councilors, Stoughton, Winthrop, Shrimpton, Browne, and Gedney; four merchants of Boston, former non-freemen; Adam Winthrop, a distant relative of Wait Winthrop, and five Puritan ministers, among them Cotton Mather.[29] Andros demanded the reason of their meeting and of the "tumultuous arming" of the people. They answered by placing him under arrest.

By this time, the rapidly increasing mob was threatening to storm the fort and put to the sword the fourteen men of the garrison, if they did not surrender. To prevent the shedding of blood, the mob leaders sought

[28] *Andros Tracts*, II, 209, 210, 211-212; III, 145; note, 234; *Cal. State Pap. Col.*, 1689-1692, §§181, 285, 510, 901; Hutchinson, *Hist. of Mass.*, I, 380-381, note; 4 Mass. Hist. Soc. *Col.*, V, 190, 198.

[29] *Cal. State Pap. Col.*, 1689-1692, §§152 (p. 47), 285; 4 Mass. Hist. Soc. *Col.*, V, 194. Palmer thought the ministers led the revolt, as is shown by the postscript to his "Impartial Account," which is addressed to the clergy. *Andros Tracts*, I, 62.

through the council to obtain from Andros an order for surrender of the garrison. He refused, whereupon they clapped a pistol to Randolph's head and ordered him on threat of death to go to Fort Hill and tell the garrison there that the governor had ordered them to deliver up the fort. The garrison then capitulated. Randolph was next ordered to deliver the same message to the garrison on Castle Island. The soldiers there were suspicious and refused to obey. The mob renewed its threats to Andros to force him to give the order to evacuate, but without avail. Not until the next day, when a delegation of the pacifiers went to Castle Island and urged submission, would the garrison give way and then only on promise of liberty. The promise was immediately broken, and the troops of the garrison were clapped into prison. The governor was confined in the fort, while Dudley and Randolph, the two most hated officers of government, were lodged in the common jail. The other officials, civil and military, were imprisoned in the castle. To prevent the prisoners from escaping by water, the sails of H. M. S. *Rose* were removed from the vessel and hidden on shore.[30]

After two days of mob dictation, the town-house pacifiers appear to have been thoroughly frightened as to the possible consequences of the revolt,—the chaos in government in the months to follow and the attitude of England toward it.[31] They took the first step in the process of reconstruction by forming a council of safety on April 20, and by inviting twenty-two gentlemen to join them, five of whom were of the government of 1686, while the rest were for the most part Boston merchants and

[30] See above, note 27. Of the twenty-six who were imprisoned Dudley was the only Massachusetts Puritan. The list is given in *Andros Tracts*, III, 94, and in *Rhode Island Col. Recs.*, III, 257, note.

[31] *Cal. State Pap. Col.*, 1689-1692, §181; Hutchinson, *Hist. of Mass.*, I, 380-381, note.

former non-freemen. On May 1 agitation arose in council meeting over the necessity of making some temporary settlement of government, until orders should come from England. With great difficulty the council reached the decision to ask the towns of the colony to send representatives, not to exceed two from each, to Boston, on May 9, to consider what should be done about the government, and, in order to unite all factions in support of the revolution, suggested to the towns that they extend the right of voting to all freeholders.[32] Most of the towns responded at once, by calling meetings of the "freemen and inhabitants" to vote on sending delegates to a general convention and to draft instructions to these delegates how to vote on the governmental settlement and on the extension of freedom.[33] On May 9, sixty-six persons from forty-four towns appeared. A few of the most theocratic delegates expressed a preference for a new election, in order to eliminate the moderates in the government of 1686, while the pro-Dominion representatives supported the council of safety and favored its continuation, until instructions should come from England. The majority, however, voted to commit the government to the governor, magistrates, and deputies who had been chosen in 1686, and, regardless of the opposition of the council of safety, sent the invitation. The governor and former magistrates, aware of the dissension, thought the expression of opinion was not general enough, and desired "that the People of the Said several Towns and

[32] Mass. Arch., vol. 107, p. 21; Court Records, VI, 2, 3, 11-12. (These are the manuscript records of the provisional government, and are to be found in the archives at the state house in Boston.)

[33] Mass. Arch., vol. 107, pp. 8a, 14, 14a, 15, 15a, 16a, 17a, 20, 21, 22, 22a, 22b, 23, 25. By a law passed in 1670 English inhabitants who were householders of the age of twenty-four years, in good standing, and who possessed an estate valued at £80 in a single country rate, could attend town meeting and vote on local matters. Whether or not they voted at these meetings is difficult to tell. *Mass. Col. Laws* (1887), p. 148.

Villages do more fully and expresly signify their Minds in that Matter and that the Other Towns and Places within the Said colony be Notified to Convene their Respective Inhabitants to manifest their minds relating to the Same.'' The convention, attempting to wrest the leadership from the council of safety, then voted to continue the latter until May 22, the date set for the second meeting of the representatives.[34]

The new convention, dominated by the theocrats, soon proved to be as much at odds with the council of safety as the old one. Forty-four towns voted for a reassumption of the charter government and a restoration of the officers of 1686, while nine towns wished to continue the council of safety until the king should settle the government. The former governor, deputy governor, and thirteen magistrates agreed to accept the administration "according to the rule of the charter," until directions should be received from England, on condition that "Fit Persons" be added to complete the required number of eighteen, but they wished it understood that no actual assumption of charter government was intended. Their acceptance forced the withdrawal from the council of safety of all who were not of the government of 1686, and was therefore a triumph for the theocrats. However, the theocratic convention made an attempt to mollify the moderates by choosing from their number the five assistants. Three, Wait Winthrop and Samuel Shrimpton of Boston and John Phillips of Charlestown were among those crowded out of the council of safety; a fourth, Jonathan Curwin of Salem, was probably chosen because that town disapproved of the revolution and might in this way be won over; the fifth, Jeremiah Swayne of

[34] Mass. Arch., vol. 107, pp. 8, 24, 26, 27; Gay MSS., State Papers, III, 92, 93-98; Court Records, VI, 15, 16, 17, 18; *Andros Tracts*, I, 199-200; *Cal. State Pap. Col.*, 1689-1692, §§134, 135, 901.

Reading, was a former non-freeman. In order to make the election conform as nearly as possible to charter provisions, the representatives voted to extend the freedom to "all that are not freemen In the present Government, either Majestrates or Representatives . . . In order to our Legall Proceeding in those things that may be before us." In spite of the representation which the theocrats diplomatically granted to the moderates, the latter had very little influence from this time on. They lost permanently the leadership which they had tried so hard to assume.[35]

At first, the governor and magistrates continued to be called the "council of safety," but upon the insistence of the representatives they assumed the charter name of "Governor and Council" and restored all laws that were in force in 1686. The theocracy was again in the saddle. The triumphant Puritans now waited expectantly to see if the Prince of Orange would "restore to us our dear lost Liberties & Patent Priviledgs and set up our Hedge of Government about us."[36]

News of the Boston outbreak reached New York on April 25, at the same time with a report from the north that the French were about to invade the province. Nicholson, the deputy governor of the Dominion, after consultation with the mayor and council of the city of New York, summoned the militia officers of the counties to a meeting on April 29, in order to urge upon them the importance of preparedness against a "hostile landing," and called a council meeting, notifying all councilors who were not involved in the revolt at Boston to be present.

[35] Mass. Arch., vol. 107, pp. 36a, 37, 37a, 38, 38a, 39, 39a, 39b, 40, 40a, 41, 41b, 43, 43a, 43b, 44, 44a, 44b, 45a, 45b, 46, 46a, 47, 48a, 49, 49a, 50, 50a, 51, 52, 53, 54, 67, 99; Court Records, VI, 25, 26-27, 28, 31; Hutchinson, *Hist. of Mass.*, I, 386-387.

[36] Mass. Arch., vol. 107, pp. 87, 94b, 109a, 110a, 138a, 149a, 174a; Court Records, VI, 30, 34, 42, 48; Hutchinson, *Hist. of Mass.*, I, 387.

Only Smith, Clarke, and Newbury, besides the New York members, responded. At this juncture, a forceful letter to the revolutionary government at Boston might have proved effectual, but instead of demanding Andros's immediate release, Nicholson dispatched a message of mild surprise at the arrest of Andros and of hope "that his excellency and the rest of the officers may be restored to their former stations, or at least have liberty to come hither." The council of safety at Boston answered that the soldiers were still in arms and it was not in their power to "set any persons at liberty who are confined and kept by the soldiers."[37]

Two weeks later, an order was received from Andros that Colonel Hamilton of New Jersey and Colonel Smith of Long Island be sent to Boston to demand his release. The council notified the two officers of Andros's commands, but the latter, evidently lacking the courage to face the Boston mob, made excuse that their absence might cause the people of their localities to rise. The council accepted this excuse and weakly decided to take no action, thus allowing the Boston revolt to triumph unchallenged.[38]

News of the overthrow of Andros flew "like lightning," for the revolutionary leaders at Boston immediately sent copies of their "Declaration" to all the colonies in the Dominion, urging them to cast off the yoke.[39] Plymouth, in imitation of Boston's example, seized Nathaniel Clark, the only pro-Dominion officer from that colony, and then proceeded to reassume the old colonial

[37] *New York Col. Docs.*, III, 591; Hutchinson, *Hist. of Mass.*, I, 384-386; *Cal. State Pap. Col.*, 1689-1692, §§2734, 2735, 2739.

[38] *Cal. State Pap. Col.*, 1689-1693, §§2743, 2744; *New York Col. Docs.*, III, 592.

[39] *Cal. State Pap. Col.*, 1689-1692, §§104, 2734; Hutchinson, *Hist. of Mass.*, I, 383, note; 4 Mass. Hist. Soc. Col., V, 190.

government.[40] Rhode Island likewise restored the government in operation previous to 1686, but not with the unanimous consent of the inhabitants.[41] In Connecticut, a minority of the freemen, who, it appears, were themselves only a minority of the adult males in the colony, held a meeting at Hartford on May 9 to decide what action to take concerning the revolution. Although a majority of those present opposed resumption of the charter government, the theocratic leaders insisted on installing in office the former colonial officials, on the ground that King James's proclamation restoring charters to corporations applied to Connecticut.[42] There were no disturbances in Maine and New Hampshire. Both of these provinces were again brought under the jurisdiction of Massachusetts, Maine because of having been the former propriety of Massachusetts,[43] New Hampshire because the inhabitants petitioned to be taken under her protection.[44]

Although New York for a while remained quiet, the

[40] Hutchinson, *Hist. of Mass.*, I, 383, note; *Plymouth Col. Laws*, p. 209; *Cal. State Pap. Col.*, 1689-1692, §183; *Andros Tracts*, I, 8; 4 Mass. Hist. Soc. *Col.*, V, 197.

[41] *Cal. State Pap. Col.*, 1689-1692, §§99, 746; 6 Mass Hist. Soc. *Col.*, V, 20.

[42] 6 Mass. Hist. Soc. *Col.*, V, 19; *New York Col. Docs.*, III, 849-854. Connecticut evidently barely escaped an outbreak, for it was reported that May 9 was a day of ''Public agitation'' at Hartford. Mass. Arch., vol. 107, p. 27a. The reasons given by the theocrats for resumption of charter government were not altogether logical, the proclamation being plainly limited to corporations in England. Governor Treat apparently appreciated this fact, for he wrote a letter explaining that ''the true and real grounds of the procedure of the colony in assuming the government was, salus populi est suprema lex,'' the colony being much concerned over alarms of Indian attacks at the eastward and of a French invasion of New York. Hutchinson, *Hist. of Mass.*, I, 383, note. See also *Conn. Col. Rec.*, III, 456-460.

[43] *Cal. State Pap. Col.*, 1689-1692, §1751; Mass. Arch., vol. 107, pp. 150a, 270a.

[44] *Cal. State Pap. Col.*, 1689-1692, §§885, 1418.

revolutionary infection soon spread to Long Island and thence to New York City, where racial and social causes for dissension existed.[45] The democratic element, largely Dutch, triumphed over the English aristocracy, and "up jumped hotheaded Leisler into the saddle."[46] Nicholson escaped to England to report conditions, while the councilors on the spot, who would not follow Leisler, were intimidated and finally silenced. The counties of Richmond, Ulster, and Albany held out for a long time against Leisler, but finally succumbed, probably more than anything else because of the necessity of united action against the French. New Jersey seems to have experienced no agitation against the Andros government, but to have awaited orders from England. However, having no resident councilors, the outbreak at New York left New Jersey without a government. Within a month, the Boston uprising had effected the complete overthrow of the Dominion of New England.[47]

What gave the revolutionary movement such strength? To deem it but an echo of the English revolution against James, is to cause it to lose all its significance.[48] The

[45] *New York Col. Docs.*, III, 591, 592; *Cal. State Pap. Col.*, 1689-1692, §§104, 121, 159, 160, 173, 187, 241, 285, 319. The king sent a letter to Nicholson on July 30 empowering him to take over the government of New York, but before it arrived, the revolution there had occurred. *Cal. State Pap. Col.*, 1689-1692, §§121, 307.

[46] The Leislerites protested that their movement was not as their enemies insinuated, "a Dutch plot," but there is evidence which leads one to suppose that the Dutch were very prominent in it. *Ibid.*, §§217, 690, 891, 961, 1084, 1746. The council of New York reported to the Earl of Shrewsbury that people of "sense or estate" were not participators in the outbreak. *Ibid.*, §§187, 288. See also the petition of New York merchants and of some Long Island inhabitants against Leisler, in *New York Col. Docs.*, III, 748-749, 754-756.

[47] *Ibid.*, 675, 684; *Cal. State Pap. Col.*, 1689-1692, §§216, 322, 362, 365, 598, 630, 693, 805, 899, 1373, 2763; *New York Col. Docs.*, III, 598, 646, 656.

[48] The Puritans tried to make it so appear. In "Revolution Justified,"

explanation is found in the fanaticism of the Puritan
theocrats, who were more Hebrew than English in their
thought and ideals and in their government. Like the
Jews of the Old Testament, they were the Chosen People
and the Andros administration was the period of their
captivity, inflicted upon them by a just, stern, and wrath-
ful God. Their holy men had prophesied that this captivity was approaching its end.[49] Therefore, when the
revolution occurred in England, the theocrats immediately interpreted it as God's sign that He was about to
deliver them from bondage and restore their former
judges.[50] The revolt, in spite of the words of the "Declaration," was not so much an uprising against oppression,
as a predestined event for which they had waited. The
features of Andros's administration which they had
disliked, gave them the justification for revolt against
what they considered a foreign rule, the rule of the op-
pressor. They rose against Andros, not because they
thought he governed them contrary to the laws of England, but because he was the principal instrument used in
making of New England an English province. They hated
the administration, because the laws were not of their
making, and therefore not based on the Bible as a guide;

it is maintained that "No man does really approve of the Revolution in
England, but must justifie that in New England also, for the latter was
effected in compliance with the former." *Andros Tracts*, I, 71-72. The same
idea is found also in "A Brief Relation of the Plantations of New
England," 3 Mass. Hist. Soc. *Col.*, I, 100; *Andros Tracts*, I, 207; *Cal.
State Pap. Col.*, 1689-1692, §138.

49 Morton, the minister at Charlestown, had, in a sermon in 1687, urged
patience, "for it would not be long before God restored their ancient
Magistrates." *Cal. State Pap. Col.*, 1689-1692, §510.

50 *Andros Tracts*, I, 18-19, 118-119; *Cal. State Pap. Col.*, 1689-1692, §129.
One Puritan wrote to the Bishop of London, "we are like Israel as told
of in the book of Judges," while Moody gave thanks to God "that He
had restored their judges as of old." *Cal. State Pap. Col.*, 1689-1692,
§§810, 306.

because the courts were the courts of England, and not of the theocratic "judges"; because English land law was introduced and they were forced to look to the king instead of to God as overlord; because trade was no longer free but confined to the English system, and most of all because the religious purity of their colony was contaminated by the toleration of the worship of idolaters and others not of the true faith.[51]

The theocrats could never have accomplished the revolution had they met with resistance from the moderates. That they did not meet with such resistance was due to the changed attitude of a part of the moderates toward Andros's administration. Before the Dominion was established, the non-freemen among them desired a royal government, while even the Puritan moderates wished to be released from the yoke of the theocrats. The liberal Puritan aristocracy gradually found that their interests were in most respects more like those of the aristocratic non-freemen than those of the democratic Puritan freemen, the theocrats. Prominent moderates accepted office under Dudley and Andros, not finding it such a serious matter that a representative assembly had been omitted as long as the government was committed into the hands of a wise and benevolent aristocracy—themselves. During Andros's administration dissension began. Both branches of the moderate party approved of Andros's military policy, but disliked his strict enforcement of the acts of trade and his attempt to change the tenure of their land. Toward his religious policy, however, they felt very differently. The non-Puritans were glad of the privilege of worshiping according to their own faith,

[51] *Cal. State Pap. Col.*, 1689-1692, §510. After the revolution, the Anglican church at Boston was subjected to constant abuse, because Cotton Mather told the people that its existence was the cause of all their calamities. *Ibid.*, §§742, 1217, 1239; *Andros Tracts*, II, 212.

without having to contribute to the support of a Congregational minister, but the Puritan moderates had not expected to have any interference with the religious system of the colony or with local institutions. The latter began to blame Andros personally for the features of his administration which they did not like, because he kept the government largely in his own hands instead of sharing it with the council. As soon as they awoke to the fact that they were exerting no influence on the government, they joined the opposition and, with the theocrats, began to make complaint against Andros's "illegal and arbitrary commission." When the theocrats urged revolt, the moderates opposed it, but when revolt came in spite of their opposition, they did not resist it, as they undoubtedly would have done had they been giving to Andros's administration their hearty support. Instead, those of Boston seized the leadership and co-operated with the theocrats in establishing a provisional government strong enough to preserve order. Without doubt, the revolution appeared differently to the different elements participating in it: to the theocrats, it meant a restoration of the old theocracy; to the Puritan moderates, the removal of Andros and the establishment of the charter government, modified by the reforms that the theocrats had to grant in order to win their support; to the non-Puritan moderates, who wished the preservation of the Dominion, it spelled calamity.

The Boston revolutionists faced two very important problems,—the winning of recognition for the revolution from the British government, and the maintenance of it at home against those among them who preferred a royal government. Therefore they deemed it best to imprison the chief officials of the Andros administration until definite word came from England concerning the settlement, so that these officials could do no damage among the factions in Massachusetts or send or carry to England any defense of themselves or any complaint against the rebels.[52]

The "President and Council for Safety of the People and Conservation of the Peace" sent an address to the king on May 20, thanking him "for casting off the yoke from our brethren of England and from ourselves," and telling him of the revolution at Boston, which, they asserted, was undertaken in imitation of his example. They reported the imprisonment of the Dominion officials pending the king's orders, and appealed to him for "a share in the universal restoration of charters and English liberties, that we may under the shadow of your crown enjoy our ancient rights and privileges."[53] In June the "President and Revolutionary Council of Massachusetts" sent a petition to the king, reporting their restoration of the governor, deputy governor, and assistants of 1686, and begging "for a favorable interpretation of our late action and for restoration to our undoubted rights."[54] Although the king had heard of the revolution, unofficially, before July 4 and had promised Mather to send a letter of approval to the revolutionists, no word of any kind was received from him until the last of November. The letter which arrived at that time did not in the least relieve the tension, because it completely ignored the question of government, merely ordering those persons who had seized Andros and the other officials to send them home at once to answer whatever charges there might be against them, and to treat them

[52] *Cal. State Pap. Col.*, 1689-1692, §133; *Andros Tracts*, I, 72. Randolph says the chief purpose of imprisoning him was to restore free trade with Europe. *Cal. State Pap. Col.*, 1689-1692, §949.

[53] *Cal. State Pap. Col.*, 1689-1692, §138; Court Records, VI, 22-24.

[54] *Cal. State Pap. Col.*, 1689-1692, §182; *Pub.* Mass. Col. Soc., 17, p. 24 and note.

well in the passage.[55] In spite of these orders, the provisional government made no effort to get transportation for the prisoners until after the arrival, on December 1, of a second letter from the king, authorizing those in charge of the government to continue in their work until further settlement should be decided upon.[56]

This somewhat belated sanction of the overthrow of Andros brought relief to the various provisional governments in New England, but it gave them no assurance as to what the future settlement would be.[57] All the colonies comprised in the Dominion officially petitioned for restoration of their charters and for the abandonment of the policy of consolidation. Plymouth asked for a royal charter guaranteeing the privileges which the

[55] *Cal. State Pap. Col.*, 1689-1692, §309.

[56] C. O. 5: 905, p. 108; Mass. Arch., vol. 35, pp. 100, 104; *Cal. State Pap. Col.*, 1689-1692, §§322, 709, 709-v. No orders having come from England by the time of the meeting of the revolutionary General Court on June 5, some action concerning the prisoners was necessary. Evidently all except Andros, Randolph, Dudley, Graham, West, Palmer, Farwell, and Sherlock had already been released on bail, but these having violated a capital law of the colony were declared unbailable. In July, Dudley was released on a £10,000 bond to remain at his home in Roxbury, but the mob seized him and forced him back to prison. Andros was transferred from the fort to the "castle" where Palmer and Graham were, and kept, according to Randolph, in a small room without a fireplace, so low that rain sometimes stood five or six inches on the floor. Andros was dependent upon his servants for provisions, which were difficult to obtain in bad weather, the "castle" being so far from town. Randolph himself was imprisoned in the common jail, which he grimly referred to in his letters, as "New Algiers." He complained that the jail was full of poor prisoners, among whom were wounded men, "who rot and perish for want of men to dress their wounds." Besides the personal discomfort, the prisoners, at least Randolph, experienced distress of mind through the fear that the Puritans would carry out their threats of trying them for the capital crime of attempted subversion of government. Mass. Arch., vol. 107, pp. 108, 137, 137b, 151, 151a; *Andros Tracts*, I, 174-175; III, 236; *Cal. State Pap. Col.*, 1689-1692, §§184, 286, 510, 511, 522, 644, 745, 844.

[57] Connecticut and probably Rhode Island received no authorization from England to resume their charter governments. *New York Col. Docs.*, III, 852.

colony had previously enjoyed, and although not unwilling to be under a governor-general, preferred local autonomy.[58] Connecticut asked only for a recognition of her *status quo,* her charter never having been vacated. Rhode Island likewise expected a confirmation of the old charter, "which, though submitted to the King, was not condemned nor taken from us."[59] The inhabitants of New Hampshire, realizing that they were too few and too poor to maintain an independent existence, seemed not to care whether they were under a royal or a Puritan government, provided they were protected. The proprietor, Samuel Allen, asked, however, that the colony be given local autonomy, even though subject to the superior authority of a governor-general.[60] New York petitioned against re-annexation to the Dominion, should it be restored, having "groaned under intolerable ills ever since the union of this province to Boston, when the dominion was so large, and the means of communication so difficult, that one end of it might have been destroyed before the other could have notice of it." However, realizing the military advantages in a larger unit, New York favored union with the Jerseys and with Pennsylvania or Connecticut.[61] The proprietors of the Jerseys, whom the Dominion had dispossessed of the right to govern, likewise opposed its restoration. For the present, they preferred to govern their provinces independently, but recognized the possible necessity of a union of the middle colonies in the near future, if war with France were continued.[62]

[58] Gay MSS., Plymouth Papers, II, 106; *Cal. State Pap. Col.,* 1689-1692, §183.

[59] *Cal. State Pap. Col.,* 1689-1692, §746; *Conn. Col. Rec.,* III, 463-466.

[60] *Ibid.,* §§1668, 1740, 1751.

[61] *Ibid.,* §§121, 1671, 1691, 1987, 2208.

[62] *New York Col. Docs.,* III, 838. They intended to appoint Joseph Dudley governor. *Cal. State Pap. Col.,* 1689-1692, §1373.

It was with great difficulty that the revolutionary government of Massachusetts maintained itself during the long period of delay before William decided upon a colonial policy. In the first place, it could not command the respect of the people because it had no secure legal foundation. Without a restoration of the old charter, there was a question as to whether or not the former laws of Massachusetts could be legally enforced. There were at the outset no funds, and though the burden of expense was probably heavier than at any other time in the history of the colony, it soon proved to be very difficult to raise any money by the old revenue acts. Money was needed for the war with France and for the charter campaign in England, as well as for the ordinary expenses of government. Many people, defying the authority of the government, refused to pay the rates, which made taxation fall heavier on those who did. In 1690 it was necessary to levy thirty-two and a half single country rates, a very heavy burden, because of the financial depression which had followed the decline in commerce. The government was equally impotent to do anything effective to revive trade. It was not strong enough to direct trade along new lines, and the war prevented a complete return of traffic to the old pre-Dominion channels.[63]

The provisional government likewise failed in its military policy. In order to satisfy the mutinous troops it withdrew the forces from the frontier in Maine and New Hampshire, leaving those parts exposed to the devastating attacks of the French and Indians.[64] Equally

[63] *Cal. State Pap. Col.*, 1689-1692, §§285, 311, 482, 484, 510, 511, 763, 773, 788, 885, 901, 906, 1313; Mass. Arch., vol. 107, 271a; *Andros Tracts*, I, 206-207, 208.

[64] *Andros Tracts*, I, 176-178; III, 24-25; *Cal. State Pap. Col.*, 1689-1692, §§285, 286-i, 509, 901 (p. 271), 902, 905, 906, 913.

disastrous was its plan for the invasion of Canada, which had been instigated by the agents in London for the purpose of winning favor with the king and of uniting all factions in the colony against a common enemy. It made every effort, through propaganda, to obtain the support of public opinion for the expedition, urging that there never could be any peace in New England until the French were conquered and the Indians subdued.[65] To the merchants who had suffered from attacks by French privateers, it pointed out the advantages to trade, if New France were destroyed, while to religious enthusiasts it endeavored to picture à war with the French Roman Catholics as a crusade against popery. Finally it sent an expedition to capture Port Royal, and because of its successful outcome, undertook an attack on Quebec. This second expedition failed, partly because of the cowardice and inefficiency of Phips, the commander, and partly because of the poor organization and training of the troops.[66]

Reaction against the government accompanied its general demoralization.[67] Lukewarm or indifferent sup-

[65] *Cal. State Pap. Col.*, 1689-1692, §797; *Andros Tracts*, I, 207, and note. One of the revolutionary pamphlets asks, ''Whether we had not better come to part cheerfully with all we have, even to our very Rings and Buckles and Bodkins, to defray Publick Charges, than suffer our French enemies to come and rifle us of what is nearer to us than our very Shirts, our Skins?'' *Andros Tracts*, I, 206-207.

[66] *Andros Tracts*, III, 54; *Cal. State Pap. Col.*, 1689-1692, §§741, 787, 904, 1157, 1239, 1245, 1282, 1309, 1313, 1315, 1319, 1373. Bullivant entered in his journal an item concerning the mustering of Phips's men at the town-house; ''About eighty in a body deserted with huzzas on being told that they must find their own arms. One of the officers appointed by Phips was hooted by his own company, which had chosen another captain.'' *Cal. State Pap. Col.*, 1689-1692, §885.

[67] Cuthbert Potter wrote in a journal, which he kept on a journey from Virginia to New England in August 1690, ''The people of Boston were generally much dissatisfied and blame the Government for their sufferings

porters of the revolution, among the common people, were alienated just as they had been by the Andros administration, because they were taxed and pressed into military service often without pay. Bullivant notes in his "Journal" that some soldiers returning from the frontier, disgusted at receiving no wages, "spoke very insolently to their new masters, crying out publicly in the streets, 'God bless King William, God bless Sir Edmund Andros, and damn all pumpkin States.' "[68] Sympathizers of the Andros administration, who had been silenced at the time of the revolution, openly denied the authority of the provisional government.[69] Many who supported it because the theocrats promised an extension of the suffrage, felt betrayed, when for almost a year the theocrats failed to keep their promises.[70] Moderates

which were due only to their ill management in sending away Sir Edmund Andros." *Cal. State Pap. Col.*, 1689-1692, §1164-vii.

[68] *Cal. State Pap. Col.*, 1689-1692, §§336, 482, 484, 885, 906, 1164, 1164-vii, 1313, 1857.

[69] *Ibid.*, §§482, 484, 485-iii, 513; *Andros Tracts*, I, 207, note.

[70] In January, 1690, a petition was sent to the General Court urging the "enlargement of the freemen" according to the declaration of the towns, May 24, 1689, because it would be the means of bringing the non-freemen to the support of the revolution and of the governmental settlement desired by the theocrats. In response, the General Court issued an order on February 14 repealing the clause concerning the admission of non-freemen in the suffrage act of 1673 and substituting the requirement that any inhabitant in good standing who paid four shillings besides the poll tax in a single country rate, or possessed houses or lands of the yearly value of six pounds, could be admitted to freemanship by the General Court upon the recommendation of the selectmen of his town. In March, April, and May, 1690, nearly seven hundred were made freemen, of whom about two hundred and fifty were church members in full communion, while about four hundred came in under the new property qualification. The rest cannot be classified. Even with this great extension, the theocratic voters were still in the majority because the property qualification was not required of them. Andrews, *List of Freemen of Massachusetts Bay Colony from 1630 to 1691; Twenty-ninth Report Boston Records, Miscellaneous Papers*, 157-163; *Laws of New Hampshire*, I, 355, 361, 363, 377-378, 379-380, 381, 382, 383, 384, 385, 386, 387, 388, 389, 390, 391, 392, 393, 394, 396, 397,

who expected from the theocrats reform in their old ways of governing, were disappointed to find them as arbitrary and anti-English as in the days of the charter. Moreover, they had not anticipated that the provisional government would be of such long duration.[71] The inhabitants of Maine, Pemaquid, and of Great Island, New Hampshire, were bitter against the Massachusetts government for its failure to protect them.[72] Everywhere in New England there was lack of confidence in the ability of the restored governments to save the colonies from French invasion, and the people remembered Andros's vigorous military policy with regret.[73] Reports of the pro-Dominion reaction, in the colonies outside of Massachusetts, led Andros to believe that the revolt was the work of a "few turbulent and ungovernable spirits," unsupported by the majority of the people, and this belief spurred him to attempt to escape in August, 1689, for the purpose of joining the royalists and overthrowing the revolution. Unfortunately, he fell into the hands of the revolutionists in Rhode Island before he had time to co-operate with the royalists, and after his recapture, up to the time of his departure from the colony in February, 1690, he was confined too closely to make escape or communication with confederates possible.[74] Without his leadership, the pro-

---

398, 402, 403, 404, 406, 407, 408; Sewall, *Letter Book*, I, 107; Mass. Arch., vol. 35, p. 154.

[71] *Cal. State Pap. Col.*, 1689-1692, §§311, 906.

[72] *Andros Tracts*, I, 176-178; *Cal. State Pap. Col.*, 1689-1692, §§129, 740, 883, 884. When the people at Casco Bay begged for help, Danforth answered "that Jesus Christ was king of earth as well as heaven, and that if Jesus Christ did not help them, he could not." *Cal. State Pap. Col.*, 1689-1692, §906.

[73] Even Samuel Sewall admitted in 1690 that it was necessary that "these lesser Governments be firmly compacted together in one." Sewall, *Letter Book*, I, 114-115.

[74] *Cal. State Pap. Col.*, 1689-1692, §§407, 482, 746; *Andros Tracts*, III, 95-102.

Dominion party, in spite of its growing strength, dared not attempt a forcible restoration of the Dominion. All eyes were turned toward England as the only source from which help would come. From all the New England colonies except Plymouth, petitions were sent to England praying for preservation of the Dominion and the appointment of a governor-general.[75] The royalists were becoming every day more hopeful and the theocrats more anxious, for the king's delay in making a settlement of government led to the general belief that he would restore the Dominion and punish the leaders of the revolt, as he had those in New York. Cotton Mather and others, prominent in the conspiracy against Andros, already fearful that Leisler's fate would be theirs, were terrified anew by the report that Andros and Randolph were coming from Barbados with a regiment of foot, and they began to make preparations for flight.[76] But for the arrival of favorable news from England, the tottering provisional government would probably have fallen.

[75] Mass. Arch., vol. 35, pp. 35b, 53, 54, 65, 77a, 110, 287; vol. 107, pp. 50a, 75; *Cal. State Pap. Col.*, 1689-1692, §§129, 181, 242, 306, 311, 336, 482, 484, 511, 740, 741, 742, 743, 773, 788, 883, 884, 885, 906, 1157, 1282, 1313, 1373, 1374, 1465, 1534, 2476, 2477; *Andros Tracts*, I, 176-178, 198; III, 191, 194, 203, 204; 6 Mass. Hist. Soc. *Col.*, V, 20; *New York Col. Docs.*, III, 849-854. One Connecticut petition paints the reaction there very vividly, ''Some at first very hot for this Govnt, now grow weary of it; theire charet-wheeles are taken off, and they draw very heavily, yet (being engaged) they will drag on still.'' *New York Col. Docs.*, III, 853.

[76] *Cal. State Pap. Col.*, 1689-1692, §482. Francis Foxcroft wrote to Francis Nicholson, October 26, 1691, ''Cotton Mather, the great pulpit buffoon, is said to be bound over, also some other leaders of the late rebellion.'' A few days later, another letter from New England reached Nicholson bearing the report that ''young Mather, Dr. Winthrop and Several others are on the wing for England fearful that when the Governor arrives, they may be brought to the test.'' *Ibid.*, §§1857, 1875.

CHAPTER XI

ABANDONMENT OF THE POLICY OF CONSOLIDATION

The first official expression of the policy of the new dynasty toward New England was in William's acceptance of the recommendation of the Lords of Trade, of February 26, 1689, that for a temporary settlement Andros be recalled and a provisional government established without the power to levy taxes; and that for a permanent settlement, a charter be granted guaranteeing the rights and liberties of the people, but safeguarding the king's interests. The significance of this report is that the Dominion was to be preserved, but with certain reforms,—a representative assembly and a new governor. Although the king expressed a preference for a commission of two in the provisional government, in place of the governor-general, the outbreak of war with France and the consequent necessity of placing the colonies in a state of defense forced the Lords of Trade to override the king's judgment and to insist upon the immediate appointment of a governor-general of New England, New York and the Jerseys.[1] When the agents of Massachusetts were consulted concerning a suitable candidate, they immediately protested against the continuation of the Dominion at all; and maintained that the appointment of a royal governor would be a violation of their charters,

[1] *Cal. State Pap. Col.*, 1689-1692, §§69, 72, 75, 90, 102; *Acts, Priv. Coun. Col.*, II, §§278, 283; *Andros Tracts*, III, 151, note.

only one of which, they said, was now not in operation and even that was about to be restored, the House of Commons having voted in favor of the corporation bill. They insisted further that the continuation of the Dominion would be a hindrance rather than a help in defense against the French, "as is manifest in that when they enjoyed their charter, they easily subdued their enemies, but since that it has been otherwise."[2] The second argument, although untrue, was the most effective one which they could have used with William, who cared for little else than the humiliation of his arch enemy Louis. The king, appreciating that the situation would be embarrassing and inconvenient if suddenly, after the appointment of a Dominion governor, parliament should pass the corporation bill and legal opinion should declare a royal governor contrary to the terms of the old charter, called a council meeting and asked the attorney-general and solicitor-general to attend and "give his Majesty the best information they can concerning the Grants and Charters of these colonies, and of His Majesty's right to appoint a Governor for those parts if his Majesty shall soe thinke fit." He also invited "the Merchants Inhabitants and other concerned in New England, New York and the New Jerseys" to this meeting, that they might express their opinions concerning the appointment of a governor.[3]

Before a decision was reached concerning the settlement of the government of New England, news came, unofficially, of the revolution at Boston.[4] William appears to have been somewhat annoyed at the presumption of

---

[2] Andros Tracts, III, 151-152, note; Sewall, Diary, I, 251.

[3] Acts, Priv. Coun. Col., II, §288.

[4] Sewall, Diary, I, 261. The report on the review of the proceedings against the charter of Massachusetts was not made until October 30, when opinion was given that it had been legally vacated. Cal. State Pap. Col., 1689-1692, §525.

the Puritans. On July 4, Mather, anxious to ascertain how the king received the news, hastened to ask him if he had been informed of the service done him by his subjects in New England. William replied that he had seen some letters which spoke of it, and he accepted what they had done. Mather then urged him to let them know his attitude, for it would be "a great Encouragement," and evidently noting the coolness of the king's tone, pointed out that the people of New England could make him the emperor of America if he but restored their charters.[5] Although William took no immediate action, Mather had brought before his eyes the time-old temptation of empires and power, which in the end triumphed over his judgment in regard to colonial policy. Not until August 12, however, did he send word to the anxiously waiting revolutionists that their work had been acceptable.[6]

The king having acknowledged the revolution, the bill for restoring charters having previously passed the House of Commons, and "there not being then any apparent Hazard but that it would be carried on unto Perfection," Mather considered his work completed and prepared to return to Boston.[7] He was prevented from sailing by the illness of his son, and returning to London "found such a Turn of Affairs as fulfill'd what his Friends told him when they welcomed him upon his Return, That the Gracious God had stop'd his Voyage in Great Mercy to his Country." While the corporation bill was still pending, the Convention Parliament was unexpectedly prorogued on January 27, 1690, and dis-

[5] *Andros Tracts,* III, 154; Sewall, *Diary,* I, 263.

[6] C. O. 5: 75, no. 3; *Cal. State Pap. Col.,* 1689-1692, §332.

[7] *Andros Tracts,* III, 153, and note; Sewall, *Diary,* I, 251. Rumor reached the colony in October that Mather had obtained the charter, whereupon the theocrats began to talk of trying Andros and Randolph and others for the capital crime of attempting subversion of government. *Cal. State Pap. Col.,* 1689-1692, §511.

solved a few days later. Mather soon found that nothing
in New England's favor was to be expected from the
new parliament and that if charters were restored it
must be through the king, who might be induced to grant
a new and more liberal charter than the old one.[8]

While Mather was doing his utmost to restore the
former governments in New England, the Lords of
Trade were trying to persuade the king that necessity
demanded the immediate re-establishment of the Dominion. As proof, they pointed to the breach of the acts
of trade, the devastation of the frontiers, the chaos and
lawlessness in Massachusetts due to the weak provisional government there, and the royalist petitions for
a governor-general.[9] The matter was brought to an issue
by the arrival early in April, 1690, of Andros and the
other Dominion officers. The agents were ordered to
draw up their charges against the prisoners, and both
sides were heard at a meeting of the Lords of Trade.
The whole trial proved, however, to be a fiasco because
the agents refused to sign the charges. Andros and his
officers presented answers, point for point, to the accusa-
tions, and Andros listed his instructions, with statements in parallel columns as to how he had carried
them out. Practically all of the charges were complaints
against actions which Andros had been instructed to
take. The refusal of the agents to sign the charges, together with the satisfactory answers of the officials,
resulted in the dismissal of the latter, and the complete
exoneration of the Andros administration.[10] No longer
could Andros's misgovernment be used as an argument

[8] *Andros Tracts*, III, 154, and note, 155, 180-181.

[9] *Cal. State Pap. Col.*, 1689-1692, §§306, 336, 468, 482, 509, 510, 513,
524, 741, 742, 743, 745, 773, 788, 797, 798, 801, 906, 994, 1157, 1164-vii,
1282, 1373, 1534; Mass. Arch., vol. 107, p. 75.

[10] *Cal. State Pap. Col.*, 1689-1692, §§817, 828, 830, 844, 846, 862, 908,
939, 940; *Andros Tracts*, III, 41-43.

for abolishing the Dominion. Nevertheless the king would not order its re-establishment. It is difficult to tell whether his delay in deciding on a colonial policy was due to deliberate vacillation or to preoccupation with more important matters. Perhaps he failed to appreciate the significance of the New England situation. Because of the war with France, he was more concerned with preserving the colonies from the clutches of Louis than he was in the problem of how those colonies should be governed. He found the news of Phips's successful expedition to Port Royal of greater interest than the complaints that the trade of New England was ruined and the government in disorder.

The year 1690 passed without action concerning the colonial policy, in spite of periodic attempts of the agents on the one hand and of the Dominion delegation on the other, to force the issue. Finally on January 1, 1691, the agents, thinking that because of Phips's high favor with the king the time was propitious for a forward movement, presented the king with proposals concerning a new charter. By an order in council, William referred the petition to the Lords of Trade for report.[11] While this request was under consideration, a petition from the pro-Dominion element in Boston and Charlestown arrived, laying the blame of all of New England's troubles to the "tumultuous removal of Sir Edmund Andros." It dwelt upon the disintegration of the Dominion into ten impotent little parts incapable of resist-

---

[11] 4 Mass. Hist. Soc. *Col.*, II, 301; *Cal. State Pap. Col.*, 1689-1692, §§1309, 1276, 1277. Phips knew how to paint his exploits so that they would appear at their best. In June, when proposing the conquest of Canada, he mentioned that in the preceding year, he "succeeded in reducing Nova Scotia, which would be well worth while for the crown to keep, as it has plenty of masts and naval timber, as well as copper and other rich mines." *Cal. State Pap. Col.*, 1689-1692, §1600.

ing the enemies' attacks, and upon the vast destruction
of property and lives on the frontier, the insignificance
of achievement from the Port Royal expedition, the
failure of the Canadian invasion, and the burden of debt.
As a relief from these troubles, the petitioners begged
for a royal government.[12] This petition was likewise
referred to the Lords of Trade, who summoned the
agents to answer the charges made therein against the
provisional government. The agents, as usual, placed the
blame for all the ills of New England on the Andros
administration, and appreciating that it was the psycho-
logical time to strike for the restoration of the charter,
again promised a Canadian expedition, the success of
which they maintained would depend on a satisfactory
settlement of government.[13] The Lords of Trade, believing that if the long deadlock of inactivity were broken
they must abandon hope of continuing the Dominion,
decided to save what they could from the wreckage of
their colonial policy. They therefore asked the agents
if they would accept a new charter, in which provision
for a representative assembly should be made, but in
which the right to choose the governor and council should
be left to the king. The agents answered by presenting
a draft of the kind of charter they desired. Before reporting on the plan, the Lords of Trade, in order to
establish a working basis, asked the king to instruct
them how he wished the governor to be chosen. He
answered that he would appoint the governor himself,

12 *Cal. State Pap. Col.*, 1689-1692, §§1390, 1393, 1404; 4 Mass. Hist. Soc.
Col., II, 301-302.

13 *Cal. State Pap. Col.*, 1689-1692, §§1391, 1404, 1418. The agents tried
to belittle the importance of the petition by saying that the men were
persons of little or no fortune. The representatives of the pro-English
element, who were in England at the time, answered this by a report on
the value of the estates of the signers, which, they said, ranged from two
thousand to twelve thousand pounds. *Ibid.*, §1439.

and ordered the lords to prepare a charter upon that foundation.[14]

Forced to accept the king's appointment of a governor, the agents now endeavored to reduce the power of that official as much as possible. They requested that the deputy governor be chosen by the council, and the council, like the representatives, by the freemen and freeholders; that the governor have no veto on elections and appointments; that courts be erected and all officers appointed by the General Court; that admiralty jurisdiction remain with the colony, as in the old charter; and that the governor and council have control of the militia, but that inhabitants should not be moved out of the colony without the consent of the assembly. Such provisions, had they been adopted, would have placed the government in the hands of the representatives of the voting population, the majority of whom would have been Puritans, for the terms "freemen" and "freeholders" would have eliminated those of the non-free aristocracy, whose wealth was invested in commerce. In this way the theocracy would have been restored.[15]

The Lords of Trade ignored all of these demands except those concerning the assembly's appointment of minor officials and its ultimate control of the militia, refusing to make any changes which would jeopardize the king's interests or shut out the non-Puritans from a share in the government. When Mather objected to their draft of the charter, he received the reply that the agents from New England were not plenipotentiaries of a sovereign state, and that if New England refused to submit to the terms of the charter, the king would settle the country as he pleased. Nothing

[14] *Cal. State Pap. Col.*, 1689-1692, §§1420, 1431, 1432, 1440, 1443; 4 Mass. Hist. Soc. Col., II, 302; *Andros Tracts*, III, 163, and note, 164.
[15] *Cal. State Pap. Col.*, 1689-1692, §1574.

further that Mather could say altered the final decision, and the charter passed the great seal on October 7, 1691.[16]

By the decision to grant a charter to Massachusetts, the idea of a political consolidation of New England was abandoned. Connecticut and Rhode Island were restored to their former status as independent corporations and autonomous governments, and New Hampshire, thanks to the influence of the Mason heirs at court, was made an independent royal colony. 'Maine, Pemaquid, Plymouth, and Nova Scotia (captured from the French), were added to Massachusetts. A mere shadow of the Dominion remained, in the power given the governor of Massachusetts to command the militia of all the New England colonies, by which means the Lords of Trade hoped to preserve the military strength of the former consolidation.[17]

The charter of 1691[18] largely determined the British policy toward New England in the eighteenth century. Although many features of the Dominion were abandoned, the colony did not win that freedom of action which it hoped to attain by the restoration of the old charter supplemented by additional grants of power. As in the royal colonies, the king appointed the governor, whose administration of affairs he guided by means of instructions on general policy and specific issues.

Legislative power was vested in a General Court consisting of two houses, the executive council acting as

[16] *Cal. State Pap. Col.*, 1689-1692, §§1483, 1500, 1570, 1571, 1572, 1573, 1596, 1606, 1631, 1650, 1658, 1665; *Andros Tracts*, III, 165.

[17] Phips's commission is in *Pub.* Col. Soc. Mass., II, 75. A personal union was also established in the middle colonies. Fletcher was appointed captain-general and governor-in-chief of New York and, by a separate commission, of Pennsylvania and the Lower Counties. He was to command the militia of those provinces and of East and West Jersey. *New York Col. Docs.*, III, 830, 859-860.

[18] The Massachusetts charter of 1691 is printed in Thorpe, *Federal and State Constitutions*, III, 1870-1886.

the upper, and the representatives of the people comprising the lower house. All laws were subject to the absolute veto of the governor and to the royal disallowance. Contrary to the usual custom in royal colonies, the council members were to be chosen annually by the General Court, a procedure which allowed the deputies to select men in sympathy with them. The governor, however, by his veto power, could refuse to confirm the election of those of whom he disapproved. Had the office of governor been quite independent of popular control, this right of confirming the election of councilors might have developed into the practice of governmental dictation of choice, so that the share of the General Court in the election would have been merely the exercise of the nominating power. Such a development would have brought over to the governor the support which the upper house usually gave to the executive in the royal colonies. That the trend of development should have been away from increased power in the hands of the governor was due to a great omission,—the failure on the part of the Lords of Trade to make provision for a permanent fund out of which the salaries of officials could be paid. This omission was of great significance, for it gave to the representatives of the people the means of controlling the governor. By threat of withholding his salary, they were able to override his veto and, at least temporarily, to pass and put into operation laws derogatory to the interest of the mother country, although such laws might ultimately be disallowed. By this means, the representatives were able in time to make the office of governor more like that of prime minister, responsible to themselves for his actions. They could not, of course, remove him, but by withholding his salary they could force him to submit or to ask the king for his recall. Thus the principle of responsible ministry, which was not officially introduced into England's colonial policy until the middle of the nineteenth century, might almost seem to have been developed in this early period. If the Dominion had proved to be a successful experiment in colonial policy and the other colonies had been formed into similar groups, the control of the executive by the assembly in each group would have been rendered impossible.

The charter did not adequately provide for royal supervision of courts of justice. The General Court was given the power to erect "judicatories and Courts of Record," thus offering an opportunity for such divergences from English custom as the colonists cared to make. In cases of personal action, exceeding the value of three hundred pounds sterling, appeals could be taken to the king in council and there the case could be reviewed according to English law and procedure, but otherwise there was no means of controlling the judicial system. Probate matters, however, were left with the governor and council instead of being restored to the General Court. Likewise the appointment of all judicial officials was left with the governor and council, but again the lack of a settled fund for payment of their salaries gave to the assembly, in time, the opportunity to usurp the power of appointment. On the question of land law, England yielded completely, allowing the New England custom to prevail. The charter confirmed all grants previously made, even those which had "defect of Form," and omitted the stipulation that new patents should be taken out in the king's name. No requirement of quit-rents was made on land to be granted in the future, although holders of land already bound by quit-rent reservations were not released from their obligations. The General Court was empowered to grant lands in Massachusetts, Plymouth, or Maine, but north and east of Sagadahoc, all grants had to have the royal approval.

Liberty of conscience was granted to all except papists. This privilege in itself would have been of little value to the non-Puritans had it not been guaranteed by another provision which prevented the complete restoration of the old theocratic "hedge." The charter particularly specified that the suffrage should be given to all possessing freeholds worth forty shillings annually or other property to the value of forty pounds sterling. By this provision, practically all property holders, whether Puritan freeholders or non-Puritan business men, could vote, and political domination passed from the theocrats to the aristocratic moderates of the large towns.[19] Henceforth, it was impossible legally for the theocrats to force the non-Puritans to attend services at a Puritan meeting-house.

There is every indication to show that the Lords of Trade expected the abolition of the Dominion to make very little if any difference in the regulation of the trade of New England. The royal appointment of the governor placed the execution of the navigation acts in the hands of one whose own interests would best be served by careful regard for those of England, and who would be guided by his instructions. Vice-admiralty jurisdiction

---

[19] Cotton Mather insisted in his "Parentator" that the theocracy could still be maintained under the new charter. "Religion is forever Secured," he wrote, "A Righteous and Generous Liberty of Conscience Established. And the General Assembly may by their Acts give a Distinguishing Encouragement unto that Religion which is the General Profession of the Inhabitants. They may still have their Judges as at the first, and their Counsellors as at the Beginning if the Fault be not their own. As long as their Principal Magistrates, and Justices, favour and express Piety, and abhor and punish Wickedness, tis to be hoped, Religion will be kept in Heart. And if they have not such, the Fault will not be in the New Charter, but in Themselves. Behold, A wall of Defence about the Vineyard!" *Andros Tracts*, III, 170-171.

was reserved to the crown, thereby allowing the mother country to erect a vice-admiralty court, with authority over the whole of New England. The Lords of Trade, perceiving that New England was a natural economic unit, believed that the political disintegration of the Dominion would not affect exchanges of products in that region. Connecticut, Rhode Island, and New Hampshire had been dependent upon Massachusetts as a commercial centre before the Dominion was established, and would so continue, while the rest of New England was now annexed to Massachusetts. In this large royal province, staples, they thought, could be as easily encouraged as in the Dominion. Reports from many sources of the unlimited natural supplies of naval stores in New England inspired more confidence than ever that in the future trade expansion lay in that direction. To safeguard the king's right to forests on ungranted lands, the charter reserved for the navy all trees of the diameter of twenty-four inches. Reports on the possibility of developing the minerals in New England seem not to have been so favorable, for instead of granting any of the petitions for monopoly rights to work the mines, which was the most certain way of insuring the investment of capital for their development, the king by the charter granted all mineral rights to the colony.

It has been often pointed out that the charter of 1691 was a compromise between the old charter and the royal type of government. To be more accurate, it was a compromise between a practically independent theocracy, which had developed out of the primitive government of the trading company, and the Dominion of New England, representing England's latest ideas on colonial policy. As Cotton Mather remarks in his "Parentator," if the demands of the theocrats for their old charter had been granted, Massachusetts would have found herself a tiny

province confined between the three-mile limit north of
the Merrimac River on one side and Plymouth, Connecticut, and Rhode Island on the other, with a government
that had no power to call a representative assembly, to
tax non-freemen, or to try capital cases. Since the colony,
like all others which had originated through trading
companies, had outgrown its charter, it could not have
"comfortably or Tolerably Subsisted" without exercising the powers which it had simply usurped in the
process of its development. That the colony was granted
as much freedom as was given to it by the new charter
was due to the Boston revolution and to Mather's successful diplomacy. Without these factors, the king would
have carried out the plan he announced in April, 1689,
of appointing a governor-general for New England, New
York, and the Jerseys. But to the theocrats, who in their
blind faith had expected the re-establishment of the
theocracy, the new charter was a great disappointment.

To the Lords of Trade and to the non-Puritan element
in New England, the governmental settlement was likewise a disappointment. They had found the Dominion
experiment satisfactory on the whole. Union had created
a formidable defense against the French, which without
doubt delayed the opening of a period of warfare. The
navigation laws had been enforced, and although trade
was still at the ebb, there were already evidences of the
readjustment of the merchants to the new economic conditions. The arbitrary rule of the Puritan theocracy had
been broken, and liberty of conscience for all sects established. Control of legislation and of the courts had made
colonial laws conformable to the laws and interests of
the mother country. The revenue policy had not been
worked out, but probably would have been in time, for,
up to the very last, Andros was trying to establish a

general system of quit-rents, which, with import duties, would have given to the government sufficient funds for expenses and would have made unnecessary the levying of direct taxes. Had the effort been successful, even a representative assembly, had it been granted, could not have tyrannized over the governor, who would have been financially independent.

If the Dominion was satisfactory to England, and for the most part, to the colonists, why should it have been abandoned? The fault lay with William, who chose to gratify the wishes of the Puritans in order to win their support in the war with France. By his choice, England lost the only opportunity she ever had of carrying out a consistent policy in New England, for in the eighteenth century the local institutions of the colonies in that region were too deeply rooted to make consolidation possible. William could easily have continued the work so well begun, redressing the most obvious grievances by the establishment of a representative assembly, safe-guarded by some provision for a permanent fund for the support of government, and by the appointment of an-other governor more acceptable to the Puritans than Andros had been and better fitted by temperament and experience for constructive statesmanship. Such a settle-ment would have gone a long way toward quieting the general unrest. The war with France would have drawn the various parts of the Dominion more closely together and united them more firmly to the mother country. The passing of the generation of Puritans who had lived under the theocracy, would soon have removed that fanatical and independent flavor which rigid Puritanism had given to New England.

It was not long before the new dynasty was aware of the fatal error. The attempt to unite the militia under one command proved to be most ineffective, for the colonists refused to march outside the bounds of the colony in which they lived, and the commander-in-chief was powerless to force them to obey. Trade laws were as little enforced as before 1684, while the growing independence of the New England governments gave ample cause for a justifiable concern. Furthermore, there continued to be a great deal of unrest in New England due to the discontent of non-Puritans with the abandonment of the Dominion. The policy of the eighteenth century, beginning with the establishment of the Board of Trade in 1696, centred in the effort, long persisted in, to establish once more the relationship between the colonies and the mother country which had existed under the Dominion. The various attempts in 1701, 1702, 1706, 1715, and in 1722 to royalize the proprietary and corporate colonies by act of parliament, the many suggestions of union advanced by Englishmen and by colonists, the isolated parliamentary enactments concerning coinage, paper money, manufactures, and commerce, and especially the reforms in the colonial policy after 1763, show belated and more or less unsuccessful efforts to handle what could have been so easily managed through the Dominion government, had the policy of consolidation and royalization survived and been extended to the other colonies. It is, of course, idle to speculate on what evils might have been avoided if the events of history had taken some other course. It is obvious, nevertheless, that the relationships established between the colonies and the mother country in the eighteenth century were quite different from what they would have been had the Dominion survived and its system of government been revised. Perhaps the loss of the continental colonies south of Canada might have been avoided, or if not, the seceding colonies might have been fewer and larger, corresponding to the natural economic, political, and social sections, which have always existed and still persist, even to the present. In conclusion, one may say that because of its potentialities, the experiment of the Dominion of New England was the most important piece of constructive statesmanship in the field of British colonial policy that had been brought into being before the issue of Lord Durham's report and the subsequent adoption of his two suggestions of union and responsible ministry.

BIBLIOGRAPHICAL NOTE

British Manuscript Sources

For a study of the Dominion as a feature of British seventeenth-century colonial policy, the most comprehensive body of material to be found on this side of the water is the large collection of transcripts from the Colonial Office Papers in the Public Record Office, made under the direction of Mr. Albert Matthews, editor of the publications of the Colonial Society of Massachusetts, to whose courtesy in allowing me free access to them I am greatly indebted. They are in the form of commissions and instructions, circular letters, reports, answers of governors to queries, etc. The manuscripts in classes 5 and 324 were the most useful.

Another interesting collection of transcripts from British archives is that which the late Mr. Frederick Gay had made for his own private use. The material duplicates much of that in the other collections, but is more scattered and appears to have been gathered somewhat unsystematically. Besides reports of action of the Lords of Trade, it contains copies of semi-official letters and narrative accounts, particularly of the period of the Mather and Phips agency. I found the "State Papers" and the "Phips Papers" the most useful.

American Manuscript Sources

The so-called Massachusetts Archives, in the public archives department of the state house at Boston, is a mine of manuscript material, invaluable for a study of the Andros administration. The collection contains commissions, orders, reports, letters, petitions, memorials, resolutions, etc. For this period I have found volumes 35, 107, 126, 127, 128, and 129 especially helpful. Other valuable collections in the public archives department at Boston are the "Council Records" covering both the Dudley and the Andros administrations, and the "Court Records, VI" which contains the secretary's minutes of the meetings of the council of safety and the provisional government after the revolution and before the establishment of government under the new charter. These, with the Massachusetts Archives material, furnish a splendid opportunity to follow the course of the revolutionary movement after the April outbreak. For a study of Andros's land policy, the small volume in the Boston archives entitled "Sir Edmund Andros's Land Warrants" is very illuminating and helps to counteract the distorted impression which revolutionary propagandists have usually given concerning Andros's attempts to change the tenures. The Suffolk Files in the library of the Suffolk County Court House at Boston furnished the records of a few cases of trial for breaches of the acts of trade and of land disputes.

The Jeffries Family Papers comprise a miscellaneous collection of the private papers of John Usher and of public documents in his possession, when he was treasurer of the Dominion of New England. The collection consists mostly of accounts, receipts of expenditure, tax lists, bills of lading, and letters both of a public and a private nature. It is now in the custody of the Massachusetts Historical Society, as is also "The Accounts of John Usher from July 1, 1688, to January 1, 1689,"—evidently Usher's official report of all income and expenditure for the period.

British Official Documents

Of the printed sources, the first in importance is the *Calendar of State Papers, Colonial Series,* edited by W. N. Sainsbury, J. W. Fortescue, and C. Headlam. This collection is helpful not only because of the wealth and variety of the material, but also because of its chronological arrangement, which furnishes an outline of events and simplifies the work of identifying and dating manuscripts from other collections. The worst drawback in using this material is that often official letters, reports, and journals of meetings have been so condensed as to give one an impression quite different from that received from reading the original manuscript. Fortunately much of the material herein contained is accessible in manuscript form. I also found the *Acts of the Privy Council of England, Colonial Series,* and the *Statutes at Large* indispensable.

American Official Documents

For a study of the institutional background of the colonial governments, and of the effect on the colonies of England's policy toward them after 1660, perhaps the most useful sources of information are the various colonial legislative journals: *Records of the Governor and Company of the Massachusetts Bay in New England,* edited by Nathaniel Shurtleff (Boston, 1854); *Records of the Colony of New Plymouth in New England,* edited by the same (Boston, 1855); *Public Records of the Colony of Connecticut,* 1636-1776, compiled by J. H. Trumbull and C. J. Hoadly (Hartford, 1850-1890); *Records of the Colony of Rhode Island and Providence Plantations in New England,* 1636-1792, compiled by J. R. Bartlett (Providence, 1856-1865); *Documents and Records relating to the Province of New Hampshire,*

1623-1800, edited by N. Bouton and others (Concord, 1867-1907); *Documents Relative to the Colonial History of the State of New York, Procured in Holland, England and France,* edited by E. B. O'Callaghan (Albany, 1856-1861). The last, usually cited as *New York Colonial Documents,* was especially helpful for the Andros administration because it contained in easily accessible form, Andros's commission and instructions of 1688, and many official letters and reports which could not be found so easily elsewhere or were not printed in full in the *Calendar of State Papers.* The various colonial records were supplemented by the collections of colonial statutes: *The Colonial Laws of Massachusetts,* edited by W. H. Whitmore in 1887, reprinted from the 1672 edition; *The Compact, with the Charter and Laws of the Colony of New Plymouth,* edited by William Brigham (Boston, 1836); *Acts and Laws of His Majesty's English Colony of Connecticut, in New England in America* (New London, 1769); *Laws of New Hampshire,* edited by Albert S. Batchellor (1904); *The Charter and the Acts and Laws of His Majesties Colony of Rhode Island and Providence Plantations in America,* a facsimile reprint of a 1719 edition with a bibliographical and historical introduction, edited by Sidney S. Rider (1895).

For a study of the Dominion of New England during the administrations of Dudley and Andros the printed official records are invaluable. The *Dudley Records* cover the period from May to December, 1686. They have been printed by Robert Toppan in the Massachusetts Historical Society *Proceedings,* Second Series, XIII, 226-286, and were copied from the Massachusetts Archives and the Council Records at the State House in Boston. The *Andros Records,* printed by Robert Toppan in the American Antiquarian Society *Proceedings,* New Series, XIII, pp. 239-268, cover the period from December 20, 1686, to April 13, 1687 (taken from the original minutes in the possession of the society); pp. 463 to 499, from May 4, 1687, to March 27, 1689 (taken from the Council Records of Massachusetts, Volume II, from the Massachusetts Archives, and from *Connecticut Colonial Records,* III). The laws of the two administrations have been published in *Laws of New Hampshire,* I, Province Period, as well as the royal commissions and instructions, additional instructions, and royal letters to Dudley and Andros. Dudley's and Andros's commissions are also published in "Massachusetts Royal Commissions, 1681-1774," printed in *Publications* of the Colonial Society of Massachusetts, II, together with their commissions as vice-admirals, Nicholson's commission as lieutenant-governor of the Dominion, Randolph's commission as secretary and register of the Dominion and as collector, surveyor, and searcher of the customs in New England.

Suffolk Deeds, edited by William B. Trask and others (Boston, 1880), were very useful for a study of the land system in Massachusetts, as were also *York Deeds,* edited by John T. Hull (Portland, 1887), for Maine. Additional information on the same subject was furnished by the *Farnham Papers,* 1603-1688, Volume VII of *Documentary History of the State of Maine,* compiled by Mary Frances Farnham (Portland, 1901). This volume contains patents of various sorts granted by the New England Council and their patentees and therefore shows the policy of the original holders of New England territory regarding land grants and tenures. *Boston Town Records,* 1634 to 1660, and 1660 to 1701, edited under the direction of William H. Whitmore and William S. Appleton by the Boston Record Commissioners (Boston, 1881), contain among other things accounts of land grants under quit-rent tenure. The first report of this commission, *Boston Tax Lists,* I found very useful for a comparative study of the revenue systems of Massachusetts under the charter and Dominion governments. The lists are for the years 1674, 1676, 1681, 1685, 1687, 1688, 1689 (imperfect), and 1691.

Papers, Memoirs, Letters, Lists

Perhaps the most satisfactory source for a study of British colonial policy in the period preceding the annulling of the Massachusetts charter and during the Dominion experiment, is Toppan and Goodrick's *Edward Randolph, Including his Letters and Official Papers . . . with . . . a Memoir,* a collection of the papers and letters of that most hated of British officials, beginning with his tour of investigation in New England in 1676. Randolph was the best gleaner of information and diagnostician of colonial ills of any official in the continental colonial service, and his reports and ideas were most influential in shaping British colonial policy toward New England after 1675. A few letters, duplicated elsewhere, have been printed under the title "Randolph Letters," in the Massachusetts Historical Society *Proceedings,* XVIII, 254-261.

In many ways, the best collection of colonial official papers is that entitled *Collection of Original Papers relative to the History of the Colony of Massachusetts Bay,* compiled by Thomas Hutchinson (Boston, 1769), and reprinted by the Prince Society under the title *Hutchinson Papers* (Albany, 1865). This material is very valuable, because a part of it is not now available in any other form, many of the documents having been burned in the fires which destroyed two state houses at Boston. Another collection bearing the same name, *Hutchinson Papers,* is printed in the Massachusetts Historical Society *Collections,* Third Series, I, 1 to 150. It contains letters of the king to Massachusetts, arguments against giving up the charter, an "Account of New England, 1689," and other material of like nature, which Hutchinson did not include in his *Collection of Original Papers.* Hutchinson's *History of the Colony of Massachusetts Bay* should be classed with the sources because it was based on material which has since been destroyed in the Boston fires and quotes some of this material in the footnotes. *Papers Relative to the Period of Usurpation in New England,* printed in the Massachusetts Historical Society *Collections,* Third Series, VII, 150-196, comprises miscellaneous material which is not indispensable, because most of it can be found more conveniently elsewhere.

Several collections of papers of a semi-official character have come down to us from this period. Most of them were the property of colonial officials, who evidently kept their official and private papers together. Among these collections are the *Danforth Papers,* printed in the Massachusetts Historical Society *Collections,* Second Series, VIII, 46-112, which contain letters, petitions, sign manuals, etc.; and the *Hinckley Papers,* in *ibid.,* Fourth Series, V, 1 to 309, which is the best material available for information on the workings of the Dominion in the Plymouth Colony. The *Winthrop Papers* printed in *ibid.,* Fifth Series, VIII, 3 to 571, and Sixth Series, II, 3 to 423, is a private collection of letters mostly to and from Wait and Fitz-John Winthrop, councilors during the Andros administration. These letters are of interest because they throw light on the attitude of the moderate Puritans (to which group these men belonged) toward the theocracy and toward England.

Of journals, memoirs, and diaries, an important source for the early period is *Winthrop's Journal,* 1630 to 1649, printed in *Original Narratives of Early American History.* It is of interest because it shows the ideals of government of the early Puritans and gives a valuable institutional background for a study of the colony in the Restoration period. *Bradstreet's Journal,* 1664 to 1683, printed in the *New England Historical and Genealogical Register,* VIII, 325 to 333, and in corrected form in IX, 43 to 51, is too fragmentary to be much of a contribution, but it contains a few items of interest concerning the period preceding the annulling of the charter. Thomas Lechford's *Plaine Dealing; or Newes from New England,* printed in the Massachusetts Historical Society *Collections,* Third Series, III, 55 to 129, is a sort of history of Massachusetts, containing much information concerning government, the charter, the militia, the schools, etc., with Lechford's criticisms. John Dunton, in his *Life* and *Errors,* printed in the Massachusetts Historical Society *Collections,* Second Series, V, 97 to 125, gives an interesting account of his visit to the colonies and of conditions in Boston in 1686, but he is not to be relied upon. Chester N. Greenough, in a paper printed in the *Publications* of the Colonial Society of Massachusetts, XIV, 213 to 257, says that Dunton plagiarized from Cotton Mather, Roger Williams, Josselyn, and other writers on New England, and that he is often quite inaccurate in his statements of fact. Nowhere can one get the spirit of seventeenth-century colonial New England better than in the most delightful *Diary of Samuel Sewall,* printed in the Massachusetts Historical Society *Collections,* Fifth Series, V, VI, VII (Boston, 1878 to 1882). His *Letter Book,* printed in *ibid.,* Sixth Series, V (Boston, 1886 to 1888), is not quite so intimate and personal, but it is of interest because it gives a picture of the business relations of Sewall, the merchant.

For information concerning the personnel of the colonial offices and parties, there are many valuable lists, such as *The Massachusetts Civil List for the Colonial and Provincial Periods, 1630 to 1774,* compiled by William Whitmore, and containing names and dates of appointment of all the civil officers constituted by authority of the charters or the local government, including the officers of the transitional government and the Dominion (Albany, 1870); *Civil, Military, and Professional Lists of Plymouth and Rhode Island Colonies, comprising Colonial, County and Town Officers, Clergymen, Physicians and Lawyers, With Extracts from Colonial Laws defining their Duties, 1621 to 1700,* compiled by Ebenezer W. Peirce (Boston, 1881); *List of Freemen of Massachusetts Bay Colony, 1630 to 1691* (alphabetically arranged), compiled by H. F. Andrews (Exira, Iowa, 1906); *List of Freemen in Massachusetts,* printed in the twenty-ninth *Report of Boston Town Records,* edited by William Whitmore (Boston, 1900). In the last, the names are arranged according to the year of admission to the freedom of the colony and according to the town in which the freemen lived. Particularly helpful for a study of the personnel of the Dominion councils was Albert Matthews's *Notes on the Massachusetts Royal Commissions, 1681 to 1775,* reprinted from the *Publications* of the Colonial Society of Massachusetts, XVII. It contains a chronological list of all the councilors of the charter government, of the Dudley and Andros administrations, and of the first administration under the new charter of 1691, with copious genealogical footnotes. It also contains valuable excerpts from source material not easily accessible. These various lists often had to be supplemented by the use of Savage's *Genealogical Dictionary of the First Settlers of New England* (Boston, 1860); *The New England Historical and Genealogical Register,* edited by Rev. William Cogswell

(Boston, 1860); and *The Maine Historical and Genealogical Recorder,* published by S. M. Watson (Portland, Maine, 1884).

Contemporary Pamphlets and Books

In the long period between the April revolution in 1689 and the grant of the new charter in 1691, the theocrats of Massachusetts waged a bitter pamphlet war against the Dominion government, which they feared might be restored. By means of these pamphlets they hoped to accomplish two things: stir up a public sentiment in the colony against the Dominion, and win support in England for the restoration of the old charter and a supplementary grant of powers. These pamphlets, which were contemporaneously published both in England and in America were collected and published in book form by the Prince Society under the title *Andros Tracts* (Boston, 1868). This material is invaluable for a study of the Andros administration, but the fact that it was incendiary propaganda must never be lost sight of. Besides pamphlets, there are many depositions taken by the provisional government against Andros and his officials, when charges against them were being prepared for the use of the agents in England. Of the pro-Dominion material included in this collection, the most instructive are Andros's reports, answering charges against his administration, and Palmer's pamphlet, "Impartial Account," in defense of the British policy. This collection, since its publication in 1868, has been a most potent factor in the building up of the Andros legend, by writers of history who have not had access to British documents,—a legend in which his administration is always spoken of as though it were a usurpation, an arbitrary imposition on the New Englanders of an oppressive and illegal government. *Narratives of the In-surrection,* 1675 to 1690, edited by Charles M. Andrews in the *Original Narrative Series* (New York, 1915), dupli-cates some of the material in the *Andros Tracts,* but it is nevertheless a valuable collection. *Narratives of the Indian Wars,* 1675 to 1699, of the same series, edited by Charles H. Lincoln (New York, 1613), contains informa-tion which I found helpful in a study of Andros's policy of defense. *Colonial Currency Reprints,* 1682 to 1751, with an introduction and notes by Andrew McFarland Davis, Volume I (Boston, 1910), was useful in studying New England coinage. *Report of a French Protestant Refugee in Boston,* 1687, translated from the French by E. T. Fisher (Brooklyn, New York, 1808), is a cross-section picture of New England, particularly of Boston during Andros's administration, and contains much valu-able information, especially about trade. The anonymous individual who wrote it had evidently been sent ahead by prospective immigrants from France to spy out the land and report concerning the advisability of settling there. It is interesting to note that he did not send home a discouraging report.

INDEX

Act of 1673, 11-12, purpose of, 13; appointment of collectors of duty arising from, 15-16; effect of, on colonial trade, 63, 148; duty and bond requirement of, 136; colonial interpretation of, 155-156.

Admiralty cases, tried in local courts of the Dominion, 108. See Vice-admiralty courts.

Agents, king orders Massachusetts to send, 7; of Massachusetts, in England, 14-15, 16, 21, 22; petition James II for governmental changes, 232; petition William III for restoration of charters of New England, 234-235; protest against re-establishment of the Dominion, 262-263; present to Lords of Trade a draft of charter for Massachusetts, 267.

Alford, Benjamin, prominent non-freeman, 8 (note 7).

Allen, Captain, of H. M. S. *Quaker*, 159.

Allen, James, Congregational minister, 129 (note 13).

Allen, Samuel, proprietor of New Hampshire, 256.

Allyn, John, Dominion councilor from Connecticut, 38 (note 39), 73 (note 9); reports revolutionary spirit in Connecticut, 239 (note 19).

Andrews, John, one of Ipswich rebels, 87.

Andros, Sir Edmund, Governor of Dominion, 46, 70-73, 76-77; arrival of, in New England, 69; friendliness with moderates, 76-77; salary paid by England, 80; revenue policy of, 80-85; settles mutiny, 85-90; establishes judicial system, 104-109; appropriates a Congregational meeting-house for services of Church of England, 128-130; demands strict enforcement of navigation acts, 135; favors re-establishment of mint, 161, and raising value of all money, 164; order concerning money, 165; puts down piracy, 166; explains English land law, 193, 194, 199; policy of defense, 216-219, 226-228; conference with Iroquois, 224; at Pemaquid, 239; writes of restlessness of Massachusetts people, 240 (note 24); arrest of, 243; refuses to surrender garrison at fort, 244; orders officers to demand his release, 248; declared unbailable, 255 (note 56); is transferred to castle, 255 (note 56); attempt to escape, 260.

Anglicans, ministers' maintenance during provisional government, 60-61; use Congregational meeting-house at Boston, 61; attempt to build church of their own, 61; in majority in Maine and New Hampshire, 124; use of Congregational meeting-house for services, 129, 130.

Appeals, to king's courts, 72; Massachusetts denial of right of king

Judges, difficulty of getting men legally trained for, 110.
Judicature Act, 105-109, 117.
Juror requirements, 109, 115-116.

King's Chapel, built by Anglicans, 130.
Kirke, Colonel Percy, suggested as governor of Dominion, 45.

Land policy, of Andros, 188, 189, 192-193, 195-198, 199-201, 202-204, 210-211.
Land tenure, provisions of commission concerning, 43; of New England Council, 178; of Plymouth, 179; of Massachusetts, 179-180, 182-184, 207; of Maine, 185; of New Hampshire, 185; of Pemaquid, 186; of Connecticut, 187; of Rhode Island, 187; of New Haven, 187; need of uniform, 188; Puritan theory of, 204, 208-209; provision concerning, in Body of Liberties, 205; in other trading company colonies, 207.
Laurence, Robert, claims land in Falmouth, 189 (note 43).
Laws, royal supervision of, 71; power to make, in Dominion, 77; committee on revision of, 78, 79; divergence of Massachusetts from English, 102-103.
Leisler, Jacob, leader of revolution in New York, 250; fate of, 261.
Leverett, Thomas, grantee of Waldo patent, 180 (note 17).
Liberty of conscience, policy of, in Andros's commission, 44; in provisional government, 59.
Lidgett, Charles, prominent non-freeman, 8 (note 7); advocates production of naval stores in New England, 172 (note 97); is granted a piece of Charlestown commons, 195.

Linen manufactures, imported into the colonies directly from Europe, 145.
Liscombe, Humphrey, prominent nonfreeman, 8 (note 7).
Livestock, insufficient markets for, in British West Indies, 142.
Logwood, obtained by New England from the British West Indies, 140.
Long Island, trade of, 138.
Lords of Trade, appointed in 1675, 12; investigate Massachusetts conditions, 13; threaten her with *quo warranto* proceedings, 20, 21; consider claims of Maine and New Hampshire, 27-28; recommend appointment of a governor-general for New England, 30; draft Andros's commission, 40, 47, and instructions, 44; favor Dudley for president of the provisional government, 48; confidence of, in Randolph, 50; policy of, regarding liberty of conscience, 59; encourage trade in New England, 62; hasten work on Andros's commission, 69; attitude of, toward provisional government, 69; oppose innovations in taxation, 80; satisfaction of, with Dominion, 98; investigate New England courts, 104; religious policy of, 122; trade instructions of, 154-155, 157; Randolph's trade reports to, 158; reopen mint question, 160; receive Andros's report on mint, 161, and report of mint officers, 162; attempt to suppress piracy, 166; decide to use quit-rents for raising revenue, 175-176; desire consolidation of New England colonies for defense, 216; report of, on Massachusetts petition, 233; promise agents new charter, 234; investigate agents' charges of il-

DATE DUE

		FEB 0 8 2008	